# The Economies of the West Bank and Gaza Strip

# Westview Special Studies

The concept of Westview Special Studies is a response to the continuing crisis in academic and informational publishing. Library budgets for books have been severely curtailed. Ever larger portions of general library budgets are being diverted from the purchase of books and used for data banks, computers, micromedia, and other methods of information retrieval. Interlibrary loan structures further reduce the edition sizes required to satisfy the needs of the scholarly community. Economic pressures on the university presses and the few private scholarly publishing companies have severely limited the capacity of the industry to properly serve the academic and research communities. As a result, many manuscripts dealing with important subjects, often representing the highest level of scholarship, are no longer economically viable publishing projects--or, if accepted for publication, are typically subject to lead times ranging from one to three years.

Westview Special Studies are our practical solution to the problem. We accept a manuscript in camera-ready form, typed according to our specifications, and move it immediately into the production process. As always, the selection criteria include the importance of the subject, the work's contribution to scholarship, and its insight, originality of thought, and excellence of exposition. The responsibility for editing and proofreading lies with the author or sponsoring institution. We prepare chapter headings and display pages, file for copyright, and obtain Library of Congress Cataloging in Publication Data. A detailed manual contains simple instructions for preparing the final typescript, and our editorial staff is always available to answer questions.

The end result is a book printed on acid-free paper and bound in sturdy library-quality soft covers. We manufacture these books ourselves using equipment that does not require a lengthy make-ready process and that allows us to publish first editions of 300 to 1000 copies and to reprint even smaller quantities as needed. Thus, we can produce Special Studies quickly and can keep even very specialized books in print as long as there is a demand for them.

# About the Book and Author

The creation of Israel called for the realignment of the West Bank and Gaza Strip economies with those of Jordan and Egypt. Subsequent conflicts have fostered economic uncertainties associated with occupation status, making investment in various sectors unattractive and hampering the prospects for development. Land expropriation, the growing number of Jewish settlements, and restrictions on the tapping of water resources have all retarded agricultural potential. Investment in industry is deemed risky, municipal services have barely kept pace with population growth, and tourism income has diminished. Dr. Gharaibeh examines how political developments and the course of the Arab-Israeli dispute will determine the future economic status of the area, providing extensive data from both Israeli and Jordanian sources.

Dr. Fawzi Gharaibeh is professor and dean of the Faculty of Economics and Administrative Sciences at the University of Jordan.

# About the Text and Author

# The Economies of the West Bank and Gaza Strip

Fawzi A. Gharaibeh

Routledge
Taylor & Francis Group
LONDON AND NEW YORK

First published 1985 by Westview Press, Inc.

Published 2019 by Routledge
52 Vanderbilt Avenue, New York, NY 10017
2 Park Square, Milton Park, Abingdon, Oxon OX14 4RN

*Routledge is an imprint of the Taylor & Francis Group, an informa business*



Library of Congress Cataloging in Publication Data
Gharāybah, Fawzī.
The economies of the West Bank and Gaza Strip.
(Westview special studies on the Middle East)
Bibliography: p.
Includes index.
1. West Bank--Economic conditions. 2. Ghaza--Economic conditions. 3. Israel--Economic policy. 4. Israel-Arab War, 1967--Occupied territories.
I. Title. II. Series.
HC415.25.Z7W473 1985 330.95695 84-19541

ISBN 13: 978-0-367-29161-7 (hbk)

# Contents

# Tables

# Preface

This study is an examination of the performance of the economy of the West Bank and Gaza Strip since the Israeli occupation of the two territories in 1967. The economy of these territories has been greatly influenced by a host of factors that are either inherent in the occupation status or have been created by deliberate Israeli policies. The net effect of these forces is assessed in order to diagnose the problems faced by the economy of the occupied territories and to discern future prospects under different sets of alternatives.

Data on economic activity in the West Bank and Gaza Strip have, by necessity, come for the most part from Israeli sources. Reliance on Israeli statistics might be considered a shortcoming in any study of this sort. Israel, as an occupying power, may have a vested interest in portraying the economy of the territories as being blessed by the links that have been established with the more advanced Israeli economy. Therefore, caution is called for when dealing with Israeli published figures on the economy of the occupied territories. Another shortcoming is that data on Arab Jerusalem are not published in West Bank statistics, but are rather buried with those of Israel.

I am indebted to various Jordanian government agencies and departments for their help and cooperation. Among these are the Department of Statistics, the Economics Department of the Royal Scientific Society, Cities and Villages Development Bank, Jordan Cooperative Organization, Industrial Development Bank, Central Bank of Jordan, Agricultural Credit Corporation, Ministry of Tourism and Ministry of Occupied Territories Affairs. The University of Jordan was generous in its moral and material support, for which I am grateful.

I owe a special debt to the American Enterprise Institute for Public Policy Research and its staff for their help and hospitality and ANERA and its President Dr. Peter Gubser for his stimulating ideas and for providing me with valuable material. I also wish to thank Michael H. Van Dusen of the staff of the United States House Foreign Affairs Committee; John Vista of Amideast; Ann Lesch of the Ford Foundation; Professor Michael Hudson of the Center for Arab Contemporary Studies at Georgetown University; Merle Thorpe, Jr., Jerome Fried, Dr. Abel Salam Majali, President, Dr. Kamel Abu Jaber, Professor of Political Science, and Professor Adnan Bakhit, Dean of Research, all at the University of Jordan; Dr. Bassam Saket, Director General of the Jordan Pension Fund; and Dr. Fuad Bseisso.

*Fawzi A. Gharaibeh*
Amman

# 1
# Introduction

The geography and history of the West Bank and Gaza Strip suggest many of the hindrances and difficulties that presently beset their respective economies. The West Bank consists of around 5,700 square kilometers and borders Israel on the north, west, and south, and the Hashemite Kingdom of Jordan on the east. It is entirely landlocked, and its trade routes must pass through neighboring territories. The terrain is hilly in the north and near Jerusalem, and below sea level in a narrow belt in the Jordan Valley. The Gaza Strip, separated from the West Bank by Israeli territory, has a common border with Israel on the north and east, and with Egypt on the south. The Sinai Peninsula isolates the Strip from Egyptian population centers in the Suez Canal zone, some 200 kilometers away. The area of the Gaza Strip is less than 400 square kilometers and constitutes a narrow area on the southernmost coast line of the Mediterranean.

Geographical factors such as these are compounded by the circumstances of history. After the creation of Israel in 1948, the West Bank and Gaza Strip were the only territories of British Mandated Palestine still in Arab hands. At the outset, then, a climate of isolation was present in the existence of these territories, both of which bordered Israel and both of which represented the remaining vestiges of Palestine. Before the 1948 partition, the West Bank and Gaza Strip were economically and politically an integral part of Palestine. They enjoyed the many benefits of a unified system of administration, transportation, communications, and services. There was a common currency. The West Bank market was a natural extension of a larger domestic market, and commercial transactions took place both within and without. Many workers from the West Bank were employed in the coastal cities and other industrial centers in northern Palestine. The situation was much the same in the Gaza Strip. The town of Gaza itself had developed into a growth pole and a port handling a good deal of trade for the southern parts of Palestine.[1] The town's trade markets were a crucial component of the marketing system of the whole of Palestine, and various types of simple industry prospered, including traditional crafts such as pottery and weaving.[2]

The events of 1948 dealt the two territories a severe blow. They were now completely cut off from the major part of Palestine, which became known as Israel. Since that time neither has been economically independent. The borders with Israel were now tightly sealed, and the West Bank and Gaza Strip faced new political and economic realities. The impact of these realities for the West Bank was extremely hard to cope with. It lost markets, sources of supply, access to sea outlets, a transportation network, a communications system, and some farm land, which was sliced away by the armistice line of 1949. In addition, incomes earned by West Bank inhabitants from employment in areas that became part of the state of Israel dried up completely with the loss of employment possibilities there.[3] An influx of refugees swamped the West Bank in great numbers and thereby magnified its economic problems, pushing them beyond immediate resolution.

The economy of the Gaza Strip immediately after 1948 was reduced to a complete shambles. Like the West Bank, the Gaza Strip was severed from the rest of Palestine, destroying in the process its domestic trade links. To add to this problem, the Strip received dislocated Palestinian refugees in numbers far exceeding those of the indigenous population. The economy was much too fragile to support the burden that this dramatic increase in the population caused. Egyptian authorities took charge of the administration of the Strip, managing its economy as a unit quite distinct from that of Egypt.

The economic survival of the West Bank called for an urgent redirection of its economic links; its only possible outlet to the world was eastward, that is, with the Kingdom of Jordan. Economic and political links were formalized in April 1950 when the West Bank and the East Bank of the Jordan (Kingdom of Jordan) were united, with Amman in the East Bank as the seat of government. From 1950 until June 5, 1967, both Banks formed a single political and economic unit, through which the West Bank was able to reorient its economic ties. Whether the economy of the West Bank ever fully became integrated into that of the East Bank, or vice versa, remains very much a matter of debate. Still at issue are the questions whether the West Bank was an economic asset or a liability; whether its economy competed with or complemented that of the East Bank; whether it could have achieved better performance and standards than those already achieved by June 1967. These questions and others have been raised, and many researchers have attempted, with various degrees of success, to answer them satisfactorily.

As a result of the 1967 war, the economies of the West Bank and Gaza Strip were once again severely disrupted. When the guns fell silent on June 10, 1967, the West Bank and the Gaza Strip were under Israeli occupation. Since then their economic performance has been dominated by the policies and decisions of the occupying power. During and immediately after the war the economy of the West Bank was thrown off balance, and economic activity was considerably curtailed. As a consequence of occupation, economic relations with Jordan, other Arab countries, and the rest of the world were severed or scaled down; income and employment generated by the Jordanian civil administration and army largely ceased to accrue to the economy;[4] much of the income derived from tourism dried up as a result of the sudden halt in the inflow of Arab tourists and the annexation of Arab Jerusalem, the West Bank's major tourist attraction, to Israel. Remittances from West Bankers working abroad were reduced to a trickle due to economic disruptions and political uncertainties. Investment in economic activity was impeded by the risks associated with the occupation status and the closure of banks. One-quarter of the population fled across the Jordan River, thereby shrinking substantially the size of the domestic market and the labor force.[5] Many of the people who emigrated eastward were from among the previous 1948 refugees and skilled workers from Palestine whose absence from the West Bank affected various sectors of the economy for the worse.[6]

The problems that faced the Gaza Strip's economy as a result of occupation were even more serious than those experienced in the West Bank. Unlike the West Bank, the Strip had limited farmland, a small skilled manpower base, no significant industry and a rudimentary infrastructure. Moreover, its economy stagnated during Egyptian rule because most economic activity was directed toward servicing the troops stationed in the area, in addition to citrus production. Hence, the standard of living in the Strip was very low compared to that of the West Bank.

The 1967 war created a situation that had profound effects on the Strip's economy. The departure of the United Nations and Egyptian armies deprived the economy of incomes derived from servicing those forces, and the dissolution of the Palestine Liberation Army eliminated thousands of employment opportunities for the area's Arab inhabitants.[7] In addition, the occupation of the Strip made visits by Egyptian tourists impossible, thereby depriving the economy of a valuable source of income. The immediate effects of these developments on the local economy were to curtail substantially economic activity, virtually paralyzing trade, crafts, and services, and to increase unemployment to unprecedented levels.[8]

The occupation of the West Bank and Gaza Strip brought their economies into close contact with the much larger, more industrially advanced Israeli economy. The economies of the two territories have been subsequently reshaped by policies and decisions made by the occupation authorities in such a way as to serve Israeli interests. Because the local population does not participate in the formulation of economic and social policies, the two territories have been entirely dependent on the Israeli economy for economic growth.

The economies of the West Bank and Gaza Strip are small, unorganized, predominantly agricultural, and operate at a low level of technology, whereas that of Israel is relatively large, industrialized and technologically sophisticated. Israel's agriculture is subsidized and its industry is well protected; by contrast, agriculture and industry in the West Bank and Gaza Strip receive no protection or subsidization at all. The labor force in the two territories, contrary to that of Israel, is unorganized and hence is easily lured into ventures serving the interests of the more developed Israeli economy.[9]

The economies of the two territories are left with no planning body capable of administering economic growth; by contrast the Israeli economy is well managed and diversified. Needless to say, under the prevailing conditions the economies of the two territories cannot successfully compete with that of Israel. Expectedly, economic links that have evolved between Israel and the occupied territories in the postwar period are of the satellite type, whereby the smaller units orbit in the gravity range of the larger and more advanced one.

These satellite economies are of special interest, however. It is the purpose of this study to analyze them in some detail as they have developed under Israeli occupation. By doing so, it is hoped to suggest the means by which the occupied territories may preserve their Arab identity to withstand, and eventually overcome, hardships created by the occupation. First, the pre-1967 situation will be described so as to form a coherent background against which more recent developments can be clearly understood. But our larger concern is to analyze the economic developments in the West Bank and Gaza Strip since 1967. This analysis will shed light on the new realities and relationships that have evolved in the two economies during this crucial period and that could serve as a basis for economic measures required to reactivate economic life in the event of a political settlement.

**Notes**

1. Brian Van Arkadie, Benefits and Burdens: A Report on the West Bank and Gaza Strip Economies Since 1967 (New York: Carnegie Endowment for International Peace, 1977), p. 29.
2. Ibid.

3. Ibid., p. 23.

4. Vivian A. Bull, The West Bank: Is It Viable? (Lexington, Mass.: Lexington Books, 1975), p. 37.

5. Ibid.

6. Van Arkadie, Benefits and Burdens, p. 32.

7. E. Kanovsky, The Economic Impact of the Six Day War (New York: Frederick A. Praeger, Inc., 1970), p. 179.

8. Ibid.

9. Van Arkadie, Benefits and Burdens, p. 44-45.

# 2
# Overall Economic Performance and Structural Change

Before June 1967 the economies of the West Bank and the Gaza Strip were completely isolated from one another, each operating under entirely different conditions. Reliable and accurate information about the two economies during this period is hard to come by because statistics are scarce. For example, data for the West Bank were not kept separately but were published as part of the statistics covering the East and West Banks of Jordan together. Fortunately, it has been possible to compile West Bank data for the pre-1967 period by sifting through what was left of records, worksheets, and other documents of the Department of Statistics of Jordan and other departments and ministries. However, this information remains fragmentary. Nonetheless, its reconstruction takes us some way in identifying the overall economic picture, the general trends as well as particular components of the economy.

To reconstitute the general economic picture of the Gaza Strip is much more difficult because official data on its economy for the pre-1967 period are entirely lacking. The Strip was administered by Egypt as a separate economic unit; its economy functioned independently. Statistics for the Strip were neither published separately nor aggregated with those of Egypt. Hence, economic analysis for this period must depend on available published studies, most of which are Israeli.

Available economic data for the West Bank go back as far as 1959, when Jordan first published its national accounts. For the Gaza Strip these accounts were estimated only for 1966.

## THE PREWAR ECONOMY

### The West Bank

To determine the gross national product (GNP) and gross domestic product (GDP) for the West Bank, an analysis of the aggregate sectoral figures for Jordan must be undertaken. Many economists have tried to estimate the total share of the West Bank in the GNP and GDP of Jordan, and their estimates invariably range between 38 and 40 percent for the former and 36 to 38 percent for the latter.[1] After the June war, the Jordan Department of Statistics attempted to determine more accurately the share of the West Bank in the various economic activities of Jordan during 1959-1965, using whatever of the original material underlying the aggregate figures was available. Accordingly, the West Bank was conservatively found to account, on average, for 38 to 39 percent (GDP) and 39 to 40 percent (GNP). These figures are very similar to those estimates arrived at by other unofficial analyses. This similarity suggests, perhaps, that the figures hold some credibility and may be accepted as accurate (see Table 2.1).

TABLE 2.1
West Bank share in gross national product of Jordan, by sector, 1959-1965.

| Sector | Range (%) | Mid-Point (%) |
| --- | --- | --- |
| Agriculture | 34-40 | 37.0 |
| Manufacturing and mining | 18-20 | 19.0 |
| Construction | 30-35 | 32.5 |
| Electricity and water | 31 | 31.0 |
| Transportation | 45-50 | 47.5 |
| Wholesale and retail trade | 40-45 | 42.5 |
| Banking and finance | 35-40 | 37.5 |
| Ownership of dwellings | 41 | 41.0 |
| Public administration and defense[a] | 30-35 | 32.5 |
| Other services | 50-60 | 55.0 |
| Net factor income from abroad | 50[b] | 50.0 |
| Total | 35-40 | 37.5 |

Source: Department of Statistics, <u>The Contribution of the West Bank in Jordan's Economy</u> (Amman, 1969), p. 2.

[a]The original estimate is between 10 and 20 percent because it excluded defense. With defense included, the range would be 30 to 39 percent.
[b]Estimated at a later date.

The West Bank's GNP at factor cost grew from JD 36.1 million in 1959 to as high as JD 64.5 million by the end of 1966, an increase of 78.7 percent (see Table 2.2). The average annual rate of growth during this period was 8.8 percent, slightly lower than the 9.1 percent for the whole of the Kingdom of Jordan and 9.3 percent for the East Bank alone. By

TABLE 2.2
Gross domestic product and gross national product (at factor cost), Jordan, East and West Banks, 1959-1966
(current prices)[a]

| | Jordan | | East Bank | | West Bank | |
|---|---|---|---|---|---|---|
| Year | JD[b] million | Increase % | JD million | Increase % | JD million | Increase % |
| GDP | | | | | | |
| 1959 | 85.3 | -- | 52.0 | -- | 33.3 | -- |
| 1960 | 89.5 | 4.9 | 54.6 | 5.0 | 34.9 | 4.7 |
| 1961 | 110.8 | 23.8 | 67.8 | 24.2 | 43.0 | 23.2 |
| 1962 | 108.6 | -2.0 | 66.4 | -2.1 | 42.2 | -1.9 |
| 1963 | 117.6 | 8.3 | 72.0 | 8.4 | 45.6 | 8.1 |
| 1964 | 135.6 | 15.3 | 83.6 | 16.1 | 52.0 | 14.0 |
| 1965 | 150.9 | 11.3 | 93.6 | 12.0 | 57.3 | 10.2 |
| 1966 | 149.6 | -0.9 | 92.7 | -1.0 | 56.9 | -0.7 |
| Average annual growth | | 8.7 | | 8.9 | | 8.2 |
| GNP | | | | | | |
| 1959 | 90.9 | -- | 54.8 | -- | 36.1 | -- |
| 1960 | 96.9 | 6.6 | 58.3 | 6.4 | 38.6 | 6.9 |
| 1961 | 117.8 | 21.6 | 71.3 | 22.3 | 46.5 | 20.5 |
| 1962 | 120.5 | 2.3 | 72.3 | 1.4 | 48.2 | 3.7 |
| 1963 | 126.2 | 4.7 | 76.3 | 5.5 | 49.9 | 3.5 |
| 1964 | 147.3 | 16.7 | 89.4 | 17.2 | 57.9 | 16.0 |
| 1965 | 163.8 | 11.2 | 100.1 | 12.0 | 63.7 | 10.0 |
| 1966 | 164.9 | 0.5 | 100.2 | 0.1 | 64.5 | 1.3 |
| Average annual growth | | 9.1 | | 9.3 | | 8.8 |

Source: Department of Statistics, <u>The National Accounts, 1959-1967</u> (Amman, n.d.), p. 13.

[a]Prices were relatively stable during this period.
[b]Exchange rate: JD 1 = $2.8

and large this growth was the product of increased output in various sectors of the economy.

In 1961 the total population of Jordan was 1.7 million, of which 806,000 were inhabitants of the West Bank.[2] The total number of Jordanians working abroad was close to 63,000.[3] By the end of 1966, the population of Jordan had increased to 2.1 million people,[4] of whom 843,000 were West Bankers (assuming an annual rate of population growth of 0.9 percent, the rate recorded between the 1952 and 1961 censuses). The number of those working abroad had reached 120,000.[5] In other words, the West Bank population comprised 49 percent of the total resident population of Jordan in 1961, and 43 percent in 1966. These figures exclude those working abroad. Hence, almost one-half of the Kingdom's resident population in 1961 accounted for 39 percent of its GNP. In 1966, when West Bankers constituted only 43 percent of the total resident population, its share in the national product had remained constant at 39 percent. It seems that the stable contribution of the West Bank to the Jordanian economy is to be largely explained by the modest rate of population increase in the area and an increase in output. Although growth in the national product more than kept pace with the population increase, a population re-adjustment seems to have taken place in the West Bank through migration to the East Bank and abroad.

In 1961 per capita GNP in the West Bank amounted to JD 58 whereas that of the East Bank stood at JD 86 (excluding Jordanians working abroad). Five years later, the gap in per capita GNP between the two Banks of the Kingdom was much narrower at JD 76 for the West Bank and JD 88 for the East Bank. The inflow of people into the East Bank effectively absorbed the increase in its GNP, thus keeping the per capita figure virtually constant.

Domestic output in the West Bank jumped from JD 33.3 million in 1959 to JD 56.9 million in 1966, an increase of 59 percent. During this period, the 8.2 percent average annual growth rate in GDP in the West Bank was slightly less than the 8.7 percent for the whole of the country or the 8.9 percent for the East Bank. The lower rate achieved in the West Bank would lend some support to the belief that its overall economic performance as measured by domestically produced output lagged behind that of the East Bank, although only by a small portion.

Per capita output in the West Bank was calculated at JD 53 in 1961, and JD 67 in 1966, whereas that of the East Bank remained at JD 82 in each of the two years. The increase of 26 percent in per capita product of the West Bank was a manifestation of an expansion of economic activity that far surpassed population growth. During this same period, all economic growth in the East Bank was absorbed by the population increase. The 1961 level was maintained in the East Bank, even though our figures do not take into consideration changes in price levels, which were in fact relatively stable at this time.

Of special interest is the fact that the majority of Jordanians working abroad came from the West Bank. The 1961 population census showed that 50,000 (80 percent) of the total of 63,000 Jordanians working abroad were West Bankers.[6] These workers sent remittances to their families in the area, and hence it might be reasonable to assume that personal income was higher than the national income figures suggest.[7] This latter point explains the fact that the average annual rate of growth in GNP of the West Bank, which included unilateral transfers mainly in the form of remittances, was higher than that of the GDP, which did not include this item in its calculations.

## Structure of the West Bank Economy

The contribution of the various sectors of the economy to the GDP of the West Bank during the 1959-1966 period reveals that the service sectors were predominant and commanded a share ranging between 68 and 77 percent of GDP. Conversely, the producing sectors of the economy, that is, agriculture, manufacturing, and construction, occupied a less prominent position, and contributed less than one-third of the GDP. However, the average annual rate of growth in the service sectors (7.2 percent) was considerably less than that of the producing sectors (12.4 percent). This trend, had it been allowed to continue, could have lessened the dependence of the West Bank on services and augmented the production base of the economy. By contrast, the share of the service sectors in the East Bank in 1965 and 1966 was a consistent 57 and 59 percent of the GDP, respectively.

The relative importance of the service sectors in the West Bank during the 1959-1966 period could partly be explained by fluctuations in agricultural output due to erratic weather conditions, a weak industrial base, and an abundance of religious and tourist sites (see Table 2.3). In 1966, the West Bank accounted for 53 percent of the total number of manufacturing and mining establishments in Jordan, although almost all were of the small-scale, consumer-goods type; the West Bank accounted for 49 and 46 percent of trade and service enterprises, respectively.[8] The West Bank enjoyed a comparative advantage in tourism, accounting for 80 to 90 percent of Jordan's tourism income.[9]

The agricultural sector of the West Bank accounted for about one-third to two-fifths of agricultural output in Jordan. Of course, the proportion depended upon weather conditions. Due to the limited area of irrigated agriculture in

TABLE 2.3
Gross national product, the West Bank, 1959-1966, and the East Bank, 1965 and 1966 (current prices)

| | West Bank | | | | | | | | | | | | | | | | East Bank | | | |
|---|---|---|---|---|---|---|---|---|---|---|---|---|---|---|---|---|---|---|---|---|
| | 1959 | | 1960 | | 1961 | | 1962 | | 1963 | | 1964 | | 1965 | | 1966 | | 1965 | | 1966 | |
| Sector | JD | %[a] | JD | % | JD | % | JD | % | JD | % | JD | % | JD | % | JD | % | JD | % | JD | % |
| Agriculture | 5.6 | 16.8 | 4.5 | 15.5 | 9.4 | 21.9 | 7.7 | 18.3 | 8.2 | 18.0 | 12.6 | 24.2 | 12.6 | 22.0 | 10.2 | 17.9 | 21.5 | 23.0 | 17.4 | 18.8 |
| Manufacturing & mining | 1.2 | 3.6 | 1.3 | 3.7 | 1.7 | 3.9 | 1.5 | 3.5 | 2.0 | 4.4 | 2.4 | 4.6 | 3.1 | 5.4 | 3.3 | 5.8 | 13.1 | 14.0 | 14.0 | 15.1 |
| Construction | 1.5 | 4.5 | 1.5 | 4.3 | 1.5 | 3.5 | 2.0 | 4.7 | 2.0 | 4.4 | 1.8 | 3.5 | 2.6 | 4.5 | 3.0 | 5.3 | 5.3 | 5.7 | 6.3 | 6.8 |
| Electricity and water | 0.2 | 0.6 | 0.2 | 0.6 | 0.2 | 0.5 | 0.2 | 0.5 | 0.3 | 0.7 | 0.3 | 0.6 | 0.5 | 0.9 | 0.6 | 1.1 | 1.2 | 1.3 | 1.4 | 1.5 |
| Transportation | 5.1 | 15.3 | 5.3 | 15.2 | 6.0 | 13.9 | 5.9 | 14.0 | 6.1 | 13.4 | 5.7 | 11.0 | 6.0 | 10.5 | 6.8 | 11.9 | 6.6 | 7.1 | 7.6 | 8.2 |
| Wholesale & retail trade | 7.7 | 23.1 | 8.3 | 23.8 | 1.3 | 23.9 | 10.0 | 23.7 | 11.2 | 24.6 | 11.9 | 22.9 | 13.3 | 23.2 | 12.3 | 21.6 | 18.1 | 19.3 | 16.6 | 17.9 |
| Banking & finance | 0.3 | 0.9 | 0.3 | 0.9 | 0.5 | 1.2 | 0.6 | 1.4 | 0.5 | 1.1 | 0.6 | 1.1 | 0.8 | 1.4 | 1.1 | 1.9 | 1.3 | 1.4 | 1.7 | 1.8 |
| Ownership of dwellings | 2.6 | 7.8 | 2.9 | 8.3 | 3.3 | 7.7 | 3.5 | 8.3 | 3.9 | 8.5 | 4.1 | 7.9 | 4.4 | 7.7 | 4.6 | 8.1 | 6.3 | 6.7 | 6.6 | 7.1 |
| Public administration and defense | 4.8 | 14.4 | 5.1 | 14.6 | 5.4 | 12.6 | 5.6 | 13.3 | 5.7 | 12.5 | 6.4 | 12.3 | 7.0 | 12.2 | 7.2 | 12.7 | 14.4 | 15.4 | 14.8 | 16.0 |
| Other services | 4.3 | 12.9 | 4.6 | 13.2 | 4.7 | 10.9 | 5.2 | 12.3 | 5.7 | 12.5 | 6.2 | 11.9 | 7.0 | 12.2 | 7.8 | 13.7 | 5.8 | 6.2 | 6.3 | 6.8 |
| GDP at factor cost | 33.3 | 100.0 | 34.9 | 100.0 | 43.0 | 100.0 | 42.2 | 100.0 | 45.6 | 100.0 | 52.0 | 100.0 | 57.3 | 100.0 | 56.9 | 100.0 | 93.6 | 100.0 | 92.7 | 100.0 |
| Net factor income from abroad | 2.8 | | 3.7 | | 3.5 | | 6.0 | | 4.3 | | 5.9 | | 6.4 | | 7.6 | | 6.5 | | 7.5 | |
| GNP at factor cost | 36.1 | | 38.6 | | 46.5 | | 48.2 | | 49.9 | | 57.9 | | 63.7 | | 64.5 | | 100.1 | | 100.2 | |
| East Bank's GNP | 54.8 | | 58.3 | | 71.3 | | 72.3 | | 76.3 | | 89.4 | | 100.1 | | 100.2 | | -- | | -- | |
| Jordan's GNP | 90.9 | | 96.9 | | 117.8 | | 120.5 | | 126.2 | | 147.3 | | 163.8 | | 164.7 | | -- | | -- | |
| West Bank percentage | -- | 40 | -- | 40 | -- | 39 | -- | 40 | -- | 40 | -- | 39 | -- | 39 | -- | 39 | -- | | -- | |

Source: Department of Statistics, National Accounts, p. 10; Central Bank of Jordan, Monthly Statistical Bulletin (Amman), various issues.

[a]Percentages may not add up to 100 due to rounding.

Note: Values are derived from aggregates.

the West Bank, production fluctuated widely during the 1959-1966 period, in response to annual precipitation. Hence, the relative importance of agriculture in the GDP of the territory ranged between 15.5 percent in a bad crop year (1960), to almost one-fourth in a good crop year; agriculture's share in GDP of the East Bank was 23.0 percent in 1965 and 18.8 percent in 1966. Despite fluctuations in this sector's output, it grew at an annual rate of 13.4 percent, probably reflecting improvements in farming methods.

The industrial sector in the West Bank produced about 20 percent of Jordan's industrial production during the 1959-1966 period. According to the records of the Department of Statistics, West Bank industry contributed 28 percent (JD 4.5 million out of JD 16.2 million) of Jordan's industrial output. Its relative importance ranged between 3.5 and 5.8 percent of the GDP of the area during this period. The smallness of this sector in both absolute and relative terms clearly reflects the weakness of the industrial base in the West Bank, despite the fact that it contained the majority of the industrial establishments in Jordan in 1965 and 1966. Of course, many were small and inefficient units.[10] Because industrial output of the West Bank during the period under study was estimated on the basis of the period average, it is quite possible that this output was grossly underestimated in the later years of the period. If this is so, industrial output in the East Bank would have been overestimated. Consequently, the relative importance of the industrial sector in the East Bank was at an unbelievably high level of 14.0 percent and 15.1 percent in 1965 and 1966, respectively. However, the industrial sector in the West Bank was the fastest growing in the economy, rising by an average of 16.6 percent per annum.

The construction sector in the West Bank stagnated in absolute terms during 1959-1961 and 1962-1963, decreased in 1964 and finally picked up in 1965 and 1966. Its relative importance in the GDP fluctuated during the whole period, reaching a peak of 5.3 percent in 1966, compared with 6.8 percent for the East Bank in the same year. However, much of the gain in this sector occurred in the last two years of the period, showing an average growth rate of 11.9 percent annually.

Among the service sectors in the West Bank, trade (both wholesale and retail) figured predominantly in absolute and relative terms. Its relative importance averaged 23.4 percent, competing with and almost always surpassing agriculture as the greatest contributor to the GDP. Other major services in terms of relative importance were transportation (13.2 percent), public administration and defense (13.1 percent), other services (12.5 percent), and ownership of dwellings (8.0 percent). By contrast, the relative importance of trade in the East Bank in 1966 was 17.9 percent, transportation (8.2

percent), public administration and defense (16.0 percent), other services (6.8 percent), and ownership of dwellings (7.1 percent). With the exception of public administration and defense, all of these averages are less than those of the West Bank. The seat of government and military headquarters are located in the East Bank and this explains the exaggerated importance of the public administration and defense figure. Generally, these statistics reflect the fact that the service sectors as a whole are much smaller in the East Bank than in the West Bank.

The comparison between the East and West Banks of Jordan obviously shows an uneven division of domestic production and economic activity, with the balance tilted toward the East Bank. Several factors are thought to be responsible for this situation:

1. The East Bank started at a very low economic base at the time when the two Banks were united in 1950. Amman, in the East Bank, as the seat of government and center of political activity, required a large dose of investment in public buildings and facilities to cope with the expanded demand created by the civil service.[11]
2. The influx of a large number of refugees into the East Bank in 1948 and immediately after called for a parallel expansion in public services and made a host of private services a lucrative business to initiate and develop.[12]
3. Several business enterprises, including banks, whose base of operations was in Jerusalem in the West Bank, chose to relocate their headquarters in Amman in the East Bank.[13]
4. The rapidly growing Jordanian Army depended, in the early stages of its formation, on recruits from the East Bank and was based there. Consequently, a good portion of Army wages and salaries, equipment, and infrastructure were paid and located in the East Bank.[14]
5. With the loss of the Palestinian ports on the Mediterranean in 1948, both the East and West Banks had to reorient their trading routes. This called for the development of the port of Aqaba on the Red Sea together with a road network connecting it to population centers. Similarly, the road linking the East Bank with Syria had to be repaired and maintained to move imports and exports (phosphate) to and from Syrian and Lebanese ports. Transport equipment had to be acquired and related services had to be developed, buttressing in the process the transportation sector in the East Bank.[15]
6. The East Bank was better endowed with readily exploitable mineral and water resources. Investment was required to extract phosphate deposits near and south of Amman, and to utilize the Yarmouk water in expanding irrigation in the eastern part of the Jordan Valley.

For these reasons it could be said that much of the development was concentrated on the East Bank. In the words of one commentator, this is attributable to the "area's greater economic potential in such sectors as mining, hydroelectric power and transportation."[16]

However, although the conclusion that economic activity was heavily concentrated in the East Bank is undoubtedly true, it is not entirely so. It can be safely said that the Amman region, the capital, has almost exclusively monopolized economic activity in Jordan, possibly to the detriment of other areas in the East as well as on the West Bank. The location of economic activity in Amman and its vicinity was the culmination of a process that was spontaneously set into motion in the 1950s and continued through the 1960s; the trend was still unabated in the 1970s. Amman has been the center of political power and the civil service, naturally developing into a growth pole that increasingly attracted entrepreneurs who preferred to remain close to public authority. Consequently, trade, banking and finance, and industry, especially large institutions, were concentrated in the Amman region. Even as late as 1975, the Amman region was the home of the great majority of East Bank establishments employing five persons or more in various economic sectors, e.g., 97 percent of manufacturing, 80 percent of electricity, 96 percent of construction, 94 percent of transport, 100 percent of financial institutions (main offices) and 94 percent of trade establishments.[17] It is not surprising then that the Amman region accounted for 95 percent of the nonagricultural labor force employed in enterprises engaging five persons or more in the East Bank in 1975.[18]

The city of Amman itself grew very rapidly from a small town of 20,000 people in 1940[19] to as many as 108,000 in 1952.[20] This more than four-fold increase in the population of Amman is mainly attributable to the influx of Palestinian refugees in 1948, and then to migration from rural areas in the East Bank. By the time of the first census in 1961, the population of Amman had already grown to 246,000,[21] an increase of 12.8 percent per annum between 1952 and 1961. The city continued to grow very rapidly, and by the end of 1966 its population was estimated at around 350,000 people,[22] an increase of 42 percent over the 1961 figure. Much of Amman's population growth was at the expense of other areas in the Kingdom, east and west of the Jordan River.

The private sector was, to a large extent, responsible for the concentration of economic weight in Amman, and the absence of government concern about such a concentration is partly to blame. The entrepreneurs of Jordan, many of whom were actually West Bankers, had almost always initiated business enterprises and had chosen to locate in or around Amman. Even in those enterprises in which the government held some equity, private investors took the lead in their conception, organization, and choice of location.

**The Gaza Strip**

In some respects, the economic situation of the Gaza Strip before the 1967 war was substantially different from that of the West Bank. To begin, the Strip's economy was much smaller; in 1966 its GNP stood at only about 20 percent the size of that of the West Bank. The exact figure for the Strip's GNP at this time was estimated at JD 12.6 million, of which a considerable amount (JD 3.0 million, or 24 percent) came from unilateral transfers. These transfers derived from funds provided by UNRWA and other charitable organizations (JD 2.4 million) and remittances from residents working abroad (JD 0.6 million).[23] Per capita national product was JD 35 in 1966, or 46 percent of that of the West Bank. There is some disagreement, however, about the GNP figure. Kanovsky came up with an estimate of JD 18.4 million for the same year of 1966, of which JD 4.1 million (22 percent) was derived from net factor income from abroad.[24] According to Kanovsky's estimate, per capita product for the Strip reached JD 52. Table 2.4 exhibits the two alternative appraisals of the GNP and GDP of the Gaza Strip in 1966.

Domestic output in the Strip totaled JD 9.6 million in 1966 (or JD 14.3 million), or a per capita of barely JD 27 (or alternatively JD 40). The producing sectors of the economy contributed about 45 percent (or 44 percent) of total output, and services accounted for the rest. Agriculture was the largest single sector in the economy, accounting for over one-third of production; government services provided one-fourth (or 22.4 percent); and trade, commerce, and personal services together produced 27.1 percent. The smaller sectors of the economy were construction, 6.2 percent (or 4.9 percent); industry, 4.2 percent (or 4.9 percent); and transportation, 3.1 percent.

On the eve of the 1967 war, the economy of the Gaza Strip was characterized by the preponderance of services; government services and trade and commerce were the dominant activities. Agriculture, at a commanding level of 34 percent of total production, was by and large centered around the citrus fruits. On the other hand, industry was of minor importance; all industrial enterprises, save one or two, were small, outmoded, and of the workshop type, engaging in handicrafts, food processing, and a few other similar enterprises.[25] Construction and public works were on a modest scale and at a level much below the needs of the highly urbanized population of the Strip.

TABLE 2.4
Gross national product, the Gaza Strip, 1966

| | 1 | | 2 | |
|---|---|---|---|---|
| Sector | JD million | % | JD million | %[a] |
| Agriculture | 3.3 | 34.4 | 4.9 | 34.3 |
| Industry | 0.4 | 4.2 | 0.7 | 4.9 |
| Construction | 0.6 | 6.2 | 0.7 | 4.9 |
| Public services | 2.4 | 25.0 | 3.2 | 22.4 |
| Transport | 0.3 | 3.1 | 4.8 | 33.6 |
| Trade, commerce, and other services | 2.6 | 27.1 | | |
| GDP | 9.6 | 100.0 | 14.3 | 100.0 |
| Net factor income from abroad | 3.0 | | 4.1 | |
| GNP | 12.6 | | 18.4 | |

Sources: (1) Ben Shahar et al., Economic Structure and Development Prospects of the West Bank and Gaza Strip (Santa Monica: The Rand Corporation, 1971), p. 29; (2) E. Kanovsky, The Economic Impact, p. 175.

[a]Percentages do not add to 100 due to rounding.

## THE POST-1967 ECONOMY

After the 1967 Israeli occupation of the West Bank and Gaza Strip, previous economic relations with adjoining regions were either completely severed or greatly weakened. Postwar relationships with the East Bank were reshaped by Israeli policies and decisions toward the West Bank. The West Bank was no longer administratively part of the Kingdom of Jordan; the Gaza Strip was completely isolated from Egypt and administered by Israeli military government. As might be expected, both territories have gradually developed new economic links with Israel through trade, labor, and other kinds of economic relationships.

The Israeli occupation of the West Bank and the Gaza Strip had adverse effects on most economic activities of the two territories. It took several years for economic activity to pick up and regain previous levels of performance. In particular, tourism in both territories suffered more than any other sector and has never reached prewar levels. Income from tourism in the whole of Jordan peaked at an unprecedented level of JD 12 million in 1966. The West Bank in general, and

Arab Jerusalem in particular, contained most of the developed tourist sites in Jordan and hence was the center of the tourist industry in prewar Jordan. Official Jordanian estimates credited the West Bank with more than four-fifths of the country's prewar tourism income. Similarly, the Gaza Strip derived a considerable income from Egyptian tourists and soldiers and U.N. forces. The occupation of the two territories and the Israeli annexation of Arab Jerusalem in the West Bank stopped the flow of Arab tourists completely, and diverted much of the money spent by West Europeans, Americans, and others who visit religious sites in Jerusalem to Israeli tourist concerns.

Remittances sent by Jordanians working abroad, mainly in the Arab oil-producing countries, reached JD 10.6 million in the year preceding the June war. Of the 63,000 Jordanians who were working outside the country in 1961, 80 percent were residents of the West Bank.[26] Their number had almost doubled by 1966. West Bankers working abroad sent their families about JD 7 million in remittances in 1966, contributing more than one-tenth of the value of the GNP in the area. However, many of these transfers dried up immediately after the war and were later resumed at a much slower rate. This was due to the emigration to the East Bank of many families who had relatives working abroad as well as to the political uncertainties associated with the occupational status of the area. Ironically, wages earned by Arab inhabitants working inside Israel have become a dominant factor in the economy of the territories in the postwar period.

**Overall Economic Performance**

Real gross national product of each of the two territories increased substantially during the 1968-1982 period. Average growth in GNP has been 10.7 percent per annum for the West Bank and 9.7 percent annually for the Gaza Strip during the same period. Both economies attained higher annual rates of growth during the first five years immediately after occupation, but those rates slowed down considerably and fluctuated in the later part of the period (see Table 2.5). For instance, GNP of each of the territories rose at an average rate of more than 20 percent in 1968 through 1972, then decreased to a low of 7 and 5 percent for the West Bank and the Gaza Strip, respectively, during the 1973-1982 period. Apparently, some of the growth that occurred in the earlier period of occupation was nothing more than a recovery from the disruptions caused by the war to the prewar level of economic activity.[27] On the other hand, the modest growth rate witnessed in the second part of this period appears to have leveled off and it is, probably, more representative of the

TABLE 2.5
Growth in gross national product at market price, the West Bank and the Gaza Strip, 1968-1982 (in 1968 prices; IL million)

| Year | West Bank | Increase % | Gaza Strip | Increase % |
|---|---|---|---|---|
| 1968 | 344 | -- | 131 | -- |
| 1969 | 423 | 23.0 | 145 | 10.7 |
| 1970 | 466 | 10.2 | 187 | 29.0 |
| 1971 | 573 | 23.0 | 225 | 20.3 |
| 1972 | 717 | 25.1 | 274 | 21.8 |
| 1973 | 670 | -6.6 | 312 | 13.9 |
| 1974 | 893 | 33.3 | 317 | 1.6 |
| 1975 | 883 | -1.1 | 340 | 7.3 |
| 1976 | 1,012 | 14.6 | 382 | 12.4 |
| 1977 | 998 | -1.4 | 397 | 3.9 |
| 1978 | 1,150 | 15.2 | 413 | 4.0 |
| 1979 | 1,109 | -3.7 | 456 | 10.4 |
| 1980[a] | 1,310 | 18.1 | 445 | -2.4 |
| 1981 | 1,197 | -8.6 | 461 | 3.6 |
| 1982 | 1,302 | 8.8 | 459 | -0.4 |
| Average annual growth (1968-1982) | | 10.7 | | 9.7 |

Source: Central Bureau of Statistics, Statistical Abstract of Israel (various issues).

[a]The sheqel was substituted for the pound, beginning in 1980 at a rate of one sheqel for 10 pounds.

normal course of the economy.

Much of the overall growth in GNP, however, has been directly attributed to "net factor payments from abroad," a term used to describe unilateral transfers into the territories (see Table 2.6). By and large, these have been wages earned by the territories' laborers working inside Israel and remittances from Palestinians working in other countries. Net factor payments from abroad comprised around 12 and 24 percent of the GNP of the West Bank and Gaza Strip, respectively, in 1966. However, remittances constituted only 5 percent of the Strip's GNP, the rest being transfers from UNRWA.[28] Net factor payments from abroad, especially wages earned from employment in Israel, have had profound effects on the structure of the economies of the two territories in the postwar

TABLE 2.6
Contribution of earnings from abroad to gross national product (GNP), the West Bank and the Gaza Strip, 1968-1982 (IL million)

| | West Bank | | | Gaza Strip | | | Total | | |
|---|---|---|---|---|---|---|---|---|---|
| Year | GNP[a] | Net Factor Payments from Abroad | Percentage of GNP | GNP[a] | Net Factor Payments from Abroad | Percentage of GNP | GNP[a] | Net Factor Payments from Abroad | Percentage of GNP |
| 1968 | 325 | 11 | 3.4 | 128 | 0 | -- | 453 | 11 | 2.4 |
| 1969 | 420 | 42 | 10.0 | 144 | 7 | 4.9 | 564 | 49 | 8.7 |
| 1970 | 482 | 80 | 16.6 | 207 | 27 | 13.0 | 689 | 107 | 15.5 |
| 1971 | 724 | 164 | 22.7 | 288 | 42 | 14.6 | 1,012 | 206 | 20.4 |
| 1972 | 1,118 | 284 | 25.4 | 450 | 124 | 27.6 | 1,568 | 408 | 26.0 |
| 1973 | 1,340 | 358 | 26.7 | 688 | 220 | 32.0 | 2,028 | 578 | 28.5 |
| 1974 | 2,257 | 494 | 21.9 | 975 | 283 | 29.0 | 3,232 | 777 | 24.0 |
| 1975 | 3,269 | 860 | 26.3 | 1,368 | 433 | 29.5 | 4,737 | 1,293 | 27.3 |
| 1976 | 4,687 | 1,093 | 23.3 | 2,167 | 625 | 28.8 | 6,854 | 1,718 | 25.1 |
| 1977 | 6,279 | 1,536 | 24.5 | 3,102 | 846 | 27.3 | 9,381 | 2,382 | 25.4 |
| 1978 | 11,234 | 2,544 | 22.6 | 4,947 | 1,546 | 31.3 | 16,181 | 4,090 | 25.3 |
| 1979 | 19,267 | 5,007 | 26.0 | 9,786 | 3,392 | 34.7 | 29,053 | 8,399 | 28.9 |
| 1980 | 49,740 | 11,049 | 22.2 | 22,222 | 7,807 | 35.1 | 71,962 | 18,856 | 26.2 |
| 1981 | 99,796 | 26,224 | 26.3 | 53,179 | 20,233 | 38.0 | 152,975 | 46,457 | 30.4 |
| 1982 | 233,043 | 65,632 | 28.2 | 116,964 | 47,784 | 40.9 | 350,007 | 113,416 | 32.4 |
| Growth 1968-1982 | 232,718 | 65,622 | 28.2 | 116,836 | 47,784 | 40.9 | 349,554 | 113,405 | 32.4 |

Source: Central Bureau of Statistics, Statistical Abstract of Israel (various issues).

[a]Factor cost.

period. For the West Bank this factor constituted a mere 3.4 percent of the GNP in 1968, but increased at an accelerated rate and peaked at 26.7 percent in 1973. It then decreased, fluctuated, and leveled off at over one-quarter (28 percent) in 1982. The contribution of this component to the GNP of the Gaza Strip is much more considerable; starting at about 5 percent in 1969, it jumped to as high as 41 percent in 1982. In both territories, the indirect effect of this outside income on the growth of the local economies need not be overemphasized. Income earned abroad expanded demand for products of the various sectors of the economies, adding in the process a few percentage points to growth rates of the GNP. In recent years, however, the share of income from employment of West Bankers in the Israeli economy appears to have stagnated.

Real per capita national product rose at an average rate of 13 percent in the West Bank and 11 percent in the Gaza Strip during the 1968-1982 period. But much of this growth has been the product of an exogenous factor, i.e., wages earned in Israel, and does not accurately portray the actual performance of these economies.

Real gross domestic product has grown at 9 and less than 6 percent per annum in the West Bank and in the Gaza Strip, respectively, during 1969-1982 (see Table 2.7). This growth has been attributed to expansion in some sectors of the economy, partly in response to increased demand for locally produced goods and services created by incomes earned abroad, in Israel and other countries.[29]

The structure of the economy of the two territories has changed to some extent during the 1968-1982 period and the change has been most conspicuous in the Gaza Strip (see Table 2.8). Service sectors in both areas have declined in relative importance, from a high of 52 and 66 percent of GDP of the West Bank and the Gaza Strip, respectively, in 1968 to an average of over two-fifths in each territory in the past five years. This decrease was probably accentuated by the decline in tourism and related services and the absence of a central government and defense establishment.

Agriculture accounted for around one-third of the GDP of the West Bank, but declined to an average of over one-fifth in the Strip. However, the relative share of this sector in the economy of each territory has dropped from the high levels attained in the late 1960s and early 1970s, although agricultural production fluctuated throughout the period. Agricultural output in the West Bank has exhibited a wider variation than that of the Strip due to its dependence on unstable rainfall.

Despite this, agriculture remained the most important single branch in the economy of the West Bank and became second to construction in the Gaza Strip.

Industry has become the smallest sector in the economy of

TABLE 2.7
Gross domestic product, the West Bank and the Gaza Strip, 1968-1982 (in 1968 prices; IL Million)

| | West Bank | | Gaza Strip | |
|---|---|---|---|---|
| Year | Amount | Increase (%) | Amount | Increase (%) |
| 1968 | 333 | -- | 131 | -- |
| 1969 | 377 | 13.2 | 138 | 5.0 |
| 1970 | 411 | 9.0 | 167 | 21.0 |
| 1971 | 471 | 14.6 | 189 | 13.2 |
| 1972 | 578 | 22.7 | 195 | 3.2 |
| 1973 | 527 | -8.8 | 206 | 5.6 |
| 1974 | 688 | 30.6 | 215 | 4.4 |
| 1975 | 656 | -4.7 | 229 | 6.5 |
| 1976 | 771 | 17.5 | 256 | 11.8 |
| 1977 | 747 | -3.1 | 267 | 4.3 |
| 1978 | 878 | 17.5 | 265 | -0.7 |
| 1979 | 814 | -7.3 | 295 | 11.3 |
| 1980 | 1021 | 25.4 | 280 | -5.1 |
| 1981 | 912 | -10.7 | 283 | 1.1 |
| 1982 | 988 | 8.3 | 278 | -1.8 |
| Average annual growth (1968-1982) | | 8.9 | | 5.7 |

Source: Central Bureau of Statistics, Statistical Abstract of Israel (various issues).

the West Bank (see Table 2.9). Its relative contribution dropped from 8.3 percent of the GDP in 1968 to around 7.0 percent in 1982, whereas it grew from 3.1 percent of the GDP of the Gaza Strip in 1968 to an average of 10.0 percent in the last five years. In fact, industrial output has remained the least contributor to domestic product in the territories as a result of several factors, such as the use of traditional methods of production, inefficiencies and lack of appropriate investment in industrial plant.[30]

Construction has expanded fairly rapidly in the two territories during the 1968-1982 period. The share of construction in GDP was 3.5 and 3.1 percent in the West Bank and the Gaza Strip, respectively, in 1968; by 1982 this share had jumped to 15 and 23 percent, respectively. The extraordinary improvement in the relative position of this sector in the economy of the territories came about as a result of Arab inhabitants' increasing willingness to invest in residential building. Investment in private residential construction, and the lack of it in the other productive sectors, increased its relative importance in the economy. The people of the two territories have shown a great desire to erect their own dwellings. They are culturally predisposed to this type of activity and they also wish to establish their right to the land against Israeli takeover. Lack of alternative investment opportunities may also have played a part in the channelling of resources into building.

Public services declined in terms of relative importance in the West Bank during the 1968-1982 period from 17.8 percent of GDP in 1968 to an average of 12.2 since 1978; in the Gaza Strip the proportion remained at around one-fifth throughout the period. The share of this component in the GDP is larger in the Strip than in the West Bank probably because of a much smaller private services sector in the first. On the other hand, about one-third of the GDP in the West Bank was contributed by trade and commerce, transportation, and other services, compared with an average of one-fourth in the Gaza Strip. Altogether, the services component, public and private, generally has lost its prominent position in the two territories by contrast to the producing sectors, i.e., agriculture, industry, and construction.

Arab Jerusalem was hardest hit by occupation and its subsequent annexation by Israel in 1967. Before the war, the city "served as a market center of the West Bank, and the commercial, communication and transportation links of the West Bank focused on the city."[31] It was indeed the economic capital of the West Bank, with its holy sites attracting hundreds of thousands of Arab and foreign visitors annually, giving rise to prosperous tourist-related industries. The annexation of Arab Jerusalem has exposed its economy to several adverse effects. First, Israeli taxes applied to the Arab inhabitants and business concerns in the city, and this increased their tax burden substantially. Second, tourism and related business activities have considerably declined as a result of the interruption of the flow of Arab tourists and competition from Israeli establishments. Third, other economic activities as well have suffered from Israeli competition and at the same time lacked the protection and privileges enjoyed by Israeli concerns. Fourth, white-collar workers suffered from unemployment[32] due to the extremely limited range of job opportunities open to them in the Israeli economy and administration. Finally, wages and prices reached Israeli levels, creating additional problems for Arab establishments and inhabitants, weakening in the process their competitiveness and eroding their purchasing power.

In general, the period 1948-1982 has seen enormous and unprecedented economic disruptions and distortions in the West Bank and Gaza Strip. The two profound changes were, of course, the creation of Israel in 1948 and the June war of

TABLE 2.8
Gross domestic product at factor price, by economic branch, the West Bank, 1968-1982
(current prices; IL million)

| Sector / Year | Agri- culture | % | Industry | % | Construction | % | Public Services | % | Other Services | % | GDP (Factor Price) |
|---|---|---|---|---|---|---|---|---|---|---|---|
| 1968 | 115 | 36.6 | 26 | 8.3 | 11 | 3.5 | 56 | 17.8 | 106 | 33.8 | 314 |
| 1969 | 152 | 40.2 | 33 | 8.7 | 20 | 5.3 | 60 | 15.9 | 113 | 29.9 | 378 |
| 1970 | 141 | 35.1 | 38 | 9.5 | 25 | 6.2 | 67 | 16.7 | 139 | 34.6 | 402 |
| 1971 | 203 | 36.3 | 54 | 9.6 | 38 | 6.8 | 84 | 15.0 | 181 | 32.3 | 560 |
| 1972 | 307 | 36.8 | 68 | 8.2 | 71 | 8.5 | 109 | 13.1 | 279 | 33.5 | 834 |
| 1973 | 340 | 34.6 | 82 | 8.4 | 102 | 10.4 | 139 | 14.2 | 319 | 32.5 | 982 |
| 1974 | 796 | 45.2 | 144 | 8.2 | 201 | 11.4 | 218 | 12.4 | 404 | 22.9 | 1,763 |
| 1975 | 714 | 29.6 | 197 | 8.2 | 371 | 15.4 | 311 | 12.9 | 816 | 33.9 | 2,409 |
| 1976 | 1,243 | 34.2 | 238 | 6.5 | 511 | 14.1 | 397 | 10.9 | 1,246 | 34.3 | 3,635 |
| 1977 | 1,381 | 29.1 | 297 | 6.3 | 735 | 15.5 | 576 | 12.1 | 1,760 | 37.1 | 4,749 |
| 1978 | 3,094 | 35.6 | 615 | 7.1 | 1,221 | 14.0 | 1,004 | 11.6 | 2,756 | 31.7 | 8,690 |
| 1979 | 4,410 | 30.9 | 983 | 6.9 | 2,406 | 16.9 | 1,679 | 11.8 | 4,782 | 33.5 | 14,260 |
| 1980 | 14,896 | 38.5 | 2,618 | 6.7 | 5,284 | 13.7 | 4,071 | 10.5 | 11,822 | 30.6 | 38,691 |
| 1981 | 24,917 | 33.9 | 4,895 | 6.7 | 11,099 | 15.0 | 10,140 | 13.8 | 22,521 | 30.6 | 73,572 |
| 1982 | 52,618 | 31.4 | 11,318 | 6.8 | 23,252 | 13.9 | 22,306 | 13.3 | 57,919 | 34.6 | 167,411 |

Source: Central Bureau of Statistics, Administered Territories Statistics Quarterly (Jerusalem, various issues); later changed to Judea, Samaria and Gaza Strip Statistics.

TABLE 2.9
Gross domestic product at factor price, by economic branch, the Gaza Strip, 1968-1982
(current prices; IL million)

| Sector / Year | Agri-culture | % | Industry | % | Construction | % | Public Services | % | Other Services | % | GDP (Factor Price) |
|---|---|---|---|---|---|---|---|---|---|---|---|
| 1968 | 36 | 28.1 | 4 | 3.1 | 4 | 3.1 | 26 | 20.3 | 58 | 45.3 | 128 |
| 1969 | 39 | 26.5 | 6 | 4.1 | 9 | 6.1 | 30 | 20.4 | 63 | 42.9 | 147 |
| 1970 | 51 | 28.3 | 11 | 6.1 | 12 | 6.7 | 37 | 20.6 | 69 | 38.3 | 180 |
| 1971 | 73 | 29.3 | 14 | 5.7 | 16 | 6.5 | 49 | 19.9 | 94 | 38.2 | 246 |
| 1972 | 106 | 32.5 | 21 | 6.4 | 34 | 10.4 | 66 | 20.2 | 99 | 30.4 | 326 |
| 1973 | 135 | 28.8 | 30 | 6.4 | 66 | 14.1 | 94 | 20.1 | 143 | 30.6 | 468 |
| 1974 | 176 | 25.4 | 52 | 7.5 | 107 | 15.5 | 149 | 21.5 | 208 | 30.1 | 692 |
| 1975 | 304 | 29.4 | 98 | 9.5 | 184 | 17.8 | 225 | 21.7 | 224 | 21.6 | 1,035 |
| 1976 | 485 | 31.2 | 159 | 10.2 | 314 | 20.2 | 286 | 18.4 | 311 | 20.0 | 1,555 |
| 1977 | 685 | 30.0 | 237 | 10.4 | 381 | 16.7 | 393 | 17.2 | 591 | 25.7 | 2,287 |
| 1978 | 997 | 29.4 | 397 | 11.7 | 733 | 21.6 | 652 | 19.2 | 622 | 18.3 | 3,401 |
| 1979 | 1,500 | 23.5 | 717 | 11.2 | 1,603 | 25.1 | 1,051 | 16.4 | 1,523 | 23.8 | 6,394 |
| 1980 | 2,731 | 18.9 | 1,319 | 9.2 | 3,100 | 21.5 | 2,827 | 19.6 | 4,438 | 30.8 | 14,415 |
| 1981 | 6,899 | 20.9 | 2,670 | 8.1 | 7,873 | 23.9 | 7,266 | 22.1 | 8,238 | 25.0 | 32,946 |
| 1982 | 11,528 | 16.7 | 6,018 | 8.7 | 15,984 | 23.1 | 15,592 | 22.5 | 20,058 | 29.0 | 69,180 |

Source: Central Bureau of Statistics, *Administered Territories Statistics Quarterly* (various issues).

1967, and it is these that have caused both political and economic upheavals. It is a wonder that anything at all remains of the economic activities of the territories. The fact that it does speaks well of the resourcefulness of the Arab inhabitants. Real economic growth, in general, has taken place and at rates that (all things considered) compare well with more stable economic regions.

The events of 1948 cut off the West Bank and Gaza Strip from Palestine and required of them that they realign their economies with those of Jordan and Egypt, respectively. The figures show that this radical shift was effected relatively smoothly. Similarly, the war of 1967 and the subsequent Israeli occupation of the two territories put their economies on a radically new basis, forcing them to survive under conditions dictated by the occupying force and primarily serving Israel's interests. Some sectors of the economy suffered more than others in the process. As already demonstrated, the hardest hit has been tourism and related service industries in both territories. In the West Bank, industry has been very hard put to compete with the favored and subsidized Israeli enterprises and has suffered a relative decline. Nevertheless, such structural change has not been so profound as to completely destroy the will of the inhabitants of the territories to establish, or reestablish, their right to economic prosperity.

## Notes

1. Richard C. Ward, Don Peretz, and Evan M. Wilson, The Palestinian State: A Rational Approach (Port Washington, N.Y.: Kennikat Press, 1977), p. 123; M. Barnea, Resources, Uses and Interrelations Among Industries in the West Bank (Jerusalem: Bank of Israel, 1967), p. 9; cited in Haim Ben Shahar et al., Economic Structure and Development Prospects of the West Bank and Gaza Strip (Santa Monica: The Rand Corporation, 1971), p. 27; Oded Remba, "Why Jordan Can Survive," The New Middle East (March 1969), p. 24.

2. Department of Statistics, First Census of Population and Housing, Vol. 1 (Amman, 1964), p. 10.

3. Ibid., p. 315.

4. Department of Statistics, Statistical Yearbook (Amman, 1966), p. 2.

5. Official Estimate.

6. Department of Statistics, First Census, Vol. 1, p. 315.

7. Ben Shahar et al., Economic Structure, p. 27.

8. Department of Statistics, Study of Labor Force, 1966 (Amman, 1968), p. 20.

9. Department of Statistics, The Contribution of the

West Bank in Jordan's Economy (Amman, 1969), p. 3.

10. Department of Statistics, Industrial Survey, 1965 (Amman, 1967), p. 31; Study of Labor Force, p. 20.

11. Yusif A. Sayigh, The Economies of the Arab World: Development Since 1945 (London: Croom Helm, 1978), p. 196.

12. Ibid.

13. Ibid.

14. Ibid.

15. Ibid., p. 196-197.

16. Remba, "Why Jordan Can Survive," p. 28.

17. Department of Statistics, Employment Survey in Establishments Engaging Five Persons or More, 1975 (Amman, 1976), p. 9.

18. Ibid.

19. A. Konikoff, Transjordan: An Economic Survey (Jerusalem: Economic Research Institute of the Jewish Agency for Palestine, 1946), p. 127.

20. Department of Statistics, Housing Census, 1952 (Amman, n.d.), Table 1.

21. Department of Statistics, First Census, Vol. 1, p. 4.

22. Department of Statistics, Statistical Yearbook (1966), p. 2; Supplemented by a separate Department's estimate.

23. Ben Shahar et al., Economic Structure, p. 29.

24. Kanovsky, The Economic Impact, p. 175.

25. Elisha Efrat, "Settlement Pattern and Económic Changes of the Gaza Strip, 1947-1977," Middle East Journal (Summer 1977), p. 350.

26. Department of Statistics, First Census, Vol. 1, p. 315.

27. Van Arkadie, Benefits and Burdens, p. 122.

28. Ben Shahar et al., Economic Structure, p. 29.

29. Arie Bregman, Economic Growth of the Administered Areas, 1968-1973 (Jerusalem: Bank of Israel, 1975), p. 46.

30. Robert Pearson, "Economic and Social Development on the West Bank and Gaza Strip: Some Policy Considerations" (1981), p. 22.

31. Bull, The West Bank, p. 130.

32. Kanovsky, The Economic Impact, p. 165.

# 3
# Population, Labor Force, and Employment

## POPULATION SIZE AND COMPOSITION

In 1947 the population of the West Bank was estimated to range between 450,000 and 475,000 people.[1] In 1948, the territory was flooded with refugees coming from those parts of Palestine that had been incorporated into the state of Israel. Estimates of the number of these refugees ranged from 280,000 to as many as 400,000 people,[2] thereby almost doubling the original population. The population of the Gaza Strip in the same year was thought to be around 60,000 to 70,000,[3] but dramatically increased as a result of the influx of about 150,000 to 200,000 refugees.[4] This tripled the indigenous population in a very short time and made the area extremely densely populated indeed.

A Jordanian census in August 1952 put the population of the West Bank at 742,000 people, 56 percent of that of the whole of Jordan. Another and more detailed census carried out in November 1961 showed the population of the West Bank to be 806,000 persons, or 47 percent of the population of the Kingdom. There was no official census for the period between 1961 and the start of the June war in 1967. No census was ever taken in the Gaza Strip in the post-1948 period. However, the Egyptian administration estimated the population of the Strip at 455,000 people in 1966, although a figure in the region of 400,000 is more plausible.

Between 1952 and 1961, the population of the West Bank grew at a rate of 9 per thousand per annum, despite a high birth rate. The difference between the population growth rate and the natural rate of increase may be accounted for by the high rate of emigration to the East Bank and other Arab countries. On the assumption that the previous rate of growth is applicable to the 1961-1967 period, the population of the West Bank at the end of May 1967 may be estimated at 846,000 people, and in September of the same year, the time Israel carried out a census there, 848,000.

During the 1967 war and in the months after, a large

number of West Bankers took refuge in the East Bank of Jordan. Dislocations of the population continued, although at a decreasing rate, until the end of 1968, when it leveled off. The Israeli census of September 1967 showed the remaining population of the West Bank to be about 664,500;[5] this implies that a minimum of 184,000 West Bankers fled to the East Bank between June and September of 1967, more than one-fifth of its prewar population.

The population of the Gaza Strip was around 354,000 persons in September 1967, excluding residents of the southern part of Rafah, which is located in North Sinai.[6] The number of people who fled the area between June and September of 1967 was small. The 1967 Israeli census showed that the population of the Strip was highly urbanized; 92 percent lived in urban settlements, large refugee camps, or in large villages.[7] On the other hand, the urban population in the West Bank did not exceed one-half (48 percent) of the inhabitants.[8]

The two territories contained many camps that housed persons who were displaced as a result of the creation of Israel. In September 1967, the Israeli census showed that 13 percent of the West Bank population (more than two-fifths of its refugee population) and 48 percent of the Strip's were still living in refugee camps.[9] In fact, refugees constituted the majority of the population in the Strip,[10] but they accounted for one-fifth of the inhabitants in the West Bank. Refugees were defined in the census to include those households whose heads were born in pre-1948 Palestine.

The population of the two territories continued to decline rapidly due to emigration during the last few months of 1967 and into 1968. This trend leveled off in 1969 and by the end of this year the population of the West Bank stood at its September 1967 level. The population of the Strip started to increase slowly in 1969, but did not reach its September level until 1973 (see Table 3.1). By the end of 1982, the population of the West Bank stood at a level slightly higher than that of 1961. By contrast, the population of the Gaza Strip had increased by about two-fifths. Despite a high natural growth rate, the West Bank's population has grown at an average of 1.7 percent (1970-1982) per annum, compared with a much higher average of 2.8 percent for the Strip. Noteworthy is the fact that in both territories the real growth of population has been less than the natural population increase, although this is more pronounced in the West Bank. Emigration out of the territories has been easier for West Bankers than for the inhabitants of the Strip because all West Bankers retained their Jordanian citizenship. This explains, perhaps, the growth in the population of the Strip as compared to the relative stability of the West Bank's population.

The West Bank lost 147,000 people since September 1967 through emigration, an average of more than 9,000 persons each

TABLE 3.1
Population of the West Bank and the Gaza Strip, by age group, 1961 and 1967-1982 (in thousands)

| Year | Total | Age Group | | | | | Males/1000 Females |
|---|---|---|---|---|---|---|---|
| | | 0-14 | 15-29 | 30-44 | 45-64 | 65+ | |
| **West Bank** | | | | | | | |
| 1961[a] (Nov.) | 805.5 | 363.8 | 203.2 | 106.1 | 90.1 | 42.1 | 978 |
| 1967 | 595.9 | 286.6 | 119.7 | 82.7 | 64.6 | 39.1 | 985 |
| 1968 | 581.7 | 283.4 | 121.8 | 79.4 | 61.5 | 35.6 | 988 |
| 1969 | 595.2 | 287.9 | 131.0 | 80.8 | 62.0 | 33.5 | 995 |
| 1970 | 603.9 | 290.0 | 137.3 | 82.3 | 62.5 | 31.8 | 995 |
| 1971 | 625.6 | 305.0 | 145.4 | 83.0 | 62.4 | 29.8 | 1005 |
| 1972 | 629.0 | 301.4 | 147.7 | 80.0 | 65.4 | 34.5 | 995 |
| 1973 | 657.4 | 319.7 | 159.0 | 81.7 | 64.9 | 32.0 | 1008 |
| 1974 | 661.6 | 314.3 | 168.1 | 83.7 | 65.7 | 29.8 | 1006 |
| 1975 | 665.1 | 313.4 | 172.9 | 84.2 | 66.7 | 27.9 | 1005 |
| 1976 | 670.9 | 315.6 | 178.9 | 84.0 | 66.9 | 25.5 | 1006 |
| 1977 | 681.2 | 316.0 | 183.4 | 77.8 | 72.0 | 32.0 | 1006 |
| 1978 | 690.4 | 314.5 | 194.2 | 80.0 | 72.3 | 29.4 | 1005 |
| 1979 | 699.6 | 315.2 | 201.7 | 82.0 | 73.4 | 27.3 | 1002 |
| 1980 | 704.0 | 315.2 | 206.3 | 82.3 | 74.9 | 25.3 | 996 |
| 1981 | 707.3 | 317.5 | 208.9 | 82.3 | 75.1 | 23.3 | 991 |
| 1982 | 747.5 | 344.0 | 222.8 | 72.8 | 76.9 | 30.0 | 993 |
| **Gaza Strip** | | | | | | | |
| 1967 (Sept.) | 389.7 | 194.6 | 83.2 | 55.6 | 34.9 | 18.3 | 943 |
| 1968 | 355.9 | 177.4 | 81.6 | 49.6 | 31.4 | 15.9 | 940 |
| 1969 | 362.2 | 179.0 | 87.3 | 49.7 | 31.6 | 14.6 | 946 |
| 1970 | 367.7 | 180.4 | 91.8 | 50.4 | 31.5 | 13.6 | 948 |
| 1971 | 381.8 | 189.0 | 97.9 | 50.8 | 31.5 | 12.6 | 954 |
| 1972 | 383.5 | 184.2 | 99.0 | 49.4 | 35.9 | 15.0 | 957 |
| 1973 | 405.4 | 197.5 | 107.5 | 50.4 | 36.2 | 13.8 | 974 |
| 1974 | 408.5 | 194.8 | 113.0 | 50.6 | 37.3 | 12.8 | 970 |
| 1975 | 418.5 | 201.1 | 111.3 | 54.8 | 39.3 | 12.0 | 972 |
| 1976 | 429.0 | 204.5 | 120.6 | 54.1 | 38.6 | 11.2 | 976 |
| 1977 | 441.3 | 209.1 | 123.1 | 50.3 | 43.9 | 14.9 | 980 |
| 1978 | 450.2 | 209.0 | 130.1 | 53.0 | 44.4 | 13.6 | 983 |
| 1979 | 432.6 | 201.0 | 125.4 | 52.0 | 42.5 | 11.7 | 986 |
| 1980 | 441.9 | 203.8 | 128.8 | 54.5 | 43.8 | 11.0 | 988 |
| 1981 | 451.6 | 210.4 | 130.5 | 56.2 | 43.9 | 10.4 | 988 |
| 1982 | 476.3 | 227.5 | 138.5 | 50.7 | 46.2 | 13.4 | 988 |

Sources: Department of Statistics, First Census of Population and Housing, Vol. 1 (Amman, 1964), p. 41-44; Central Bureau of Statistics, Statistical Abstract of Israel (various issues).

[a]Including Jerusalem (60,000 people).

year. The Gaza Strip, on the other hand, lost 91,000 people during the same period, 45,000 of whom left in 1967 and 1968, or about 6,000 persons annually. The total number of inhabitants who have emigrated from the territories since the war has reached 424,000, over one-third of the 1982 combined population of the areas.

After the initial very high levels of emigration, the rate declined considerably. In 1975 and the years after, when the Israeli economy was in recession, the emigration rate for the West Bank picked up again and occasionally equaled the levels experienced immediately after the war. There seems to be a correlation between the rate of emigration from the West Bank and economic conditions in Israel; that is, when the Israeli economy slows down and job opportunities decrease, the emigration rate increases. This is not the case with the Gaza Strip where levels of emigration have remained stable and not so susceptible to the economic conditions of Israel.

In short, emigration from the West Bank has been highly sensitive to the level of economic activity in Israel due to employment factors and the accessibility of the East Bank. For instance, when the Israeli economy boomed in the early 1970s, emigration was at a low level; but when it slowed down into a recession in 1975-1976, the number of emigrants reached a high of about 15,000 a year.

In the prewar period, migration of West Bankers to Arab and other countries was in great measure confined to the educated and skilled workers. The 1961 Jordan census showed that there were 50,000 people (out of a total of 63,000) from the West Bank working abroad, of whom as many as 35,000 persons were economically active. Of the economically active portion of the emigrants, close to two-thirds had had more than twelve years of schooling or technical training.[11] The Israel census of 1967 also indicated that approximately one-third of the households in the West Bank and one-quarter of those in the Gaza Strip had some of their members abroad.[12]

The 1967 census revealed the great emphasis on education among the population of the two territories. Almost all people in the young age group had had some years of schooling. Over two-thirds of the men who had attended school in the West Bank and over one-half of them in the Strip received eight years of schooling or less. In addition, more than one-third of the male adults who had had formal education in the West Bank and less than one-half in the Strip spent nine years or more at school.[13] Consequently, the proportion of university graduates in the territories is expected to be one of the highest in the region and comparable to that in many developed countries.[14] More than one-quarter of West Bank emigrants left to pursue their college education.

Birth rate in the two territories is one of the highest in the world. Thus, the population is characterized by the preponderance of people below fifteen years of age. The 1961 census of Jordan showed that 45 percent of the population of the West Bank was less than fifteen years old.[15] In September 1967, this proportion exceeded 48 and 51 percent for the West Bank and the Gaza Strip, respectively.[16] It has leveled off at around 45 percent for the West Bank and 46 percent for the Strip in the last three years.

The large-scale adult male emigration has distorted the distribution of the population of the two territories. The continuous outflow of young men, who are more than likely to leave, has altered the demographic characteristics of the population. Indeed, females outnumber males in the 20 to 54 years age group, and it is clear that this manpower loss will eventually retard development potential in the two territories.

## LABOR FORCE

The labor force in the territories accounts for a modest proportion of the total population. According to the 1961 Jordanian census the labor force constituted 21 percent of the total population of the West Bank. In the postwar period, the labor force rose from 16 percent of the population in 1968, the year in which employment of the area's Arab labor in Israel was permitted, to a peak of 21 percent in 1974. It then decreased and leveled off at less than one-fifth of the population in 1982 (see Table 3.2). Viewed from another angle, the labor force in the West Bank comprised 39 percent of the total 1961 population in the 14 plus age group. After the occupation this proportion increased from 30 percent in 1968 to its highest level of 39 percent in 1974, then declined to around one-third in the last few years.

The labor force commanded a lower proportion of the total population in the Gaza Strip than in the West Bank, accounting for 15 percent of this total in 1968. It grew gradually to 18 percent in 1974, and has fluctuated at around this figure since then. As a proportion of the total population aged 14 years and older, the labor force has remained in the neighborhood of one-third, about the same as the West Bank.

Classification of the labor force along sex lines reveals that the male labor participation rate was almost one-half of the total male population aged five years and above in the West Bank in 1961. This rate was 56 percent of the total population 14 years and older in 1968, rising to two-thirds in 1973 and 1974, but then decreasing to its lowest postwar level of 57 percent in 1979. It later rose to 60 percent in 1982. Figures for the Gaza Strip show an increase from almost 59 percent in 1968 to as high as 66 percent in 1982. On the other hand, the female participation rate has remained very

TABLE 3.2
Population annual growth rate, the West Bank and the Gaza Strip, 1967-1982 (in thousands)

| | West Bank | | | | Gaza Strip | | | |
|---|---|---|---|---|---|---|---|---|
| Year | Population[a] End of Period | Natural Increase | Outflow | Growth (%) | Population[a] End of Period | Natural Increase | Outflow | Growth (%) |
| 1967 | 585.9 | 3.0 | 13.0 | -- | 380.8 | 3.3 | 12.2 | -- |
| 1968 | 583.1 | 13.0 | 15.8 | -0.5 | 356.8 | 8.3 | 32.3 | -6.3 |
| 1969 | 537.9 | 13.5 | -1.3 | 2.5 | 363.9 | 10.0 | 2.9 | 2.0 |
| 1970 | 607.8 | 14.9 | 5.0 | 1.7 | 370.0 | 9.4 | 3.3 | 1.7 |
| 1971 | 622.6 | 17.3 | 2.5 | 2.4 | 378.8 | 11.2 | 2.4 | 2.4 |
| 1972 | 633.7 | 18.4 | 7.3 | 1.8 | 387.1 | 12.3 | 4.0 | 2.2 |
| 1973 | 652.4 | 18.4 | -0.3 | 3.0 | 401.5 | 12.7 | -1.7 | 3.7 |
| 1974 | 663.7 | 20.1 | 2.8 | 2.7 | 414.0 | 14.3 | 1.8 | 3.1 |
| 1975 | 675.2 | 20.6 | 15.1 | 0.8 | 425.5 | 15.0 | 3.5 | 2.8 |
| 1976 | 683.3 | 22.5 | 14.4 | 1.2 | 437.4 | 16.1 | 4.2 | 2.8 |
| 1977 | 655.8 | 22.7 | 10.2 | 1.8 | 450.8 | 16.3 | 2.9 | 3.1 |
| 1978 | 708.0 | 21.6 | 9.4 | 1.8 | 463.0 | 16.9 | 4.7 | 2.7 |
| 1979 | 718.7 | 23.3 | 12.6 | 1.5 | 444.7 | 16.5 | 4.8 | 2.5 |
| 1980 | 724.3 | 22.9 | 17.3 | 0.8 | 456.5 | 16.9 | 5.1 | 2.7 |
| 1981 | 731.8 | 23.2 | 15.7 | 1.0 | 468.9 | 17.7 | 5.3 | 2.7 |
| 1982 | 747.5 | 23.6 | 7.9 | 2.1 | 476.3 | 17.5 | 3.1 | 3.1 |
| Total Emigration | | | 147.4 | | | | 90.8 | |

Source: Central Bureau of Statistics, Statistical Abstract of Israel, 1983, p. 758.

[a]Revised estimates.

low in the two territories due to cultural factors. Female participation in the labor force rose from 8 percent of the total female population aged 14 years and more in the West Bank in 1968 to a peak of 14 percent in 1974, and settled at 12 percent in 1982. It is interesting to note that this rate has decreased from 6 percent in the Gaza Strip in 1968 to 3 percent in 1982, reflecting a lower overall rate for this territory. The lower female participation rate in the labor force in the Strip may be attributed to the fact that male emigration is smaller and is less dependent on employment in Israel. Most of those who lose their jobs in Israel try to find alternative employment in the Strip rather than emigrate, reducing opportunities open to women or the need for their labor. In general, the overall labor participation rate in the two territories has remained at a relatively low level because of the large proportion of young people in the population, the high rate of school attendance, emigration of adults[17] and the low labor participation rate among women.

Expansion of the labor pool in the two territories in the postwar period has come about through the drawing of additional people into the work force to meet the increasing Israeli demand for labor. The size of the labor force in the two territories rose steadily between 1968 and 1974, the period of Israeli boom. When economic activity in Israel cooled off, the size of the work force was reduced, especially in the West Bank, with no corresponding increase in unemployment levels. This phenomenon implies that those who lose their jobs in Israel either cease to be part of the labor force or tend to emigrate. The latter is the more likely alternative in the West Bank in view of yearly statistics on total population outflow. The Gaza Strip's labor force fell slightly in 1971 and 1975 and resumed its growth in the following years. Apparently, the scale of labor emigration in the Strip has not been large and workers who are not employed in Israel are reabsorbed into the domestic economy, or cease to seek employment.[18] Indeed, it is more difficult for the Strip's inhabitants to emigrate either to Jordan or to other countries because they do not hold Jordanian (or any other) citizenship.

## EMPLOYMENT

Total employment in the occupied territories expanded appreciably in the postwar period, from 117,000 in 1968 to 223,000 in 1982 (see Table 3.3). Much of this increase of approximately 90 percent of the original number of employed persons has been a direct result of expansion of employment in Israel. In 1982, the territories' labor working in the Israeli economy accounted for over one-third of their total

TABLE 3.3
Population aged 14 years and over, by labor force characteristics, the West Bank and the Gaza Strip, 1961 and 1968-1982 (in thousands)

| Year | Population Aged 14+ | Not in Labor Force | Labor Force: Total | Labor Force: Employed | Labor Force: Not Employed | % Labor Force of Population Aged 14+ | % Labor Force in Total Population | % Employed in Labor Force |
|---|---|---|---|---|---|---|---|---|
| West Bank | | | | | | | | |
| 1961[a] | 441.7 | 269.6 | 172.1 | 160.3 | 11.8 | 39.0 | 21.4 | 93.1 |
| 1968 | 308.6 | 215.6 | 93.0 | 82.9 | 10.1 | 30.1 | 16.0 | 89.2 |
| 1969 | 313.7 | 199.1 | 114.6 | 109.9 | 4.7 | 36.5 | 19.3 | 95.9 |
| 1970 | 322.9 | 204.5 | 118.4 | 114.6 | 3.8 | 36.7 | 19.6 | 96.7 |
| 1971 | 330.0 | 210.3 | 119.7 | 116.8 | 2.9 | 36.3 | 19.1 | 97.6 |
| 1972 | 336.6 | 210.0 | 126.6 | 125.2 | (1.4) | 37.6 | 20.1 | 98.9 |
| 1973 | 341.6 | 213.9 | 127.7 | 126.4 | (1.3) | 37.4 | 19.4 | 99.0 |
| 1974 | 355.2 | 216.2 | 139.0 | 137.5 | (1.5) | 39.1 | 21.0 | 98.9 |
| 1975 | 366.9 | 233.0 | 133.9 | 132.3 | (1.6) | 36.5 | 20.1 | 98.8 |
| 1976 | 371.0 | 239.7 | 131.3 | 129.7 | (1.6) | 35.4 | 19.6 | 98.8 |
| 1977 | 379.4 | 250.6 | 128.8 | 127.3 | (1.5) | 33.9 | 18.9 | 98.8 |
| 1978 | 389.7 | 256.9 | 132.8 | 131.5 | (1.3) | 34.1 | 19.2 | 99.0 |
| 1979 | 398.6 | 264.5 | 134.1 | 132.8 | (1.3) | 33.6 | 19.2 | 99.0 |
| 1980 | 401.0 | 263.8 | 137.2 | 134.8 | 2.4 | 34.2 | 18.9 | 98.3 |
| 1981 | 402.9 | 267.6 | 135.3 | 133.4 | (1.9) | 33.6 | 18.5 | 98.6 |
| 1982 | 405.9 | 263.1 | 142.8 | 140.9 | (1.9) | 35.2 | 19.1 | 98.7 |
| Gaza Strip | | | | | | | | |
| 1968 | 182.6 | 129.0 | 53.6 | 44.5 | 9.1 | 29.3 | 15.1 | 83.1 |
| 1969 | 189.0 | 130.8 | 58.2 | 52.9 | 5.3 | 30.8 | 16.1 | 90.9 |
| 1970 | 196.8 | 134.4 | 62.4 | 58.7 | 3.7 | 31.7 | 17.0 | 93.9 |
| 1971 | 200.7 | 138.9 | 61.8 | 59.7 | 2.1 | 30.8 | 16.2 | 96.6 |
| 1972 | 205.1 | 140.5 | 64.6 | 63.6 | (1.0) | 31.5 | 16.8 | 98.4 |
| 1973 | 210.4 | 141.8 | 68.6 | 68.1 | (0.5) | 32.6 | 16.9 | 99.4 |
| 1974 | 218.6 | 145.1 | 73.5 | 73.0 | (0.5) | 33.6 | 18.0 | 99.3 |
| 1975 | 225.0 | 152.3 | 72.7 | 72.4 | (0.3) | 32.3 | 17.4 | 99.6 |
| 1976 | 235.5 | 155.2 | 76.3 | 76.1 | (0.2) | 33.0 | 17.8 | 99.7 |
| 1977 | 239.5 | 162.2 | 77.3 | 77.2 | (0.1) | 32.3 | 17.5 | 99.9 |
| 1978 | 249.8 | 169.0 | 80.8 | 80.4 | (0.4) | 32.3 | 17.9 | 99.5 |
| 1979 | 243.0 | 163.2 | 79.8 | 79.6 | (0.2) | 32.8 | 18.5 | 99.7 |
| 1980 | 242.7 | 161.4 | 81.3 | 80.9 | (0.4) | 33.5 | 17.8 | 99.5 |
| 1981 | 247.1 | 164.3 | 82.8 | 82.5 | (0.3) | 33.5 | 17.7 | 99.6 |
| 1982 | 246.4 | 164.0 | 82.4 | 82.0 | (0.4) | 33.4 | 17.3 | 99.5 |

Sources: Department of Statistics, First Census, Vol. 2, p. 4-5; Central Bureau of Statistics, Statistical Abstract of Israel (various issues).
[a]Including Jerusalem, figures are for people 5 years of age and older.

TABLE 3.4
Employed persons by place of work, the West Bank and the Gaza Strip, 1970-1982 (in thousands)

| Year | Employed in Israel | | Employed in the Territories | | Total | |
|---|---|---|---|---|---|---|
| | Number | Percent | Number | Percent | Number | Percent |
| 1968 | 5.0 | 4.3 | 112.4 | 95.7 | 117.4 | 100.0 |
| 1969 | 9.0 | 5.5 | 153.8 | 94.5 | 162.8 | 100.0 |
| 1970 | 20.6 | 11.9 | 152.7 | 88.1 | 173.3 | 100.0 |
| 1971 | 33.8 | 19.2 | 142.7 | 80.8 | 176.5 | 100.0 |
| 1972 | 52.4 | 27.8 | 136.3 | 72.2 | 188.7 | 100.0 |
| 1973 | 61.3 | 31.5 | 133.4 | 68.5 | 194.7 | 100.0 |
| 1974 | 68.7 | 32.7 | 141.7 | 67.3 | 210.4 | 100.0 |
| 1975 | 66.3 | 32.4 | 138.6 | 67.6 | 204.9 | 100.0 |
| 1976 | 64.9 | 31.5 | 140.9 | 68.5 | 205.8 | 100.0 |
| 1977 | 63.0 | 30.8 | 141.4 | 69.2 | 204.4 | 100.0 |
| 1978 | 68.2 | 32.3 | 142.7 | 67.7 | 210.9 | 100.0 |
| 1979 | 74.1 | 34.9 | 138.0 | 65.1 | 212.1 | 100.0 |
| 1980 | 75.1 | 34.8 | 140.6 | 65.2 | 215.7 | 100.0 |
| 1981 | 75.8 | 35.1 | 140.1 | 64.9 | 215.9 | 100.0 |
| 1982 | 79.1 | 35.5 | 143.6 | 65.5 | 222.7 | 100.0 |

Source: Central Bureau of Statistics, Statistical Abstract of Israel (various issues).

combined labor force, and well over one-half of those employed inside the two territories (see Table 3.4).

The number of persons employed in the West Bank was 160,000 workers in 1961; the unemployment level reached 12,000 or 7 percent of the labor force.[19] The total number of West Bank laborers employed in the territory and in Israel was estimated at 83,000 in 1968, jumped to a peak of more than 137,000 in 1974, an increase of close to two-thirds, then fluctuated downwards before reaching a high of 141,000 in 1982 (see Table 3.5). Employment of West Bank labor in Israel climbed from 5,000 persons in 1968 to more than 42,000 in 1974, accounting for 69 percent of the total increase during this period. At the same time, the unemployment rate diminished from about 11 percent in 1968 to a mere 1.3 percent in 1982. Recession in the Israeli economy in 1975 and the years immediately after reduced the total employment figures. But as the Israeli economy recovered, the employment level rose moderately but gradually. Despite this fluctuation in employment, the rate of unemployment has remained quite constant at 1.0 to 1.5 percent between 1975 and 1982. Labor emigration to the booming economies of Jordan and the Gulf states has re-

TABLE 3.5
Employed persons by place of work, 1970-1982 (in thousands)

| | Employed in Israel | | Employed in the Territories | | Total | |
|---|---|---|---|---|---|---|
| Year | Number | Percent | Number | Percent | Number | Percent |
| **West Bank** | | | | | | |
| 1970 | 14.8 | 12.8 | 99.8 | 87.2 | 114.6 | 100.0 |
| 1971 | 25.6 | 21.9 | 91.2 | 78.1 | 116.8 | 100.0 |
| 1972 | 34.9 | 27.9 | 90.3 | 72.1 | 125.2 | 100.0 |
| 1973 | 38.6 | 30.5 | 87.8 | 69.5 | 126.4 | 100.0 |
| 1974 | 42.4 | 30.9 | 95.0 | 69.1 | 137.5 | 100.0 |
| 1975 | 40.4 | 30.5 | 91.9 | 69.5 | 132.3 | 100.0 |
| 1976 | 37.1 | 28.6 | 92.6 | 71.4 | 129.7 | 100.0 |
| 1977 | 35.5 | 27.9 | 91.9 | 72.1 | 127.4 | 100.0 |
| 1978 | 36.8 | 28.1 | 94.0 | 71.9 | 130.8 | 100.0 |
| 1979 | 39.8 | 30.1 | 92.5 | 69.9 | 132.3 | 100.0 |
| 1980 | 40.6 | 30.1 | 94.3 | 69.9 | 134.9 | 100.0 |
| 1981 | 39.9 | 29.9 | 93.5 | 70.1 | 133.4 | 100.0 |
| 1982 | 43.0 | 30.6 | 97.5 | 69.4 | 140.5 | 100.0 |
| **Gaza Strip** | | | | | | |
| 1970 | 5.9 | 10.0 | 52.9 | 90.0 | 58.8 | 100.0 |
| 1971 | 8.2 | 13.7 | 51.5 | 86.3 | 59.7 | 100.0 |
| 1972 | 17.5 | 27.6 | 46.0 | 72.4 | 63.5 | 100.0 |
| 1973 | 22.7 | 33.2 | 45.6 | 66.8 | 68.3 | 100.0 |
| 1974 | 26.3 | 36.0 | 46.7 | 64.0 | 73.0 | 100.0 |
| 1975 | 25.9 | 35.7 | 46.7 | 64.3 | 72.6 | 100.0 |
| 1976 | 27.8 | 36.5 | 48.3 | 63.5 | 76.1 | 100.0 |
| 1977 | 27.5 | 35.7 | 49.5 | 64.3 | 77.0 | 100.0 |
| 1978 | 31.4 | 39.2 | 48.7 | 60.8 | 80.1 | 100.0 |
| 1979 | 34.3 | 43.0 | 45.5 | 57.0 | 79.8 | 100.0 |
| 1980 | 34.5 | 42.7 | 46.3 | 57.3 | 80.8 | 100.0 |
| 1981 | 35.9 | 43.5 | 46.6 | 56.5 | 82.5 | 100.0 |
| 1982 | 36.1 | 43.9 | 46.1 | 56.1 | 82.2 | 100.0 |

Source: Central Bureau of Statistics, Statistical Abstract of Israel (various issues).

duced excess labor supply and maintained the West Bank economy at full employment.

Employment in the Gaza Strip was estimated at 63,000 in 1965.[20] In 1968, employed persons numbered 45,000, all of whom were domestically employed, employment in Israel not being permitted until 1969. At the same time, unemployment ran at about 17 percent of the labor force. Employment of Gaza Strip residents in Israel became possible in 1969 and since then employment has risen steadily and stabilized at about 82,000 persons. Simultaneously, unemployment dropped dramatically and has been virtually eliminated. Employment inside Israel has been responsible for absorbing the unemployed workers of the Gaza Strip. It appears that total employment in the Strip, unlike that in the West Bank, is not sensitive to economic conditions in Israel. Indeed, there has been no appreciable decline in the number of the Strip's workers employed in Israel in any year during the postwar period.

Female employment constituted about 9 percent of total employment in the West Bank in 1961. This figure was 16 percent in 1968 and since then has fluctuated at between 15 and 20 percent (see Table 3.6). Conversely, women's employment in the Gaza Strip dropped sharply from 9 percent in 1968 to just 6 percent in 1969; it has remained stable at around this figure. There exist no data to explain the higher female employment rate in the West Bank during the postwar period. It could be that more women have been involved in the growing

TABLE 3.6
Employed males and females in the West Bank and the Gaza Strip, 1968-1982 (percentages)

| | West Bank | | Gaza Strip | |
|---|---|---|---|---|
| Year | Male | Female | Male | Female |
| 1961 | 91.5 | 8.5 | n.a. | n.a. |
| 1968[a] | 84.3 | 15.7 | 90.6 | 9.4 |
| 1969 | 80.3 | 19.7 | 94.0 | 6.0 |
| 1970 | 79.4 | 20.6 | 93.0 | 7.0 |
| 1971 | 81.6 | 18.4 | 93.3 | 6.7 |
| 1972 | 84.7 | 15.3 | 94.0 | 6.0 |
| 1973 | 84.8 | 15.2 | 93.8 | 6.2 |
| 1974 | 81.2 | 18.8 | 93.0 | 7.0 |
| 1975 | 82.0 | 18.0 | 93.2 | 6.8 |
| 1976 | 81.3 | 18.7 | 93.3 | 6.7 |
| 1977 | 81.7 | 18.3 | 93.4 | 6.6 |
| 1978 | 80.5 | 19.5 | 94.2 | 5.8 |
| 1979 | 81.9 | 18.1 | 94.5 | 5.5 |
| 1980 | 81.4 | 18.6 | 93.4 | 6.6 |
| 1981 | 82.8 | 17.2 | 94.3 | 5.7 |
| 1982 | 81.7 | 18.3 | 95.0 | 5.0 |

Sources: Department of Statistics, First Census, Vol. 2, p. 4-5; Central Bureau of Statistics, Statistical Abstract of Israel (various issues).
n.a. = Not available.
[a]August-December

activity of subcontracting and some females may have entered the labor force to substitute for migrant workers.

## OVERALL SECTORAL EMPLOYMENT

Agriculture was the largest single employer in the economy of the West Bank in 1961, engaging two-fifths of the employed labor force. Next in importance were the service sectors whose share of employment stood at 36 percent. Manufacturing and mining and construction absorbed less than a quarter of total employment in the same year. During the postwar period, the structure of employment in the territory (and in Israel) has changed. Agricultural employment, although remaining the largest in the economy, steadily declined in importance to around a quarter of total employment. The service sectors maintained their relative share of employment at about 30 percent. Construction gained in relative importance by about 5 percent of total employment. Industrial employment stood at around 17 percent during this period (see Tables 3.7 and 3.8).

In 1965, agriculture accounted for over one-third of the labor force in the Gaza Strip, whereas services and construction engaged over 60 percent of the work force. Industrial employment was negligible. In the postwar period, agriculture has lost its predominant position as the largest employer; its relative importance has steadily fallen to about 18 percent of total employment. Industry and construction increased their share considerably to about 20 percent for industry in 1980 (declining to 16 percent in 1982), and to more than a quarter for construction. Services became less important than before the war, employing approximately 40 percent of the employed labor force.

The restructuring of the occupied territories' labor force has been achieved at the expense of agricultural employment, which has declined in relative and absolute terms. The increase in construction came about through an increase in construction within the Israeli economy. Apparently, many farm workers have found employment on construction sites in Israel, reducing the number of farm laborers, and at the same time increasing the construction employment figure.

## SECTORAL EMPLOYMENT IN THE TERRITORIES

The number of workers employed within the West Bank declined from almost 100,000 in 1970 to barely 88,000 in 1973; the number stood at 98,000 in 1982 (see Tables 3.9 and 3.10). The structure of employment has changed, with agriculture giving way to services as the most important sector. For instance, agricultural employment declined from 42,000 workers in 1970 to 31,000 in 1982. Consequently, agriculture's share in domestic employment has fallen by about 10 percent between 1970 and 1982. Employment in the service sectors, on the other hand, has risen by more than 15 percent during the same period. Employment in other sectors of the economy, namely industry and construction, has stagnated. Industrial employment stood at 14,600 workers in 1970, and rose to 15,500 in 1982, thereby maintaining a share of approximately 16 percent of the total employment figure. The share of the construction industry's employment has risen a little from 8 percent of total employment in 1970 to about 11 percent in 1982. It seems that the decline in agricultural employment has not resulted in a general rise in employment figures for the other sectors of the economy. Apart from the service sectors, employment rates per sector of the economy have remained constant, implying that the Israeli economy absorbed much of the reduction in farm workers.

Similarly, the total domestically employed labor force in the Gaza Strip has shrunk from 53,000 workers in 1970 to 46,000 in 1982, a reduction of more than 13 percent. Agriculture suffered the greatest fall, about half of its workers, in fact. Employment in industry stagnated at around 12 percent of total employment, although it did experience a temporary rise in 1978 to 19 percent. Construction employed about 4,500 workers in 1970 (or about 9 percent of total employment), but this dwindled measurably in the early and mid-1970s, finally recovering to 9 percent in 1982. Services employed about one-quarter of domestic employment throughout the period, but its relative share increased from 48 percent in 1970 to 59 percent in 1982. The general shift in employment has been from jobs in the Strip, especially in agriculture, to those offered in the Israeli economy.

## LABOR PRODUCTIVITY

Agriculture in the West Bank engaged 43 percent of domestic employment and contributed 35 percent of gross product in 1970. This means that agricultural workers produced less than their equal share in production terms. This was either because of low productivity or underemployment in the sector, or both. However, by the end of 1982 this gap between employment and productivity had been bridged through the elimination of disguised unemployment and improved production methods. Likewise, productivity in agriculture in the Gaza Strip was originally somewhat higher than in the West Bank, accounting for 32 and 28 percent of domestic employment and product, respectively. By the end of 1982, this difference had been eliminated.

TABLE 3.7
Employed persons, by economic branch, the West Bank and the Gaza Strip, 1968-1982 (in thousands)

| Sector | 1961[1] | 1968[a] | 1969 | 1970 | 1971 | 1972 | 1973 | 1974 | 1975 | 1976 | 1977 | 1978 | 1979 | 1980 | 1981 | 1982 |
|---|---|---|---|---|---|---|---|---|---|---|---|---|---|---|---|---|
| West Bank | | | | | | | | | | | | | | | | |
| Total | 160.3 | 82.9 | 109.9 | 114.6 | 116.8 | 125.2 | 126.4 | 137.0 | 132.5 | 129.7 | 127.3 | 131.5 | 132.8 | 134.8 | 133.4 | 140.9 |
| Agriculture | 64.6 | 32.3 | 49.2 | 45.0 | 39.9 | 38.5 | 33.4 | 40.5 | 36.3 | 35.8 | 35.4 | 36.7 | 33.4 | 35.3 | 32.2 | 35.5 |
| Industry | 19.6 | 12.4 | 14.6 | 16.5 | 17.6 | 19.7 | 22.4 | 22.3 | 22.0 | 21.5 | 22.0 | 23.1 | 24.3 | 22.8 | 21.9 | 23.2 |
| Trade, restaurants & hotels | 13.9 | 10.3 | 12.9 | 12.8 | 13.9 | 14.2 | 14.5 | 15.4 | 15.7 | 16.8 | 17.3 | 16.4 | 16.7 | 17.2 | 16.6 | 16.7 |
| Construction | 17.9 | 10.5 | 13.1 | 16.3 | 20.2 | 26.3 | 28.6 | 30.6 | 30.0 | 27.6 | 25.1 | 27.3 | 29.9 | 30.5 | 31.9 | 33.8 |
| Transport | 4.3 | 3.9 | 4.1 | 4.7 | 4.7 | 5.4 | 5.4 | 5.6 | 6.0 | 6.2 | 5.8 | 5.5 | 5.9 | 6.0 | 6.5 | 6.4 |
| Public & community services | 25.5 | 9.0 | 11.3 | 14.6 | 15.7 | 15.8 | 15.7 | 16.7 | 17.6 | 17.3 | 16.7 | 17.0 | 17.1 | 17.9 | 19.0 | 19.6 |
| Other | 14.5 | 4.3 | 4.7 | 4.2 | 4.8 | 5.3 | 6.1 | 5.8 | 4.9 | 4.5 | 5.0 | 5.5 | 5.5 | 5.1 | 5.3 | 5.7 |
| Gaza Strip | 1965[2] | | | | | | | | | | | | | | | |
| Total | 63.0 | 44.5 | 52.9 | 58.7 | 59.8 | 63.6 | 68.1 | 72.9 | 72.6 | 76.1 | 77.2 | 80.4 | 79.6 | 80.9 | 82.5 | 82.0 |
| Agriculture | 22.0 | 11.4 | 17.5 | 19.2 | 20.2 | 19.4 | 20.0 | 20.2 | 17.4 | 18.2 | 18.2 | 17.5 | 16.4 | 15.1 | 14.3 | 14.4 |
| Industry | 2.0 | 7.2 | 6.6 | 6.9 | 7.1 | 8.4 | 8.8 | 9.5 | 10.3 | 11.6 | 11.6 | 13.9 | 15.8 | 15.8 | 14.3 | 13.0 |
| Trade, restaurants & hotels | 15.0 | 8.4 | 9.6 | 9.5 | 9.7 | 9.0 | 9.4 | 9.8 | 10.2 | 10.4 | 10.5 | 10.9 | 10.0 | 11.3 | 11.7 | 11.3 |
| Construction | | 4.4 | 5.1 | 7.3 | 5.5 | 8.1 | 11.5 | 14.1 | 16.1 | 16.5 | 16.0 | 17.2 | 18.3 | 18.7 | 21.8 | 22.3 |
| Transport | 24.0 | 3.5 | 3.8 | 3.5 | 3.2 | 4.5 | 4.9 | 5.4 | 5.3 | 4.9 | 5.3 | 5.5 | 5.0 | 5.3 | 5.5 | 5.1 |
| Public & community services | | 6.5 | 7.4 | 9.0 | 9.5 | 10.4 | 10.2 | 10.0 | 9.6 | 10.6 | 11.3 | 10.9 | 9.6 | 10.5 | 10.6 | 11.1 |
| Other | | 3.0 | 2.9 | 3.3 | 3.6 | 3.8 | 3.2 | 3.9 | 3.8 | 3.9 | 4.3 | 4.5 | 4.5 | 4.2 | 4.3 | 4.8 |

Sources: (1) Department of Statistics, First Census, Vol. 2, p. 16-18; (2) Ben Shahar et al., Economic Structure, p. 21; Central Bureau of Statistics, Statistical Abstract of Israel (various issues).

[a]August-December.

TABLE 3.8
Employed persons by economic branch, the West Bank and the Gaza Strip, 1961 and 1968-1982 (percentages)

| Sector | 1961 | 1968 | 1969 | 1970 | 1971 | 1972 | 1973 | 1974 | 1975 | 1976 | 1977 | 1978 | 1979 | 1980 | 1981 | 1982 |
|---|---|---|---|---|---|---|---|---|---|---|---|---|---|---|---|---|
| West Bank | | | | | | | | | | | | | | | | |
| Total - thousands | 160.3 | 82.9 | 109.9 | 114.6 | 116.8 | 125.2 | 126.4 | 137.0 | 132.5 | 129.7 | 127.3 | 131.5 | 132.8 | 134.8 | 133.4 | 140.9 |
| - percentages | 100.0 | 100.0 | 100.0 | 100.0 | 100.0 | 100.0 | 100.0 | 100.0 | 100.0 | 100.0 | 100.0 | 100.0 | 100.0 | 100.0 | 100.0 | 100.0 |
| Agriculture | 40.3 | 39.0 | 44.8 | 39.3 | 34.2 | 30.8 | 26.5 | 29.6 | 27.4 | 27.7 | 27.8 | 27.8 | 25.3 | 26.2 | 24.1 | 25.2 |
| Industry | 12.2 | 15.0 | 13.3 | 14.2 | 15.1 | 15.7 | 17.7 | 16.3 | 16.6 | 16.6 | 17.3 | 17.6 | 18.3 | 16.9 | 16.4 | 16.5 |
| Trade, restaurants & hotels | 8.7 | 12.4 | 11.7 | 11.1 | 11.9 | 11.3 | 11.5 | 11.2 | 11.8 | 19.2 | 13.6 | 12.5 | 12.7 | 12.7 | 12.5 | 11.9 |
| Construction | 11.2 | 12.7 | 11.9 | 14.7 | 17.3 | 21.0 | 22.3 | 22.4 | 22.6 | 21.3 | 19.7 | 20.7 | 22.6 | 22.6 | 24.0 | 24.0 |
| Transport | 2.7 | 4.8 | 3.7 | 4.1 | 3.9 | 4.3 | 4.2 | 4.1 | 4.5 | 4.8 | 4.6 | 4.2 | 4.4 | 4.5 | 4.9 | 4.5 |
| Public & community services | 15.9 | 10.9 | 10.3 | 12.7 | 13.6 | 12.7 | 12.5 | 12.2 | 13.3 | 13.3 | 13.1 | 13.0 | 12.8 | 13.3 | 14.2 | 13.9 |
| Other | 9.0 | 5.2 | 4.3 | 3.8 | 4.1 | 4.2 | 4.9 | 4.2 | 3.7 | 3.4 | 3.9 | 4.2 | 3.9 | 3.8 | 3.9 | 4.0 |
| Gaza Strip | | | | | | | | | | | | | | | | |
| Total - thousands | 63.0[a] | 44.5 | 52.9 | 58.7 | 59.8 | 63.6 | 68.1 | 72.9 | 72.6 | 76.1 | 77.2 | 80.4 | 79.6 | 80.9 | 82.5 | 82.0 |
| - percentages | 100.0 | 100.0 | 100.0 | 100.0 | 100.0 | 100.0 | 100.0 | 100.0 | 100.0 | 100.0 | 100.0 | 100.0 | 100.0 | 100.0 | 100.0 | 100.0 |
| Agriculture | 34.9 | 25.6 | 33.1 | 32.7 | 33.8 | 30.5 | 29.4 | 27.7 | 24.0 | 24.0 | 23.4 | 21.9 | 20.4 | 18.5 | 17.3 | 17.7 |
| Industry | 3.2 | 16.2 | 12.5 | 11.8 | 11.9 | 13.1 | 13.0 | 13.0 | 14.2 | 15.3 | 15.0 | 17.3 | 19.8 | 19.5 | 17.2 | 15.9 |
| Trade, restaurants & hotels | 23.8 | 18.9 | 18.1 | 16.2 | 16.2 | 14.2 | 13.8 | 13.5 | 14.0 | 13.9 | 13.6 | 13.5 | 12.5 | 14.0 | 14.2 | 13.7 |
| Construction | | 9.9 | 9.6 | 12.4 | 9.2 | 12.8 | 16.9 | 19.3 | 22.1 | 21.6 | 20.8 | 21.4 | 23.0 | 23.1 | 26.5 | 27.2 |
| Transport | | 7.9 | 7.2 | 6.0 | 7.0 | 7.1 | 7.2 | 7.4 | 7.3 | 6.3 | 6.9 | 6.8 | 6.4 | 6.6 | 6.8 | 6.2 |
| Public & community services | 38.1 | 14.6 | 14.0 | 15.3 | 15.9 | 16.4 | 14.9 | 13.7 | 13.2 | 13.9 | 14.7 | 13.5 | 12.1 | 13.0 | 12.8 | 13.5 |
| Other | | 6.7 | 5.5 | 5.6 | 6.0 | 5.9 | 4.8 | 5.4 | 5.2 | 5.0 | 5.6 | 5.6 | 5.8 | 5.3 | 5.2 | 5.8 |

Source: Derived from Table 3.7.

[a] 1965.

TABLE 3.9
Employed persons in the West Bank and the Gaza Strip, by selected economic branch, 1970-1982 (in thousands)

| Year | Total | Agriculture | Industry | Construction | Other |
|---|---|---|---|---|---|
| **Total** | | | | | |
| 1970 | 152.7 | 59.1 | 21.1 | 12.8 | 59.7 |
| 1971 | 142.7 | 52.5 | 19.7 | 8.0 | 62.5 |
| 1972 | 136.3 | 45.7 | 18.9 | 8.5 | 63.2 |
| 1973 | 133.4 | 41.8 | 20.1 | 8.5 | 63.0 |
| 1974 | 141.7 | 47.9 | 19.8 | 8.8 | 65.2 |
| 1975 | 138.6 | 44.1 | 20.1 | 10.1 | 64.6 |
| 1976 | 140.9 | 44.2 | 20.3 | 11.6 | 64.8 |
| 1977 | 141.4 | 43.1 | 20.1 | 12.9 | 65.3 |
| 1978 | 142.7 | 42.5 | 21.7 | 13.6 | 64.9 |
| 1979 | 138.0 | 38.6 | 23.2 | 13.9 | 62.2 |
| 1980 | 140.6 | 39.9 | 22.9 | 13.5 | 64.3 |
| 1981 | 140.1 | 36.8 | 22.4 | 15.0 | 65.9 |
| 1982 | 143.6 | 39.6 | 22.4 | 14.2 | 67.5 |
| **West Bank** | | | | | |
| 1970 | 99.8 | 42.4 | 14.6 | 8.4 | 34.4 |
| 1971 | 91.2 | 36.7 | 13.4 | 5.6 | 35.6 |
| 1972 | 90.3 | 34.3 | 12.3 | 6.5 | 36.3 |
| 1973 | 87.8 | 30.0 | 14.4 | 6.7 | 36.7 |
| 1974 | 95.0 | 36.0 | 14.3 | 6.7 | 38.0 |
| 1975 | 91.9 | 31.8 | 14.5 | 7.7 | 37.9 |
| 1976 | 92.6 | 31.4 | 13.3 | 9.3 | 38.2 |
| 1977 | 91.9 | 30.7 | 13.9 | 9.6 | 37.8 |
| 1978 | 94.0 | 32.3 | 14.3 | 10.2 | 37.1 |
| 1979 | 92.5 | 29.1 | 14.7 | 10.9 | 37.7 |
| 1980 | 94.3 | 31.3 | 14.3 | 10.1 | 38.6 |
| 1981 | 93.5 | 28.5 | 14.7 | 11.1 | 39.2 |
| 1982 | 97.5 | 31.3 | 15.5 | 10.3 | 40.4 |
| **Gaza Strip** | | | | | |
| 1970 | 52.9 | 16.7 | 6.4 | 4.5 | 25.3 |
| 1971 | 51.5 | 16.0 | 6.3 | 2.4 | 26.8 |
| 1972 | 46.0 | 11.4 | 5.8 | (1.9) | 26.9 |
| 1973 | 45.6 | 11.7 | 5.8 | 1.8 | 26.3 |
| 1974 | 46.7 | 11.6 | 5.7 | 1.9 | 27.5 |
| 1975 | 46.7 | 12.3 | 5.6 | 2.4 | 26.4 |
| 1976 | 48.3 | 12.8 | 6.5 | 2.2 | 26.8 |
| 1977 | 49.5 | 12.4 | 6.2 | 3.3 | 27.6 |
| 1978 | 48.7 | 10.3 | 7.5 | 3.4 | 27.5 |
| 1979 | 45.5 | 9.6 | 8.3 | 3.2 | 24.4 |
| 1980 | 46.3 | 8.7 | 8.6 | 3.4 | 25.6 |
| 1981 | 46.6 | 8.4 | 7.7 | 3.9 | 26.6 |
| 1982 | 46.1 | 8.4 | 6.8 | 3.9 | 27.1 |

Source: Central Bureau of Statistics, Statistical Abstract of Israel (various issues).

TABLE 3.10
Employed persons in the West Bank and the Gaza Strip, by economic branch, 1970-1982 (percentages)

| Year | Total(1000) | Agriculture | Industry | Construction | Other |
|---|---|---|---|---|---|
| Total | | | | | |
| 1970 | 152.7 | 38.7 | 13.8 | 8.4 | 39.1 |
| 1971 | 142.7 | 36.8 | 13.8 | 5.6 | 43.8 |
| 1972 | 136.3 | 33.5 | 13.9 | 6.2 | 46.4 |
| 1973 | 133.4 | 31.3 | 15.1 | 6.4 | 47.2 |
| 1974 | 141.7 | 33.8 | 14.0 | 6.2 | 46.0 |
| 1975 | 138.6 | 31.8 | 14.5 | 7.3 | 46.6 |
| 1976 | 140.9 | 31.4 | 14.4 | 8.2 | 46.0 |
| 1977 | 141.4 | 30.5 | 14.2 | 9.1 | 46.2 |
| 1978 | 142.7 | 29.8 | 15.2 | 9.5 | 45.5 |
| 1979 | 138.0 | 28.0 | 16.8 | 10.1 | 45.1 |
| 1980 | 140.6 | 28.4 | 16.3 | 9.6 | 45.7 |
| 1981 | 140.1 | 26.3 | 16.0 | 10.7 | 47.0 |
| 1982 | 143.6 | 27.6 | 15.5 | 9.9 | 47.0 |
| West Bank | | | | | |
| 1970 | 99.8 | 42.5 | 14.6 | 8.4 | 34.5 |
| 1971 | 91.2 | 40.2 | 14.7 | 6.1 | 39.0 |
| 1972 | 90.3 | 38.0 | 14.6 | 7.2 | 40.2 |
| 1973 | 87.8 | 34.2 | 16.4 | 7.6 | 41.8 |
| 1974 | 95.0 | 37.9 | 15.1 | 7.0 | 40.0 |
| 1975 | 91.9 | 34.6 | 15.8 | 8.4 | 41.2 |
| 1976 | 92.6 | 33.9 | 14.9 | 10.0 | 41.2 |
| 1977 | 91.9 | 33.4 | 15.1 | 10.4 | 41.1 |
| 1978 | 94.0 | 34.4 | 15.2 | 10.9 | 39.5 |
| 1979 | 92.5 | 31.5 | 15.9 | 11.8 | 40.8 |
| 1980 | 94.3 | 33.2 | 15.2 | 10.7 | 40.9 |
| 1981 | 93.5 | 30.5 | 15.7 | 11.9 | 41.9 |
| 1982 | 97.5 | 32.1 | 15.9 | 10.6 | 41.4 |
| Gaza Strip | | | | | |
| 1970 | 52.9 | 31.6 | 12.1 | 8.5 | 47.8 |
| 1971 | 51.5 | 31.1 | 12.2 | 4.6 | 52.1 |
| 1972 | 46.0 | 24.8 | 12.6 | (4.1) | 58.5 |
| 1973 | 45.6 | 25.7 | 12.7 | 3.9 | 57.7 |
| 1974 | 46.7 | 24.8 | 12.2 | 4.1 | 58.9 |
| 1975 | 46.7 | 26.3 | 12.0 | 5.1 | 56.6 |
| 1976 | 48.3 | 26.5 | 13.5 | 4.6 | 55.4 |
| 1977 | 49.5 | 25.1 | 12.5 | 6.7 | 55.7 |
| 1978 | 48.7 | 21.1 | 15.4 | 7.0 | 56.5 |
| 1979 | 45.5 | 21.1 | 18.2 | 7.0 | 53.7 |
| 1980 | 46.3 | 18.8 | 18.6 | 7.3 | 55.3 |
| 1981 | 46.6 | 18.0 | 16.5 | 8.4 | 57.1 |
| 1982 | 46.1 | 17.9 | 14.8 | 8.5 | 58.8 |

Source: Central Bureau of Statistics, Statistical Abstract of Israel (various issues).

Productivity in industry in both territories has declined during the postwar period. In 1970, industry accounted for about 15 percent of the labor force but contributed less than 10 percent of gross product; in the Gaza Strip it engaged 12 percent of the work force and accounted for only 6 percent of gross product. This gap has increased, an indication of increased inefficiency in this sector due to lack of investment in established firms and a lack of establishment of new ones.

However, there has been substantial improvement in productivity in construction in the two territories during the 1970-1982 period, with the improvement being more pronounced in the Gaza Strip. The concentration of private investment in the construction of residential buildings has been instrumental in enhancing productivity of this sector. On the other hand, productivity in the service sectors has fallen off in each of the territories, with services in the Strip suffering the greater decline. It should be noted that relative employment in these sectors has increased considerably during this period and at the same time their relative position in domestic production has been somewhat eroded.

## OCCUPATIONAL STRUCTURE OF EMPLOYMENT

An analysis of employment by occupation reveals that highly educated personnel such as scientists, academics, professionals, technicians, managers, administrators, and clerical workers comprised a small proportion of the total number of persons employed throughout the postwar period. (More than three-quarters of West Bankers who graduate from universities outside the area do not go back home.) The percentage of those employed in these occupations was 9 and 11 percent for the West Bank and Gaza Strip, respectively, in 1969. The figures for 1982 stood at 12 and 11 percent (see Table 3.11). Similarly, the relative share of sales and service workers remained stagnant at around 16 percent in the West Bank, and in the Strip it dropped from about 25 percent in 1969 to about 20 percent in 1982. The share of agricultural employment dropped dramatically for both the West Bank and the Gaza Strip. The proportion of skilled and unskilled workers in total employment expanded by almost one-half in the West Bank and by 65 percent in the Strip.

Of particular interest is the relatively small yet constant share of jobs that require advanced levels of education and training and, as in the case of the West Bank, the modest growth in skilled labor employment. This implies that the range of employment opportunities open to highly qualified persons is extremely limited. The lack of investment in industry, which has remained at a very low level of technol-

TABLE 3.11
Employed persons, by occupation, the West Bank and the Gaza Strip, 1961 and 1969-1982 (percentages)

| Occupation | 1961[1] | 1969 | 1970 | 1971 | 1972 | 1973 | 1974 | 1975 | 1976 | 1977 | 1978 | 1979 | 1980 | 1981 | 1982 |
|---|---|---|---|---|---|---|---|---|---|---|---|---|---|---|---|
| West Bank | | | | | | | | | | | | | | | |
| Total - thousands | 172.2 | 109.9 | 114.6 | 116.8 | 125.2 | 126.4 | 137.0 | 132.5 | 129.7 | 127.3 | 131.5 | 132.8 | 131.3 | 133.4 | 140.9 |
| - percentages | 100.0 | 100.0 | 100.0 | 100.0 | 100.0 | 100.0 | 100.0 | 100.0 | 100.0 | 100.0 | 100.0 | 100.0 | 100.0 | 100.0 | 100.0 |
| Scientific, academic, professional, and technical workers | 4.8 | 6.4 | 7.2 | 7.7 | 7.8 | 8.0 | 7.9 | 8.0 | 8.1 | 8.1 | 8.0 | 7.8 | 7.7 | 8.8 | 8.6 |
| Administrators, managers, clerical, and related workers | 3.6 | 2.6 | 3.2 | 3.1 | 3.5 | 3.5 | 3.1 | 3.6 | 3.5 | 3.3 | 3.0 | 3.1 | 3.5 | 3.7 | 3.5 |
| Sales workers | 7.1 | 9.2 | 9.4 | 10.0 | 9.3 | 9.1 | 8.5 | 9.4 | 10.2 | 10.6 | 9.5 | 9.7 | 10.1 | 9.5 | 9.0 |
| Service workers | 5.6 | 6.6 | 5.6 | 5.7 | 6.1 | 6.2 | 6.1 | 6.4 | 6.6 | 7.0 | 6.9 | 7.0 | 6.7 | 6.8 | 6.9 |
| Agricultural workers | 37.7 | 44.1 | 39.0 | 34.2 | 30.4 | 26.5 | 29.7 | 27.3 | 27.8 | 27.6 | 27.7 | 25.4 | 26.3 | 24.6 | 25.3 |
| Skilled workers in various economic sectors | 35.4 | 31.1 | 35.6 | 39.2 | 23.2 | 26.4 | 23.7 | 24.8 | 24.2 | 23.9 | 25.7 | 26.6 | 25.1 | 26.3 | 26.2 |
| Other and unskilled workers | 5.8 | | | | 19.7 | 20.3 | 21.1 | 20.6 | 19.6 | 19.5 | 19.2 | 20.4 | 20.6 | 20.3 | 20.5 |
| Gaza Strip | | | | | | | | | | | | | | | |
| Total - thousands | -- | 52.9 | 58.7 | 59.8 | 63.6 | 68.2 | 72.9 | 72.6 | 76.1 | 77.2 | 80.4 | 79.6 | 79.8 | 82.5 | 82.0 |
| - percentage | -- | 100.0 | 100.0 | 100.0 | 100.0 | 100.0 | 100.0 | 100.0 | 100.0 | 100.0 | 100.0 | 100.0 | 100.0 | 100.0 | 100.0 |
| Scientific, academic, professional, and technical workers | -- | 7.0 | 6.8 | 6.7 | 8.2 | 7.3 | 7.5 | 6.7 | 7.2 | 7.4 | 7.0 | 6.6 | 6.9 | 7.0 | 7.5 |
| Administrators, managers, clerical, and related workers | -- | 4.2 | 4.1 | 4.3 | 4.4 | 3.6 | 3.8 | 3.6 | 3.7 | 4.0 | 3.1 | 2.7 | 3.1 | 3.0 | 3.7 |
| Sales workers | -- | 15.5 | 14.9 | 15.1 | 12.9 | 12.6 | 12.2 | 12.3 | 12.2 | 11.7 | 11.1 | 9.9 | 11.3 | 11.1 | 11.3 |
| Service workers | -- | 9.7 | 7.7 | 7.8 | 7.7 | 7.5 | 7.8 | 8.6 | 8.1 | 8.6 | 7.6 | 7.6 | 8.4 | 7.9 | 7.5 |
| Agricultural workers | -- | 31.4 | 31.4 | 32.7 | 29.1 | 28.8 | 26.8 | 22.7 | 23.0 | 22.6 | 21.5 | 19.8 | 18.1 | 17.0 | 16.9 |
| Skilled workers in various economic sectors | | 32.1 | 35.1 | 33.4 | 22.6 | 22.4 | 25.9 | 24.7 | 23.7 | 24.7 | 28.4 | 31.7 | 31.1 | 31.6 | 30.9 |
| Other and unskilled workers | -- | | | | 15.1 | 17.8 | 16.0 | 21.5 | 22.1 | 21.0 | 21.3 | 21.7 | 21.1 | 22.4 | 22.2 |

Source: Central Bureau of Statistics, Statistical Abstract of Israel (various issues).

[1] Department of Statistics, First Census, Vol. 2, p. 70.

ogy, the absence of modern forms of business organization and the smallness of the local civil service have severely restricted demand for educated and skilled labor. In addition, the high salaries that have been paid in oil-producing Arab countries have encouraged much of this labor to emigrate. As a result, the labor force in the territories has and will become increasingly dominated by the unskilled, less educated and less enterprising categories of the population.[21] Investment in higher education in the two territories has had only a limited impact on economic development thus far, because of the continued emigration of the better educated segment of the labor force.[22]

**EMPLOYMENT IN ISRAEL**

Initially, the Israeli authorities did not allow people from the occupied territories to work inside Israel for fear of aggravating the unemployment situation there. But when the Israeli economy began to expand and the labor market grew tight in 1968, workers from the territories were allowed to seek work in Israel. As a result, the areas' work force began to commute daily to work sites in Israel in increasing numbers, returning in the evening to their homes.

Workers were recruited through Labor Exchanges operated in the territories by the Israeli Ministry of Labor and Social Affairs. Initially, these exchanges were intended to place laborers mainly in jobs in the local communities, but in fact they have ended up channeling almost all recruits into menial work in Israel. Once a worker had been hired, the Labor Exchange issued him a temporary permit of short duration without which he could not commute to his new job in Israel; whenever this permit expired a revalidation from the employment service was needed. Workers from the territories are not allowed to stay overnight in Israel and must commute to their jobs on a daily basis. Although staying overnight in Israel is not allowed, it does, of course, occur. Originally, these workers were transported to and from work sites free of charge, but later charges for transportation were imposed.

Soon after occupation, the number of territory workers in Israel was small, and did not exceed 5,000 and 9,000 persons in 1968 and 1969, respectively (see Table 3.12). This number had doubled by 1970 and grew to 79,000 in 1982 (or 6 percent of the total Israeli work force).

The number of West Bank laborers working in Israel was about 15,000 in 1970, compared to 6,000 for the Strip. In 1982, the respective figures were 44,000 and 36,000--a phenomenal increase of 198 and 500 percent. Employment of Arab territory workers in Israel equaled more than two-fifths of the domestically employed labor in the West Bank, and three-

TABLE 3.12
Employed persons working in Israel, by selected economic branch, 1970-1982 (percentages)

| Year | Total(1000) | Agriculture | Industry | Construction | Other |
|---|---|---|---|---|---|
| **Total** | | | | | |
| 1970 | 20.6 | 24.4 | 11.6 | 54.3 | 9.7 |
| 1971 | 33.8 | 22.3 | 14.8 | 52.3 | 10.6 |
| 1972 | 52.4 | 23.1 | 17.1 | 49.5 | 10.3 |
| 1973 | 61.3 | 19.3 | 18.1 | 51.7 | 10.9 |
| 1974 | 68.7 | 19.1 | 17.5 | 52.5 | 10.9 |
| 1975 | 66.3 | 14.3 | 18.4 | 54.4 | 12.9 |
| 1976 | 64.9 | 15.4 | 19.7 | 50.3 | 14.6 |
| 1977 | 63.0 | 16.2 | 21.3 | 45.3 | 17.2 |
| 1978 | 68.2 | 16.8 | 22.2 | 44.8 | 16.2 |
| 1979 | 74.1 | 14.8 | 22.8 | 46.2 | 16.2 |
| 1980 | 75.1 | 13.7 | 20.9 | 47.4 | 18.0 |
| 1981 | 75.8 | 12.7 | 18.2 | 51.0 | 18.1 |
| 1982 | 79.1 | 12.8 | 17.7 | 52.8 | 16.7 |
| **West Bank** | | | | | |
| 1970 | 14.7 | 17.7 | (12.9) | 57.2 | 12.2 |
| 1971 | 25.6 | 12.9 | 16.8 | 57.0 | 13.3 |
| 1972 | 34.9 | 12.3 | 18.6 | 56.8 | 12.3 |
| 1973 | 38.6 | 8.8 | 20.7 | 56.8 | 13.7 |
| 1974 | 42.4 | 10.6 | 19.3 | 56.1 | 14.0 |
| 1975 | 40.4 | 10.9 | 18.6 | 55.0 | 15.5 |
| 1976 | 37.1 | 12.2 | 20.9 | 49.6 | 17.3 |
| 1977 | 35.5 | 12.7 | 22.5 | 44.2 | 20.6 |
| 1978 | 36.8 | 11.4 | 23.6 | 46.0 | 19.0 |
| 1979 | 39.8 | 10.3 | 23.9 | 47.7 | 18.1 |
| 1980 | 40.6 | 9.9 | 21.0 | 50.1 | 19.0 |
| 1981 | 39.9 | 9.3 | 18.1 | 52.7 | 19.9 |
| 1982 | 43.0 | 9.4 | 17.9 | 54.1 | 18.6 |
| **Gaza Strip** | | | | | |
| 1970 | 5.9 | 40.7 | (8.5) | 47.4 | 3.4 |
| 1971 | 8.2 | 51.2 | (8.5) | 37.8 | (2.5) |
| 1972 | 17.5 | 45.0 | 14.7 | 36.0 | 4.3 |
| 1973 | 22.7 | 37.0 | 13.6 | 43.2 | 6.2 |
| 1974 | 26.3 | 32.7 | 14.8 | 46.4 | 6.1 |
| 1975 | 25.9 | 18.5 | 18.1 | 53.3 | 10.1 |
| 1976 | 27.8 | 19.6 | 18.5 | 51.8 | 10.1 |
| 1977 | 27.5 | 20.4 | 19.6 | 46.5 | 13.5 |
| 1978 | 31.4 | 23.2 | 20.4 | 44.3 | 12.1 |
| 1979 | 34.3 | 20.1 | 21.6 | 44.3 | 14.0 |
| 1980 | 34.5 | 18.3 | 20.9 | 44.0 | 16.8 |
| 1981 | 35.9 | 16.2 | 18.4 | 49.5 | 15.9 |
| 1982 | 36.1 | 16.9 | 17.4 | 51.2 | 14.5 |

Source: Central Bureau of Statistics, Statistical Abstract of Israel (various issues).

quarters of that of the Gaza Strip in 1982. There was a drop in the number of West Bankers employed in Israel in the mid- and late 1970s. This reduction was a response to the economic slow-down in Israel, the narrowing of wage differentials, and full employment status reached in the West Bank.[23] On the other hand, employment of the Strip's labor in Israel has risen consistently and it does not seem sensitive to downturns in the Israeli economy.

The construction sector in Israel has continued to provide employment for around one-half of the commuting workers, although there was a drop in this trend between 1977 and 1980. However, construction has remained the largest employer of territory workers: 51 percent of the total Israeli employment in this sector in 1982. The concentration of West Bank labor in Israeli projects may be attributed to the proximity of many Israeli construction sites to the workers' homes (especially in new settlements in and around Jerusalem).

Employment of territory workers in Israeli agriculture has declined in importance in the last decade to 9 and 17 percent for the West Bank and Gaza Strip, respectively, in 1982, from the 1970 levels of 18 and 41 percent. The percentage of migrant workers employed in industry and services has increased. In industry it has risen by 5 percent in the West Bank and 9 percent for the Gaza Strip between 1970 and 1982. The service sectors have seen a similar increase.

Official Israeli statistics on the number of Arab territory workers in Israel have been grossly underestimated because they keep track only of those registered with the Labor Exchanges. Many employees, and employers, prefer to bypass official placement centers to evade taxes and other wage deductions. Israeli authorities have estimated the number of unofficially employed workers at 25 to 30 percent of those legally employed.[24]

Initially, many of the Arab workers drawn to Israel were from the ranks of the unemployed and underemployed, especially in agriculture. These were attracted by high wages. This labor pool was soon exhausted and further expansion of Arab territory workers in Israel was achieved at the expense of employment in the domestic economies, creating labor shortages and pushing up wages. With full employment and higher labor participation rates in the territories, any additional employment in Israel must reduce the number of those working in the territories,[25] or must be confined to a portion of population growth.[26]

So far, Arab territory workers employed in the Israeli economy have been concentrated in the unskilled and semi-skilled occupations. They are employed at the "lower end of the occupational scale, in many of the more menial temporary or seasonal jobs to which the Israeli labor force seems less and less attracted."[27] Unfortunately, this division of labor has been along ethnic lines,[28] and has reduced the role of the territories to that of supplying the Israeli economy with cheap labor.[29]

The territories stood to gain from the transfer of labor to the Israeli economy. Unemployment among the unskilled and semi-skilled sector of the labor force was reduced appreciably; many more male adults became active in the labor force; wages earned by this labor force were sent back home, thereby improving the standard of living of the population;[30] and demand for a wide range of products was expanded, giving rise to modest investment in the economies.[31]

Labor movement, however, has not been without its shortcomings. The massive emigration of workers has created some labor scarcity in certain economic sectors in the territories. This has pushed up wages in these sectors.[32] Arab workers in Israel tend to hold low-skill jobs and are concentrated in certain economic activities. Thus, in the event of economic slow-down or recession they are more liable to adverse effects. The confinement of this labor to menial work may well create a sense of social deprivation, especially when the worker compares his conditions with those of his privileged, better paid, well-positioned, and unionized Israeli counterpart.[33]

Incomes earned from employment in Israel have undoubtedly been one of the major contributing factors to economic growth in the territories. But domestic economic activity has failed to expand due to the very low level of investment. Therefore, too few new jobs were created in the domestic economies, especially in the West Bank, to absorb the increments in the active population or the laborers who lose their employment in Israel when economic conditions become unfavorable.[34] In fact, many unskilled and semi-skilled workers, in addition to the educated and skilled ones, have emigrated in increasing numbers since the 1975 recession in Israel. At the same time, the economies of Jordan and oil-producing countries, booming and labor short, provided alternative employment for the territories' labor.

## VOCATIONAL TRAINING

The Israeli authorities have opened 25 centers for vocational training in the occupied territories (18 in the West Bank and 7 in the Gaza Strip), operated by the Ministry of Labor and Social Affairs. (In addition, there is a number of private and governmental vocational schools that receive assistance from Jordan, West Bankers living in Jordan and the Arab Gulf, and private voluntary organizations.) The number of people completing courses at these centers reached 50,000 at the end of 1982.[35] Initially, these centers were established to provide Arab inhabitants with some basic skills in construction to prepare them for employment in the Israeli construction sector. A trainee would attend a course for six months, after which he was eligible for employment.

Recently, there has been some effort to diversify training into other skills in order to attract certain segments of the population, namely young people and women.[36] Longer courses were substituted for the shorter ones, and these now cover a wider range of skills such as manufacturing, car repair, welding, sewing, etc. In 1982, some 4,000 persons completed courses at these training centers, of whom 53 percent were from the West Bank. Courses in industry make up almost one-quarter of the total in 1982-83, compared to less than 10 percent in construction and about one-third in the transport sector.[37]

At present, training programs are set up to satisfy the needs of the Israeli economy. Indeed, there exist close links between these centers and the employment service to channel their trainees into the Israeli labor markets. This type of relationship overshadows the development needs of the territories and minimizes the benefits that can be directly derived from the increase in the supply of trained manpower.[38]

## WAGES

Agriculture was one of the lowest paying sectors in the economies of the occupied territories at the beginning of the 1970s. But thanks to higher wages paid in Israel, scores of laborers moved there to work. As a result, the labor force became fully employed and the supply of labor grew short, thereby pushing up wages in the territories in various economic sectors (see Table 3.13). The gap between wages paid in the territories and in Israel has narrowed considerably, increasing from about 50 percent of daily wages paid in Israel to more than 93 percent in 1982 (see Table 3.14). Wages paid to migrant workers in Israel were highest for construction and lowest for agricultural jobs. The areas' laborers still occupy the lowest paid jobs in the Israeli wage scale.[39]

Wages earned by Arab workers in Israel are subject to deductions for tax and social security purposes. These deductions are governed by tax law and national insurance legislation and may account for 30 percent of earnings. Laborers working in Israel pay their share to all branches of the National Insurance Scheme, yet they are not entitled to benefits accrued on the basis of residency such as old-age and survivors' benefits, invalidity benefits, unemployment benefits, and children's allowances.[40] (The latter was partially compensated for in the form of a special allowance for the first two children.)[41] Pension payments were first paid in

TABLE 3.13

Average daily wage per employee, by economic branch, the West Bank and the Gaza Strip, 1970-1982 (IL)

| Year | Total | Agriculture | Industry | Construction | Commerce Restaurants & Hotels | Transport | Public & Community Services | Other |
|---|---|---|---|---|---|---|---|---|
| West Bank | | | | | | | | |
| 1970 | 7.9 | 5.8 | 6.6 | 10.3 | 5.6 | 7.8 | 8.7 | 5.5 |
| 1971 | 10.3 | 8.1 | 8.9 | 14.2 | 7.2 | 10.8 | 10.0 | 6.8 |
| 1972 | 13.7 | 11.8 | 12.7 | 18.2 | 10.3 | 14.1 | 11.8 | 9.7 |
| 1973 | 17.9 | 16.2 | 16.3 | 23.3 | 13.6 | 17.1 | 15.9 | 13.2 |
| 1974 | 25.3 | 21.9 | 23.0 | 30.8 | 19.8 | 23.9 | 23.9 | 18.8 |
| 1975 | 39.6 | 33.3 | 34.9 | 47.2 | 32.7 | 35.1 | 39.2 | 30.4 |
| 1976 | 50.0 | 41.3 | 43.4 | 58.2 | 43.3 | 45.4 | 52.5 | 43.1 |
| 1977 | 68.0 | 56.0 | 60.0 | 79.1 | 59.8 | 61.9 | 71.4 | 55.3 |
| 1978 | 105.5 | 86.1 | 94.3 | 120.2 | 96.4 | 99.7 | 110.1 | 79.6 |
| 1979 | 181.7 | 143.8 | 166.3 | 215.9 | 169.4 | 169.3 | 173.2 | 135.4 |
| 1980 | 364.0 | 287.0 | 329.0 | 426.0 | 331.0 | 321.0 | 360.0 | 285.0 |
| 1981 | 1,040.0 | 706.0 | 892.0 | 1,220.0 | 921.0 | 923.0 | 1,084.0 | 808.0 |
| 1982 | 2,310.0 | 1,830.0 | 201.0 | 2,660.0 | 2,060.0 | 2,040.0 | 2,370.0 | 1,860.0 |
| Gaza Strip | | | | | | | | |
| 1970 | 6.5 | 5.8 | 5.3 | 7.0 | (3.7) | (6.2) | 7.7 | (3.9) |
| 1971 | 8.2 | 8.0 | 6.9 | 10.0 | (4.6) | (6.5) | 8.8 | (5.5) |
| 1972 | 12.8 | 13.0 | 13.8 | 17.3 | (8.5) | (10.6) | 11.2 | (9.2) |
| 1973 | 19.6 | 19.6 | 20.3 | 25.3 | (19.7) | (16.9) | 16.0 | (15.1) |
| 1974 | 27.2 | 23.0 | 27.2 | 32.9 | 24.4 | 25.5 | 26.9 | 25.4 |
| 1975 | 38.7 | 29.2 | 36.8 | 44.6 | 35.8 | 35.7 | 43.6 | 30.3 |
| 1976 | 49.6 | 41.3 | 45.8 | 56.6 | 45.2 | 46.7 | 54.1 | 42.9 |
| 1977 | 65.6 | 53.9 | 61.1 | 73.2 | 64.5 | 62.1 | 73.2 | 53.0 |
| 1978 | 102.9 | 82.3 | 96.7 | 118.2 | 92.9 | 97.3 | 113.3 | 79.5 |
| 1979 | 199.2 | 160.1 | 195.1 | 241.9 | 192.0 | 177.2 | 180.3 | 172.9 |
| 1980 | 392.0 | 322.0 | 355.0 | 465.0 | 381.0 | 389.0 | 385.0 | 322.0 |
| 1981 | 1,025.0 | 757.0 | 850.0 | 1,129.0 | 861.0 | 1,003.0 | 1,267.0 | 749.0 |
| 1982 | 2,420.0 | 1,780.0 | 2,170.0 | 262.0 | 2,200.0 | 2,120.0 | 2,870.0 | 2,030.0 |

Source: Central Bureau of Statistics, Statistical Abstract of Israel (various issues).

TABLE 3.14
Average daily wage per employee for employees working in Israel, by selected economic branch, 1970-1982 (IL)

| Year | Total | Agriculture | Industry | Construction | Other |
|---|---|---|---|---|---|
| **Total** | | | | | |
| 1969 | 10.3 | 8.3 | 9.3 | 11.5 | 9.5 |
| 1970 | 11.8 | 10.0 | 11.1 | 13.0 | (10.6) |
| 1971 | 13.4 | 11.5 | 12.3 | 14.7 | 11.9 |
| 1972 | 17.2 | 15.4 | 15.6 | 19.1 | 14.8 |
| 1973 | 22.9 | 20.6 | 21.6 | 25.1 | 19.1 |
| 1974 | 29.1 | 23.7 | 28.7 | 32.2 | 27.0 |
| 1975 | 43.4 | 33.9 | 42.1 | 47.4 | 40.1 |
| 1976 | 53.4 | 42.7 | 51.6 | 58.2 | 50.9 |
| 1977 | 71.0 | 56.7 | 69.2 | 77.7 | 69.2 |
| 1978 | 110.8 | 86.6 | 110.2 | 120.5 | 108.5 |
| 1979 | 209.3 | 158.0 | 202.2 | 231.4 | 200.7 |
| 1980 | 405.0 | 319.0 | 387.0 | 447.0 | 377.0 |
| 1981 | 1082.0 | 767.0 | 994.0 | 1204.0 | 1035.0 |
| 1982 | 2470.0 | 1900.0 | 2360.0 | 2700.0 | 2310.0 |
| **West Bank** | | | | | |
| 1970 | 11.8 | 9.0 | (10.9) | 13.0 | 10.5 |
| 1971 | 13.5 | 10.7 | 12.1 | 15.0 | 11.8 |
| 1972 | 17.0 | 14.3 | 14.2 | 19.0 | 14.2 |
| 1973 | 21.8 | 17.7 | 20.1 | 24.2 | 17.7 |
| 1974 | 28.7 | 22.7 | 27.2 | 31.5 | 24.4 |
| 1975 | 44.6 | 35.0 | 42.3 | 48.4 | 39.6 |
| 1976 | 53.5 | 40.9 | 51.1 | 58.7 | 50.0 |
| 1977 | 72.0 | 55.0 | 69.7 | 79.7 | 68.0 |
| 1978 | 112.1 | 84.8 | 110.4 | 120.8 | 108.8 |
| 1979 | 198.7 | 141.7 | 190.7 | 219.5 | 185.0 |
| 1980 | 394.0 | 290.0 | 377.0 | 432.0 | 361.0 |
| 1981 | 1121.0 | 729.0 | 1010.0 | 1249.0 | 1057.0 |
| 1982 | 2480.0 | 1930.0 | 2260.0 | 2710.0 | 2270.0 |
| **Gaza Strip** | | | | | |
| 1970 | 11.7 | 10.7 | (11.6) | 12.5 | (11.9) |
| 1971 | 12.9 | 12.3 | (13.7) | 13.4 | (13.4) |
| 1972 | 17.6 | 16.0 | (17.5) | 19.5 | (18.8) |
| 1973 | 24.6 | 21.7 | 25.2 | 26.8 | 24.8 |
| 1974 | 30.4 | 24.8 | 31.2 | 33.8 | 30.9 |
| 1975 | 41.9 | 32.9 | 41.4 | 45.4 | 40.2 |
| 1976 | 53.5 | 44.2 | 52.4 | 57.6 | 52.8 |
| 1977 | 69.8 | 58.2 | 68.5 | 74.9 | 71.5 |
| 1978 | 109.2 | 87.7 | 110.0 | 120.0 | 107.8 |
| 1979 | 222.4 | 168.5 | 217.5 | 247.3 | 224.3 |
| 1980 | 420.0 | 337.0 | 399.0 | 469.0 | 402.0 |
| 1981 | 1038.0 | 791.0 | 978.0 | 1151.0 | 1004.0 |
| 1982 | 2470.0 | 1870.0 | 2490.0 | 2680.0 | 2370.0 |

Source: Central Bureau of Statistics, Statistical Abstract of Israel (various issues).

early 1980 to the few construction workers who had completed ten years' service and had reached retirement age. Other social benefits such as sickness leave, compensation for dismissal, clothing allowance, wife allowance, and mutual benefit insurance were disbursed to laborers in various economic sectors.[42]

The general trends that emerge regarding population and the size and nature of the work force in the West Bank and Gaza Strip are what we might expect given the social and political circumstances. Fluctuations in the overall size of the population, although more marked in the West Bank than in the Gaza Strip, have at times been extreme with a fairly steady stream of emigrants heading toward Jordan and other Arab countries. The fact that the size of the population has remained consistent in both territories is to be accounted for, as we have seen, by high birth rates. But the mere consistency of the size of the population is in itself misleading because the general trend has been for the skilled and educated to emigrate and not to return. In this sense, we can speak of a depletion of qualified human resources. Those who remain have tended to be the relatively unskilled, whose absorption into the Israeli economy, although economically beneficial to the individual in the short run, carries with it many attendant dangers. Chief among these is the lack of investment, in human and economic terms, in the local Arab economies. Stagnation in domestic industry has resulted from this. An added danger is the susceptibility of Arab migrant workers to fluctuations in the Israeli economy. Lastly, the trend for many Arabs to work in Israel in inferior, unskilled jobs reinforces unpleasant attitudes that are racially based. In short, Arab workers from the territories become "second-class citizens" in the work place and are seen as such by themselves as well as by the Israelis.

## Notes

1. Jamil Hilal, The West Bank: Its Social and Economical Structure, 1948-1974 (Beirut: Palestine Liberation Organization, 1974), p. 18.

2. See Edward Hagopian and A. B. Zahlan, "Palestine's Arab Population: The Demography of the Palestinians," Journal of Palestine Studies (Summer 1974), p. 53; United Nations estimate cited in "Palestinian Emigration and Israeli Land Expropriation in the Occupied Territories," Journal of Palestine Studies (Autumn 1973), p. 110; and Van Arkadie, Benefits and Burdens, p. 22.

3. Efrat, "Settlement Pattern," p. 349.

4. Ibid.; and Hagopian and Zahlan, "Palestine's Arab Population," p. 54.

5. Central Bureau of Statistics, Census of Population of the West Bank of Jordan, Gaza Strip, Northern Sinai and Golan Heights (Jerusalem, 1967), p. ix.

6. Ibid., p. xx.

7. Ibid., p. x.

8. Ibid.

9. Ibid.

10. Efrat, "Settlement Pattern," p. 350.

11. Department of Statistics, First Census, Vol. 1, p. 327.

12. Van Arkadie, Benefits and Burdens, p. 56.

13. Central Bureau of Statistics, Census of Population, p. xi.

14. Haim Darin-Drabkin, "The Economic Viability of a Palestinian State in the West Bank and Gaza Strip," New Outlook (April 1978), p. 47.

15. Department of Statistics, First Census, Vol. 1, p. 41-43.

16. Central Bureau of Statistics, Census of Population, p. xiii.

17. Van Arkadie, Benefits and Burdens, p. 59.

18. Arie Bregman, The Economy of the Administered Territories, 1974-1975 (Jerusalem: Bank of Israel, 1976), p. 29-30.

19. Department of Statistics, First Census of Population and Housing, Vol. 2 (Amman, 1964), p. 37-39.

20. Ben Shahar et al., Economic Structure, p. 21.

21. Committee of Foreign Affairs, U.S. House of Representatives, The West Bank-Gaza Economy: Problems and Prospects (Washington, D.C., 1980), p. 42.

22. Ibid., p. 34-35.

23. Ibid., p. 14.

24. International Labor Office, Report of the Director General, Appendices (Geneva, 1981), p. 25.

25. Bull, The West Bank, p. 118.

26. Van Arkadie, Benefits and Burdens, p. 73-74.

27. International Labor Office, Action Taken on the Resolutions Adopted by the International Conference at its 64th Session, Supplement to the Report of the Director-General (Geneva, 1979), p. 30.

28. Ibid.

29. Van Arkadie, Benefits and Burdens, p. 142.

30. Ibid., p. 64.

31. Ibid., p. 69.

32. Ibid., p. 47.

33. Avigdor Haselkorn, Mordecai Kurz, and Abraham Wagner, Trade and Economic Links in the Transition Phase: the West Bank and Gaza Strip (Marina del Rey: Analytical Assessments Corporation, 1978), p. 77-78.

34. International Labor Office, Action Taken, p. 43.

35. International Labor Office, Report of the Director

_General, Appendices_ (Geneva, 1983), p. 40.

36. Ibid. (1981), p. 32-33.
37. Ibid. (1983), p. 40.
38. Ibid. (1981), p. 32-33.
39. Van Arkadie, _Benefits and Burdens_, p. 65.
40. International Labor Office, _Report_ (1981), p. 37.
41. Ibid.
42. Ibid.

# 4
# Agriculture

Agriculture is the backbone of the West Bank and the Gaza Strip economies. Its contribution to gross domestic product and employment in the West Bank has been the highest of all economic sectors, except trade and commerce. In the prewar period, agriculture's share in the GDP of the West Bank ranged from a low of less than 20 percent in drought years to a high of about 25 percent in good harvest seasons; its share in employment was two-fifths of the total in 1961. On the eve of the war in 1967, agriculture provided a living for 45 percent of the total population of the West Bank.[1] Similarly, agriculture was the largest single activity in the Gaza Strip in 1966, comanding over one-third of domestic production and employment.

The importance of agriculture has been reinforced in the postwar economy of the West Bank; its share in domestic production and employment has been a full one-third and more. By contrast, agriculture's position in the Strip's economy was relatively weakened in terms of output and employment, although it remained the most important of all sectors.

## LAND

The total area of the West Bank is 5,572 square kilometers,* including Jerusalem whose area is about 67 square kilometers. Agricultural potential of the West Bank is governed by its topography; e.g., the soil is thin in the hilly areas confining farming there to terraced land and to tree cultivation; land is irrigated in the narrow valley along the Jordan River; the small plains are used for dry farming. Dry farming depends heavily on a widely variable annual precipitation of up to 600-700 millimeters in good rainy years. Therefore, although the cultivated acreage in the West Bank varied

----------

*Excluding the area of the Dead Sea.

in response to rainfall, cultivable land accounted for almost one-half of the total area. The Gaza Strip is much smaller than the West Bank, having an area of 367 square kilometers, of which about 210 (57 percent) are cultivable. Agriculture in the Strip is by and large dependent on the intensive cultivation of irrigated land.

Since the occupation of the West Bank and the Gaza Strip in 1967, Israeli authorities have expropriated, seized, or closed off large tracts of land. In addition, some land has come into the possession of Israeli companies and individuals through purchases. It is extremely difficult to arrive at an up-to-date figure for the total area of land that has been expropriated or otherwise confiscated, especially because it has been expanding fairly rapidly and quietly. Altogether, more than 1,500,000 dunums in the West Bank[2] (27 percent of its total area) and 119,000 dunums in the Gaza Strip[3] (about one-third of the total) have come under Israeli control for civilian or military purposes by the end of 1980. The figure for 1982 in the West Bank is probably as high as 40 percent of its total area.

Israeli-acquired land in the West Bank included those areas that had previously belonged to the government of Jordan or to absent owners. State-owned land was confiscated despite the fact that it was cultivated or utilized by nearby villagers for many generations. The Israelis, contrary to traditions and practices in the region, do not recognize villagers' claims to this land.[4] Rather, they assert their right to seize it for various purposes such as civilian settlements, military camps, or any other purpose. Total area of confiscated state land has been estimated at about 750,000 dunums. In addition, about a half million dunums of absentee and "abandoned" land (owned by those persons who lived outside the West Bank at the time of the September 1967 census or who fled the area during and immediately after the war) were seized on the pretext that their registered owners live outside.[5] And a few hundred thousand dunums were either purchased by Israeli individuals, businesses, or institutions or seized (or fenced off) for military or other reasons such as proximity to certain roads, settlements, or army camps.[6]

Some of the expropriated land is allocated for the construction of the ever-increasing Jewish settlements or for the "fattening" of old ones. Altogether, by the end of 1982 there were more than one hundred Jewish settlements (including a few approved ones) on the West Bank, excluding developments in and around Arab Jerusalem, housing around 25,000 Jews; there are eleven settlements in the Gaza Strip, with two urban centers under construction. (Estimates of the number of Jewish settlements vary, but the figures here were collected from the Israeli press.)

Land expropriation has adversely affected agriculture in

the territories because as a result, much land has been withdrawn from farming; the amount of such land is not exactly known. Suffice to mention the large tracts of pasture that were sealed off, depriving livestock from natural grazing grounds. The land, water, and rights acquired by Israeli settlers are out of proportion to their numbers.[7] For instance, the few thousand settlers in the Jordan Valley have control over 70 to 80 percent of the area[8] and much of the water, cultivating over one-half of all irrigated land in the West Bank.[9] Likewise, Jewish settlements in the Gaza Strip are all based on irrigated farming and compete with the indigenous population for available water. Therefore, it is not at all surprising that the reduction of cultivable land and the diversion of water for settlers' use have driven many farmers in the territories out of business and transformed them into wage laborers in nearby settlements and in Israel. Evidence of the past decade attests to an accentuation of this trend, especially in the West Bank. In 1970, there were 33,800 land owners and 11,200 farm laborers in the West Bank and 6,200 land owners and 13,000 workers in the Gaza Strip. In 1982, the number of landed farmers dwindled to 29,600 in the West Bank and remained the same in the Strip. On the other hand, the number of farm laborers working in the areas dramatically declined to only 5,900 and 8,200 in the West Bank and the Gaza Strip, respectively.[10]

Another reason for the reduction in the cultivated area is owners' abandonment of farms due to the limited resources at their disposal; political uncertainty concerning land tenure;[11] high cost of farm labor; poor returns on investment, especially in dry farming; and the prospects of higher incomes from employment in Israel.

According to the agricultural census of 1953, total cultivated area was put at 2,435,000 dunums in the West Bank, comprising about 30 percent of all agricultural land in Jordan.[12] This area, however, fluctuated in the prewar period between 1,800,000 and 2,200,000 dunums annually, depending on the amount of precipitation. The Israelis put the cultivated land at 1,700,000 dunums in the West Bank in 1967/68, or 47 percent of the total area. On average, total cultivated area in the past two decades has been as follows:

| | Dunums |
|---|---|
| 1961-1966[13] | 2,030,000 |
| 1968-1971[14] | 1,746,000 |
| 1976-1979[15] | 1,594,000 |
| 1980-1982[16] | 1,636,000 |

Evidently, the cultivated area in the West Bank has declined by 14 percent during 1968-1971, 21 percent in 1968-1979, and 19 percent in 1980-1982 from the prewar level. The cultivated area in the Gaza Strip was estimated at 198,000 dunums in 1968, or 55 percent of the total area. It has declined to 177,000 dunums in 1981 and 165,000 in 1982.[17]

Irrigation remains confined to a small proportion of the cultivated area in the West Bank. Irrigated land has been estimated at between 92,000 and 98,000 dunums,[18] or 6.0 percent of the cultivated area. This, however, compares unfavorably with Israel and Jordan where irrigated agriculture accounts for 43 and 13 percent, respectively, of the area under cultivation.[19] On the other hand, irrigation is the backbone of agriculture in the Gaza Strip, where it is practiced intensively in 90,000 dunums, or 45 percent of the total cultivated area.[20]

Surface irrigation is the most widely used method in the two territories whereby spring or well water flows through open channels and floods dirt ditches alongside the plants. This method, however, is extremely inefficient and wasteful, resulting in losses of up to 50 percent of the original amount of water intended for use through evaporation and seepage.[21] The more modern systems of irrigation such as sprinkling, dripping, and subsurface methods have been introduced on a very modest scale throughout the West Bank, except in the Jordan Valley where the use of new technologies is more prevalent.

## WATER

The West Bank is by and large dependent on rainfall for its water. Exploited water resources are mainly groundwater tables that are recharged by rainfall whose distribution is uneven and varies from 100 millimeters in the Dead Sea area to as much as 600-700 millimeters in the mountainous regions. However, much of the rainfall either evaporates or is lost through surface run-off or underground drainage, leaving less than one-quarter of precipitation for possible exploitation.[22]

Water potential of the West Bank is estimated at 850 million cubic meters, of which 600 million are stored underground, 45 to 50 million are surface run-off, and 200 million are in the Jordan River.[23] Some 50 million cubic meters of groundwater are brackish,[24] and much of the surface run-off is lost because no system exists to collect this water. The potential supply of water aquifers of 600 million cubic meters lies mostly under the West Bank, yet much of it plays a crucial role in providing Israel with a considerable portion of its water needs. Israel taps over one-third of its annual water requirement of 1,600 million cubic meters from the western groundwater horizon in the West Bank.[25]

There are about 300 small springs in the West Bank, fed by local aquifers of limited capacity. Some 60 large springs also exist, mostly in the Jordan Valley, and are utilized for irrigation; the others are part of the water distribution system supplying water for domestic consumption. Average output of all sweet water springs is about 50 to 60 million cubic meters annually; that of salty and unexploited springs in the Jordan Valley is around 40 to 50 million. In addition to springs, there exist some 350 wells and boreholes pumping close to 40 million cubic meters annually.[26] In 1977/78, there were 314 wells owned by Arabs in the West Bank, excluding 17 wells sunk for Jewish settlements. Total amount of water pumped from all those wells was 47 million cubic meters, of which 14 million (30 percent) was used by 20,000 Jewish settlers in the area, mainly for irrigation.[27]

At present, water consumption in the West Bank exceeds 100 million cubic meters annually, of which 14 million were for domestic use and the remainder for irrigation. On a per capita basis, domestic consumption comes to about 20 cubic meters per annum, compared with 60 cubic meters in Israel.[28]

The amount of water being exploited by West Bank Arabs is barely sufficient to support the area presently cultivated, provided a good level of precipitation exists. Hence, the only way to expand the cultivated area is to extend irrigation through the sinking of new wells to land that would otherwise remain idle. However, the Israeli authorities have severely restricted drilling of new Arab wells or even improving the capacity of already existing ones.[29] Almost all Arab applications for the sinking of new wells for irrigation purposes have been turned down by Israeli authorities.[30] Even municipalities have faced difficulties in their efforts to expand water supplies to meet increasing domestic demand. Conversely, the Israeli authorities have been active in the development of water resources for Jewish settlements in the West Bank.[31]

The ever-expanding Jewish settlements on the West Bank have threatened to greatly diminish the amount of water available for Arab farmers. Water currently consumed by these settlements is in the neighborhood of 20 million cubic meters per annum. When the planned expansion of irrigation in Jewish settlements is completed, the demand for water will more than double to 53 million cubic meters.[32] "These settlements are in direct competition with Arab farmers for the West Bank's limited water resources. The ban on the drilling of new Arab wells and the confiscation of wells belonging to absentee owners has meant that the water available to Arab agriculture has remained at or below the amount available in 1967."[33]

Arab wells in the West Bank are usually sunk to a depth of up to 100 meters, which is not enough to meet the main groundwater flow. On the other hand, the bores for Jewish settlements are 300-500 meters deep. This practice, coupled with the installation of powerful pumps, has adversely affected some existing Arab wells in the area, such as those in the villages of Bardala, and Tel Al Bada in the northern Jordan Valley.[34] The El-Auja's only spring near Jericho has run dry due to heavy pumping at new wells drilled for nearby settlements.[35]

The present water situation would certainly lead to the conclusion that should the occupation continue, water resources available to West Bank farmers will become even more scarce. The only possibility to expand the irrigated areas will be through the more efficient use of the currently available water.

In the Gaza Strip the annual consumption of water is about 100 million cubic meters,[36] as much as in the West Bank. Irrigated agriculture consumes 85 percent of this total, and the rest is used for domestic and other consumption.[37] Much of the water exploited in the Strip is pumped from more than 1,800 wells, most of which are overutilized and becoming salinated. The Israeli authorities have been more positive in facing the serious water situation in the Strip because water use there does not affect Israeli supplies. Thus, they took action to alleviate some of the water problems that faced local farmers such as metering existing wells, prohibiting the sinking of new ones, and encouraging the use of water-saving irrigation techniques, i.e., dripping and sprinkling.[38]

## FARM SIZE

Farms in the West Bank and Gaza Strip are mainly small and cultivated by the owner (see Table 4.1). Census data are available on farm size in the West Bank in 1953, 1965, and 1968. In 1953, more than two-thirds of the farms were smaller than 50 dunums, and one-third were 50 dunums or more. Between 1953 and 1965, landholdings apparently became more fragmented due mainly to inheritance laws. One-half of the farms were less than 10 dunums, and more than four-fifths were less than 50 dunums in 1965. At the same time, the proportion of the bigger farms (50 dunums and over) was cut in half. It should be noted that big farms with an area of 200 dunums and more declined from 6 percent of all landholdings in 1953 to little more than 1.0 percent in 1965.

In 1968, farms whose size was smaller than 50 dunums comprised 72 percent of all landholdings in the West Bank, compared with 84 percent in 1965; those with an area of 100 dunums or more accounted for 11 percent, versus 5 percent in 1965. Some consolidation of landholdings seems to have taken place since the 1965 census whereby the number of the smaller units was reduced. Average farm size increased by 10 dunums, from 34 dunums in 1965 to 44 dunums in 1967.[39] Farm holdings in the Gaza Strip were even more fragmented than in the West

TABLE 4.1
Farm Size, the West Bank, 1953, 1965, and 1968, and the Gaza Strip, 1968 (percentages)

| | West Bank | | | Gaza Strip |
|---|---|---|---|---|
| Dunum[a] | 1953[1] | 1965[2] | 1968[3] | 1968[3] |
| Less than 10 | 27.7 | 49.7 | 40.5 | 46.3 |
| 10-19 | 40.3 | 12.6 | | 22.4 |
| 20-49 | | 21.8 | 31.0 | 20.1 |
| 50-99 | 16.1 | 10.6 | 17.2 | 7.1 |
| 100-199 | 10.2 | 4.5 | 11.3 | 3.0 |
| 200+ | 5.7 | 1.3 | | 1.1 |

Sources: (1) Department of Statistics, Census of Agriculture, 1953 (Amman, n.d.), p. 3 and 5; (2) Department of Statistics, Census of Agriculture, 1965 (Amman, 1967), p. 91; (3) Ben Shahar et al., Economic Structure, p. 38 and 46. (Adapted.)

[a]A dunum is one-fourth of an acre.

Bank. Nearly 90 percent of all farms were smaller than 50 dunums each in 1968, and 69 percent were less than 20 dunums. However, agriculture in the Strip is largely dependent on intensive irrigation and hence productivity is much higher than in the West Bank where agriculture is mainly dependent on rainfall.

An Israeli census carried out in 1967 showed that 43 percent of the households in the West Bank owned farms, and direct employment in agriculture provided a livelihood for one-half of the population.[40] Farm population in the Strip is much smaller; only 14 percent of the total number of 66,800 households were classified as farms in 1967.[41]

## LAND USE

The area under cultivation in the West Bank fluctuated annually in the prewar period, responding to weather conditions (see Table 4.2). Generally, field crops occupied one-half of the total cultivated area, vegetables including melons, watermelons, and pumpkins occupied 12 percent, and tree

TABLE 4.2
Land use, the West Bank, 1961-1966

| Crop | 1961 | | 1962 | | 1963 | | 1964 | | 1965 | | 1966 | | 1967 | |
|---|---|---|---|---|---|---|---|---|---|---|---|---|---|---|
| | Dunum | % | Dunum | % | Dunum | % | Dunum | % | Dunum | % | Dunum | % | Dunum | % |
| Area-thousand | | | | | | | | | | | | | | |
| Field crops | 1,141.2 | 53.1 | 1,098.8 | 52.6 | 895.7 | 47.5 | 1,128.1 | 52.0 | 1,022.3 | 49.2 | 769.7 | 42.4 | 1,009.3 | 49.7 |
| Vegetables | 183.9 | 8.6 | 162.6 | 7.8 | 162.6 | 8.6 | 193.5 | 8.9 | 187.6 | 9.0 | 163.9 | 9.0 | 175.7 | 8.7 |
| Melons & watermelons | 90.5 | 4.2 | 83.9 | 4.0 | 77.5 | 4.1 | 77.8 | 3.6 | 76.9 | 3.7 | 71.8 | 4.0 | 79.7 | 3.9 |
| Olives | 477.2 | 22.2 | 486.1 | 23.3 | 500.0 | 26.5 | 514.1 | 23.7 | 535.8 | 25.8 | 536.8 | 29.6 | -- | -- |
| Citrus fruits | 11.3 | 0.5 | 11.1 | 0.5 | 10.2 | 0.6 | 11.0 | 0.5 | 12.4 | 0.6 | 13.1 | 0.7 | -- | -- |
| Other fruits | 243.8 | 11.4 | 247.1 | 11.8 | 238.7 | 12.7 | 244.1 | 11.3 | 242.6 | 11.7 | 258.7 | 14.3 | -- | -- |
| Total cultivated area | 2,147.9 | 100.0 | 2,089.6 | 100.0 | 1,884.7 | 100.0 | 2,168.6 | 100.0 | 2,077.6 | 100.0 | 1,814.0 | 100.0 | 2,030.4 | 100.0 |

Source: B. Abu Howayej, Agricultural Atlas of Jordan (Amman, Ministry of Agriculture, 1973), p. 102, 104, 106, 132, 162, and 186.

crops the rest. Wheat and barley were the major field crops in the area, using, on average, almost 30 and 12 percent, respectively, of the total annual cultivated area. Over one-half and close to one-quarter of the area devoted to field crops was usually planted with wheat and barley, respectively, and the remaining one-quarter was used for lentils, vetch, sesame, chick peas, and other crops.

Vegetables were grown on an area of more than 250,000 dunums in the West Bank in the prewar period. Most of this area, however, was devoted to melons and watermelons and tomatoes; the first covered about one-third and the second about one-quarter, with the rest used for various vegetables such as potatoes, beans, eggplants, cucumbers, onions, etc. Many of these vegetables were irrigated, especially those cultivated in the Jordan Valley.

Olives were the main fruit crop in terms of utilized area, accounting for about 30 percent of the total acreage under cultivation in the West Bank in 1966. The olive tree area expanded by 60,000 dunums (13 percent) during the 1961-1966 period. Citrus crops depended totally on irrigation and occupied 13,000 dunums in 1966, less than one percent of the total cultivated area. Other fruits accounted for 4 percent of the total area in 1966, of which grapes were predominant (7 percent), followed by figs (4 percent) and almonds (2 percent). The West Bank had about one-third of the arable land in the whole of Jordan. This constituted 80 percent of Jordan's fruit area, 45 percent of the vegetable area, and 25 percent of the field crop area.

The postwar pattern of land usage has been drastically altered in the West Bank, and to a certain extent in the Gaza Strip (see Table 4.3). The field crops area declined to no more than one-third of the total area under cultivation in the West Bank in 1982. Similarly, the land used for melons, watermelons, and pumpkins was reduced to no more than a few thousand dunums, although it has increased substantially in the last two years. On the other hand, vegetable acreage increased appreciably in the postwar period to 7 percent from 4 percent in 1968, although it never regained prewar levels. Orchards occupied considerably more than half the total cultivated area (60 percent in 1982), increasing its share by less than one-fifth; and olives accounted for about three-fourths of the fruit area.

In the Gaza Strip, the comparison between land use in 1968 and in 1982 reveals that field crops, some of which are irrigated, occupied a much smaller area in the later year, vegetables increased their absolute and relative share in total acreage, as did citrus and other fruits in relative but not in absolute terms. In 1982, orchards accounted for less than three-fourths of the total area actually cultivated, including 71,000 dunums (13 percent of this total) of citrus.

TABLE 4.3
Land use in the West Bank and the Gaza Strip, selected years

| Crop | 1968 | | 1969 | | 1970 | | 1971 | | 1973 | | 1976 | | 1977 | | 1978 | | 1979 | | 1981 | | 1982 | |
|---|---|---|---|---|---|---|---|---|---|---|---|---|---|---|---|---|---|---|---|---|---|---|
| | Dunum | % | Dunum | % | Dunum | % | Dunum | % | Dunum | % | Dunum | % | Dunum | % | Dunum | % | Dunum | % | Dunum | % | Dunum | % |
| West Bank | | | | | | | | | | | | | | | | | | | | | | |
| Area-thousand | | | | | | | | | | | | | | | | | | | | | | |
| Field crops | 890 | 52.9 | 1,072 | 57.7 | 902 | 52.3 | 915 | 53.2 | 827 | 49.2 | 539 | 33.6 | 499 | 32.2 | 530 | 32.8 | 530 | 33.0 | 544 | 33.5 | 501 | 30.1 |
| Vegetables | 70 | 4.2 | 75 | 4.0 | 85 | 4.9 | 79 | 4.6 | 80 | 4.8 | | | | | | | | | | | | |
| Melons, watermelons, and pumpkins | 43 | 2.5 | 26 | 1.4 | 26 | 1.5 | 15 | 0.9 | 10 | 0.6 | 107 | 6.7 | 107 | 6.9 | 112 | 6.9 | 98 | 6.1 | 133 | 8.1 | 139 | 8.7 |
| Citrus fruits | 20 | 1.2 | 20 | 1.1 | 22 | 1.3 | 22 | 1.3 | 24 | 1.4 | 26 | 1.6 | 29 | 1.9 | 26 | 1.6 | 26 | 1.6 | 24 | 1.5 | 25 | 1.7 |
| Other fruits | 660 | 39.2 | 665 | 35.8 | 689 | 40.0 | 689 | 40.0 | 741 | 44.0 | 931 | 58.1 | 912 | 59.0 | 949 | 58.7 | 954 | 59.3 | 925 | 56.9 | 936 | 58.5 |
| Total cultivated area | 1,683 | 100.0 | 1,858 | 100.0 | 1,724 | 100.0 | 1,720 | 100.0 | 1,682 | 100.0 | 1,603 | 100.0 | 1,547 | 100.0 | 1,617 | 100.0 | 1,608 | 100.0 | 1,626 | 100.0 | 1,601 | 100.0 |

| Gaza Strip | 1968 | | 1979 | | 1981 | | 1982 | |
|---|---|---|---|---|---|---|---|---|
| Area-thousand | | | | | | | | |
| Field crops | 56 | 28.3 | 17 | 10.0 | 20.1 | 11.3 | 17.0 | 10.3 |
| Vegetables | 22 | 11.1 | 30 | 17.7 | 30.7 | 17.3 | 29.2 | 17.8 |
| Citrus fruits | 70 | 35.3 | 72 | 42.3 | 71.6 | 40.4 | 71.5 | 43.4 |
| Other fruits | 50 | 25.3 | 51 | 30.0 | 54.7 | 31.0 | 46.9 | 28.5 |
| Total cultivated area | 198 | 100.0 | 170 | 100.0 | 177.1 | 100.0 | 164.6 | 100.0 |

Sources: For 1968-1972, Central Bureau of Statistics, Statistical Abstract of Israel, 1972, p. 665; for 1973, Brian Van Arkadie, Benefits and Burdens, p. 129; for 1976-1979 (West Bank), A. Kraisheh and Jon Ebersole, "West Bank Agricultural Cooperatives" (1980), p. 7; for 1979 (Gaza Strip), D. Instanbuli, A. Arafa, and Y. Azeh, The Agricultural Situation in the Occupied Territories and the Necessity for Development (Jerusalem: Al-Multaka Al-Fikri Al-Arabi, 1981), p. 27; for 1981 and 1982 (West Bank and Gaza Strip), Rural Research Centre, Statistical Bulletin, Vol. 2, p. 86, 95, 105 and 106; Vol. 3, p. 88, 99 and 109.

However, there were 70,000 dunums of citrus on the eve of the war, of which 40,000 dunums were planted with still young and nonbearing fruit.[42] There has been a significant decrease in the acreage of this crop during the postwar period. Other important fruits in the Strip are dates, palms, almonds, grapes, and olives.

The shift in the pattern of land use in the two territories has, by necessity, been an adaptation to new political and economic realities created by the occupation. Land expropriation, seizure, and closing off, coupled with the growing number of Jewish settlements, have considerably reduced land and water resources at the disposal of the indigenous farmers. The political risks associated with land tenure have made investment in agriculture extremely unattractive. The higher cost of farm labor caused by the availability of alternative employment opportunities in Israel has made some agricultural practices, especially marginal dry farming, much less rewarding, and has driven some farm owners out to seek jobs in Israel. The shift toward the cultivation of fruit trees appears to be a response to labor shortage because it requires less labor than field crops,[43] and a hedge against land seizure, that is, to provide the indigenous population with a visible claim to the land.

## AGRICULTURAL OUTPUT

In the prewar period, the West Bank accounted for less than one-third of Jordan's cultivable land, yet produced four-fifths of its olives, two-thirds of its fruits and vegetables, and one-third of field crops, livestock, and poultry.[44] Average agricultural production during 1961-1966 was 66,000 tons of field crops; 129,000 tons of vegetables; 70,000 tons of melons and watermelons; 44,000 tons of olives; 24,000 tons of citrus fruits; and 77,000 tons of other fruits such as grapes, almonds, and figs (see Table 4.4).

The postwar period has witnessed an increase in output of most crops in the West Bank. There have been wide fluctuations in the production of dry farmed field crops according to annual variations in precipitation. Average output of field crops, however, has not reached prewar levels because of the reduction in their acreage and structural adaptation in favor of those crops that are needed in Israel such as wheat, sesame, sorghum, lentils, etc. The shift away from subsistence to cash crops has been prevalent in vegetables and fruits since farmers were induced to expand export crops (such as onions, eggplants, beans, peppers, and the like) as well as industrial crops (such as tobacco, tomatoes, nuts, grapes, etc.).[45] Vegetable production has risen steadily and dramatically during the period and has fluctuated less due to irriga

TABLE 4.4
Agricultural output, the West Bank, 1961-1966 (thousand tons)

| Crop | 1961 | 1962 | 1963 | 1964 | 1965 | 1966 | Average 1961-66 |
|---|---|---|---|---|---|---|---|
| Field crops | 60.5 | 29.3 | 44.6 | 114.3 | 95.4 | 51.2 | 65.9 |
| Vegetables | 142.3 | 103.1 | 113.5 | 136.9 | 139.2 | 138.6 | 128.9 |
| Melons and watermelons | 68.3 | 53.7 | 70.8 | 70.3 | 125.0 | 31.5 | 69.9 |
| Olives | 97.9 | 5.6 | 30.6 | 81.2 | 23.8 | 23.6 | 43.8 |
| Citrus | 11.2 | 12.3 | 24.4 | 30.0 | 31.3 | 31.5 | 23.5 |
| Other fruits | 89.7 | 85.0 | 61.4 | 83.1 | 76.2 | 64.1 | 76.6 |

Source: Abu Howayej, Agricultural Atlas, p. 102, 104, 106, 132, 162, and 186.

tion. Production of melons and pumpkins has dropped sharply as a result of deliberate Israeli policy to reduce West Bank dependence on exports to the East Bank,[46] but has risen substantially in the last three years. Citrus production increased steadily partly because trees newly planted before 1967 matured during this period.[47] However, citrus output declined in 1980 and 1981, but increased again in 1982 (see Table 4.5).

Olive output fluctuated widely in line with its biannual yield cycle. Although it is the major crop in the area in terms of acreage, it has not shown any signficant overall increase in production.

Agriculture in the Gaza Strip has been concentrated on citrus production. On the eve of the 1967 war, there were 40,000 dunums of newly planted citrus trees, which required about five years to start bearing fruit. Therefore, much of the growth in citrus output is attributed to this factor; apparently production leveled off in the mid-1970s, and then declined in the last few years. Citrus production during 1978-1982 was much less than its 1976 level because of the lack of investment in new orchards, the growing scarcity (and salinity) of water resources, and Israeli objections to the renewal of old trees. On the other hand, vegetable production has more than doubled in the Strip during this period, thanks to the wide use of irrigation. In fact, some farmers have started growing vegetables for export on a partnership basis with Israelis. However, output of melons and pumpkins has dropped sharply; that of other fruits, including olives, fluctuated at a stagnated level.

In pre-1967 Jordan, about 33 to 37 percent of the value

TABLE 4.5

Output in agriculture, the West Bank and the Gaza Strip, 1967/68-1981/82 (in thousand tons)

| | 1967/68 | 1968/69 | 1969/70 | 1970/71 | 1971/72 | 1972/73 | 1973/74 | 1974/75 | 1975/76 | 1976/77 | 1977/78 | 1978/79 | 1979/80 | 1980/81 | 1981/82 |
|---|---|---|---|---|---|---|---|---|---|---|---|---|---|---|---|
| West Bank | | | | | | | | | | | | | | | |
| Field crops | 23.5 | 42.0 | 29.5 | 46.5 | 55.3 | 43.3 | 63.9 | 38.3 | 34.9 | 41.8 | 46.0 | 33.2 | 42.5 | 41.2 | 28.2 |
| Vegetables | 60.0 | 65.0 | 87.0 | 85.4 | 103.1 | 93.4 | 138.5 | 139.9 | 147.3 | 149.4 | 156.3 | 140.9 | 145.4 | 159.5 | 182.3 |
| Melons and pumpkins | 36.0 | 20.5 | 12.7 | 14.0 | 8.5 | 3.3 | 4.2 | 3.6 | 4.5 | 8.4 | 11.4 | 8.0 | 19.6 | 42.7 | 25.9 |
| Olives | 28.0 | 53.5 | 15.0 | 30.0 | 70.0 | 21.0 | 110.2 | 10.0 | 50.0 | 17.0 | 85.0 | 21.1 | 120.0 | 45.0 | 95.0 |
| Citrus fruits | 30.0 | 33.0 | 35.2 | 38.0 | 47.6 | 58.6 | 61.5 | 63.8 | 74.4 | 76.1 | 80.0 | 79.1 | 74.3 | 73.5 | 79.5 |
| Other fruits | 47.9 | 44.1 | 45.8 | 49.6 | 65.6 | 61.8 | 71.0 | 78.1 | 76.6 | 78.8 | 95.4 | 87.0 | 85.9 | 105.9 | 99.8 |
| Livestock: | | | | | | | | | | | | | | | |
| Meat | 10.3 | 12.9 | 15.3 | 14.0 | 18.7 | 20.2 | 22.0 | 21.4 | 22.4 | 19.2 | 19.8 | 23.5 | 23.1 | 25.7 | 26.4 |
| Milk | 30.3 | 34.9 | 37.1 | 35.0 | 43.8 | 44.3 | 44.7 | 46.0 | 41.5 | 39.6 | 39.9 | 39.4 | 36.7 | 38.8 | 41.0 |
| Eggs (million) | 25.0 | -- | -- | -- | 30.0 | 38.0 | 38.0 | 38.0 | 38.0 | 40.0 | 44.5 | 44.5 | 44.5 | 50.0 | 47.5 |
| Gaza Strip | | | | | | | | | | | | | | | |
| Field crops | -- | -- | -- | -- | -- | -- | -- | -- | -- | -- | -- | -- | -- | -- | -- |
| Vegetables | 31.8 | 33.2 | 36.4 | 36.8 | 38.9 | 40.5 | 37.9 | 46.0 | 48.0 | 54.9 | 53.4 | 51.4 | 60.0 | 72.7 | 76.6 |
| Melons and pumpkins | 12.5 | 8.0 | 7.1 | 7.9 | 4.6 | 5.0 | 6.1 | 4.7 | 3.0 | 3.7 | 2.8 | 3.6 | 5.8 | 6.1 | 3.1 |
| Citrus fruits | 91.0 | 106.2 | 142.0 | 175.0 | 178.0 | 205.2 | 207.0 | 201.4 | 243.7 | 232.3 | 180.6 | 192.2 | 171.5 | 179.3 | 199.9 |
| Other fruits/olives | 19.0 | 20.0 | 18.4 | 19.0 | 26.3 | 21.4 | 26.5 | 25.2 | 20.9 | 19.7 | 24.8 | 18.9 | 21.4 | 20.8 | 15.4 |
| Livestock: | | | | | | | | | | | | | | | |
| Meat | 1.7 | 1.9 | 2.4 | 2.6 | 3.0 | 3.5 | 3.4 | 3.7 | 4.4 | 4.3 | 4.8 | 4.8 | 5.6 | 6.2 | 6.3 |
| Milk | 6.8 | 6.9 | 7.4 | 7.2 | 9.7 | 10.2 | 11.7 | 12.9 | 12.8 | 11.7 | 14.8 | 15.5 | 4.7 | 13.9 | 12.4 |
| Fish | 3.7 | 3.8 | 3.4 | 3.2 | 4.7 | 4.6 | 3.5 | 4.8 | 4.7 | 5.1 | 4.5 | 1.5 | 1.2 | 1.4 | 1.3 |
| Eggs (million) | 10.0 | -- | -- | -- | 24.0 | 30.0 | 30.0 | 32.0 | 32.4 | 35.0 | 40.0 | 47.5 | 42.8 | 45.6 | 45.8 |

Source: Central Bureau of Statistics, Statistical Abstract of Israel (various issues).

of agricultural output originated in the West Bank.[48] About two-thirds of this value in the territory in 1966 were derived from crops, the remainder from livestock. Fruits accounted for more than one-fourth of the total value of production, vegetables over one-fifth, and field crops one-sixth.[49] Fruits were the main branch of crops, accounting for two-fifths of the total value, whereas vegetables and field crops contributed one-third and one-fourth, respectively. It should be remembered that field crops occupied one-half of the total cultivated area, yet its share in total value did not exceed one-fourth. Conversely, vegetables and fruits, which used about one-eighth and two-fifths of the arable land, contributed one-third and two-fifths of output, respectively. The intensive irrigation of vegetables was responsible for the apparent high productivity of this branch. On the other hand, almost all field crops were dry farmed and output fluctuated in response to erratic weather conditions.

The value of agricultural output has grown substantially in current prices in the two territories during the postwar period. In 1967/68 prices, however, the average annual rate of growth has been much lower: 8 percent in the West Bank and 5 percent in the Gaza Strip. The crops branch has grown at an average rate of 12 percent in real terms in the West Bank, compared with less than 5 percent in the Gaza Strip. Conversely, the average annual rate of growth in the livestock branch has been much below the overall average in the West Bank at less than 6 percent, but well above the overall average in the Gaza Strip.

On the average, crops in the West Bank comprised about two-thirds of the total value of agricultural output in the postwar period, the remainder being contributed by livestock. However, the relative importance of crops fluctuated widely during this period, ranging between 60 percent in drought years and 74 percent in good rainy years. The relative importance of crop components has remained basically unchanged, with field crops continuing to fluctuate widely, but declining appreciably in the last five years. Similarly, vegetable, citrus fruit, and other fruit shares in total value of output were relatively lower at the end of the period than at its beginning, also experiencing some fluctuations. Melons and pumpkins declined sharply in importance to a negligible proportion, and the olive share was subject to wide and erratic variations, ranging from a low of about 7 percent to a high of 38 percent (see Tables 4.6 and 4.7).

Although field crops were grown on one-third of the cultivated land in the West Bank in the postwar period, they accounted for about 5 percent of the value of agricultural output during the past five years. Vegetables occupied about 6 percent of the land, yet contributed 14 percent of output; fruits covered more than 60 percent of the area but their share fluctuated depending on the olive crop, ranging from 30 to 56 percent.

Crops in the Gaza Strip comprised three-fourths of the total value of agricultural production and have been relatively stable throughout the postwar period. The three most important branches were citrus fruits, vegetables, and other fruits, the first being at the top of the list. Field crops have never been significant, and melons and pumpkins declined in importance from about 5 percent to about 1 percent.

Citrus was the fastest growing crop, increasing by two-fifths between 1968 and 1977. However, its share has declined sharply in the last five years. The share of vegetables and other fruits in the total value fluctuated during the period, influenced by the changes in the relative share of citrus production, and averaged 14 and 12 percent of total value, respectively, in the last five years.

Field crops covered one-tenth of the cultivated area in the Strip but contributed less than 1 percent to the total value of output. Vegetables were planted on less than one-fifth of the total utilized land and added a little less to the value of production. Citrus thus far has been the largest single contributor to the value of output: more than half of the total throughout most of the postwar period (less than 50 percent since 1980) used slightly more than two-fifths of the total area. Other fruits contributed much less to output (8 and 12 percent in 1981 and 1982, respectively) than their share in total acreage. The difference in productivity among various crops may be attributed to irrigation, which has been the determining factor in this respect.

## LIVESTOCK

The stock of animals in the West Bank consisted of 35,000 head of cattle, 379,000 sheep, 272,000 goats, and 2,984,000 poultry raised on 388 farms in 1966 (see Table 4.8). At the end of 1982, there were 16,000 cattle, 261,000 sheep, 171,000 goats, about 8,000 tons of broilers, and 155,000 laying hens--all raised on 706 farms. In the Gaza Strip there were 5,000 cattle, 15,000 sheep, 21,000 goats, 2,000 tons of broilers, and 16,000 laying hens raised on 153 farms.[50]

Output of meat increased from 10,000 to 26,000 tons in the West Bank between the 1967/68 and 1981/82 periods, an increase of 7.7 percent annually; that of the Gaza Strip quadrupled from 1,700 to 6,300 tons during the same period. However, milk production fluctuated in the West Bank, growing steadily until 1975, after which it declined to around 40,000 tons annually throughout the remaining part of the period. In contrast, milk production in the Gaza Strip rose steadily throughout the period, except in the last three years. Annual

TABLE 4.6
Value of agricultural output, the West Bank and the Gaza Strip, 1967/68-1981/82 (IL million)

| | 1967/68 | 1968/69 | 1969/70 | 1970/71 | 1971/72 | 1972/73 | 1973/74 | 1974/75 | 1975/76 | 1976/77 | 1977/78 | 1978/79 | 1979/80 | 1980/81 | 1981/82 |
|---|---|---|---|---|---|---|---|---|---|---|---|---|---|---|---|
| <u>West Bank</u> | | | | | | | | | | | | | | | |
| Output - total | 135.0 | 177.0 | 169.6 | 227.4 | 347.1 | 399.5 | 885.0 | 911.0 | 1,535.1 | 1,681.3 | 3,629 | 5,367 | 17,164 | 31,072 | 66,260 |
| Crops - total | 87.9 | 121.3 | 101.7 | 147.2 | 233.3 | 253.9 | 654.9 | 558.5 | 1,058.7 | 1,126.9 | 2,688 | 3,263 | 12,688 | 18,628 | 44,071 |
| Field crops | 11.0 | 21.5 | 18.4 | 25.5 | 37.2 | 48.7 | 95.4 | 99.8 | 118.2 | 123.2 | 206 | 344 | 823 | 1,815 | 2,467 |
| Vegetables | 19.5 | 23.5 | 27.0 | 32.4 | 54.4 | 60.9 | 128.4 | 182.2 | 270.4 | 353.2 | 517 | 820 | 2,005 | 4,271 | 9,514 |
| Melons and pumpkins | 6.0 | 4.6 | 2.1 | 3.2 | 1.5 | 1.5 | 2.2 | 2.8 | 3.4 | 9.7 | 20 | 29 | 224 | 597 | 1,342 |
| Olives | 19.6 | 34.8 | 16.5 | 40.8 | 73.5 | 52.5 | 308.0 | 60.0 | 300.0 | 136.0 | 1,147 | 771 | 6,600 | 4,950 | 19,000 |
| Citrus fruits | 10.5 | 13.8 | 13.4 | 10.9 | 18.1 | 27.1 | 34.4 | 65.0 | 144.7 | 173.5 | 303 | 414 | 892 | 2,265 | 3,491 |
| Other fruits | 21.3 | 23.1 | 24.3 | 34.4 | 48.6 | 63.2 | 86.2 | 147.9 | 222.0 | 322.8 | 495 | 834 | 2,144 | 4,730 | 8,257 |
| Livestock: | 45.0 | 53.0 | 64.9 | 76.7 | 111.5 | 142.5 | 226.9 | 347.5 | 469.9 | 554.4 | 915 | 2,104 | 4,387 | 12,204 | 21,609 |
| Meat | 25.1 | 29.2 | 39.1 | 44.7 | 70.1 | 90.2 | 145.2 | 216.2 | 314.9 | 351.4 | 580 | 1,383 | 2,967 | 8,438 | 14,712 |
| Milk | 15.7 | 18.0 | 19.9 | 25.2 | 32.5 | 43.1 | 69.7 | 113.1 | 133.0 | 173.5 | 289 | 648 | 1,247 | 3,178 | 5,727 |
| Eggs | 3.2 | 5.8 | 5.9 | 6.8 | 7.0 | 7.2 | 9.9 | 16.0 | 19.0 | 26.0 | 40 | 61 | 141 | 530 | 1,045 |
| Misc. | 1.0 | -- | -- | -- | 1.9 | 2.0 | 2.1 | 2.2 | 3.0 | 3.5 | 6 | 11 | 32 | 58 | 125 |
| <u>Gaza Strip</u> | | | | | | | | | | | | | | | |
| Output - total | 53.5 | 62.0 | 75.5 | 106.5 | 149.5 | 192.2 | 278.6 | 445.5 | 691.5 | 935.3 | 1,254 | 1,923 | 3,937 | 9,562 | 17,467 |
| Crops - total | 41.3 | 48.1 | 57.8 | 83.3 | 113.8 | 140.9 | 210.3 | 328.6 | 532.3 | 726.8 | 908 | 1,448 | 2,944 | 6,926 | 12,539 |
| Field crops | 0.3 | 0.9 | 0.8 | 1.0 | 1.3 | 1.7 | 3.0 | 4.4 | 6.3 | 7.8 | 8 | 11 | 33 | 73 | 104 |
| Vegetables | 9.3 | 9.7 | 10.3 | 11.8 | 16.9 | 20.6 | 27.7 | 44.4 | 68.8 | 95.0 | 122 | 216 | 608 | 1,400 | 3,059 |
| Melons and pumpkins | 2.5 | 1.9 | 1.2 | 1.7 | 2.5 | 3.4 | 4.0 | 7.3 | 10.3 | 7.9 | 11 | 17 | 101 | 154 | 102 |
| Citrus fruits | 21.6 | 27.0 | 36.9 | 56.8 | 75.6 | 92.0 | 143.7 | 223.9 | 383.8 | 534.2 | 622 | 968 | 1,538 | 4,119 | 7,928 |
| Other fruits/olives | 7.6 | 8.6 | 8.6 | 12.0 | 17.5 | 23.2 | 31.9 | 48.6 | 63.1 | 81.9 | 146 | 227 | 664 | 1,180 | 1,346 |
| Livestock: | 10.9 | 12.6 | 15.9 | 21.7 | 33.9 | 49.5 | 66.5 | 113.6 | 154.1 | 203.4 | 342 | 475 | 978 | 2,590 | 4,819 |
| Meat | 3.6 | 4.9 | 5.8 | 9.5 | 12.7 | 17.3 | 23.6 | 35.3 | 47.5 | 64.1 | 110 | 197 | 470 | 1,300 | 2,301 |
| Milk | 3.3 | 3.6 | 3.6 | 4.3 | 7.3 | 12.2 | 16.7 | 29.1 | 41.8 | 53.5 | 103 | 148 | 294 | 662 | 1,246 |
| Fish | 2.7 | 2.3 | 4.3 | 4.8 | 9.8 | 14.6 | 19.4 | 32.7 | 45.9 | 60.9 | 85 | 35 | 58 | 198 | 354 |
| Eggs | 1.1 | 1.6 | 2.2 | 3.1 | 3.8 | 4.9 | 5.8 | 13.4 | 16.2 | 21.0 | 39 | 85 | 131 | 387 | 820 |
| Misc. | 0.2 | 0.2 | -- | -- | 0.3 | 0.5 | 1.0 | 3.1 | 2.7 | 3.9 | 6 | 10 | 15 | 52 | 98 |

Source: Central Bureau of Statistics, <u>Statistical Abstract of Israel</u> (various issues).

TABLE 4.7
Agricultural output values, the West Bank and the Gaza Strip, 1967/68-1981/82 (in percentages)

| | 1967/68 | 1968/69 | 1969/70 | 1970/71 | 1971/72 | 1972/73 | 1973/74 | 1974/75 | 1975/76 | 1976/77 | 1977/78 | 1978/79 | 1979/80 | 1980/81 | 1981/82 |
|---|---|---|---|---|---|---|---|---|---|---|---|---|---|---|---|
| West Bank | | | | | | | | | | | | | | | |
| Output - total | 100.0 | 100.0 | 100.0 | 100.0 | 100.0 | 100.0 | 100.0 | 100.0 | 100.0 | 100.0 | 100.0 | 100.0 | 100.0 | 100.0 | 100.0 |
| Crops - total | 65.1 | 68.5 | 60.0 | 64.7 | 67.2 | 63.6 | 74.0 | 61.3 | 69.0 | 67.0 | 74.1 | 60.8 | 73.9 | 60.0 | 66.5 |
| Field crops | 8.1 | 12.1 | 10.8 | 11.2 | 10.7 | 12.2 | 10.8 | 11.0 | 7.7 | 7.3 | 5.7 | 6.4 | 4.8 | 5.8 | 3.7 |
| Vegetables | 14.4 | 13.3 | 15.9 | 14.2 | 15.7 | 15.2 | 14.5 | 20.0 | 17.6 | 21.0 | 14.2 | 15.3 | 11.7 | 13.7 | 14.4 |
| Melons and pumpkins | 4.4 | 2.6 | 1.2 | 1.4 | 0.4 | 0.4 | 0.2 | 0.3 | 0.2 | 0.6 | 0.6 | 0.5 | 1.3 | 1.9 | 2.0 |
| Olives | 14.5 | 19.7 | 9.7 | 17.9 | 21.2 | 13.1 | 34.8 | 6.6 | 19.5 | 8.1 | 31.6 | 14.4 | 38.5 | 15.9 | 28.7 |
| Citrus fruits | 7.8 | 7.8 | 7.9 | 4.8 | 5.2 | 6.8 | 3.9 | 7.1 | 9.4 | 10.3 | 8.3 | 7.7 | 5.2 | 7.3 | 5.3 |
| Other fruits | 15.8 | 13.1 | 14.3 | 15.1 | 14.0 | 15.8 | 9.7 | 16.2 | 14.5 | 19.2 | 13.6 | 15.5 | 12.5 | 15.2 | 12.5 |
| Livestock: | 33.3 | 29.9 | 38.3 | 33.7 | 32.1 | 35.7 | 25.6 | 38.1 | 30.6 | 33.0 | 25.2 | 39.2 | 25.6 | 39.3 | 32.6 |
| Meat | 18.6 | 16.5 | 23.1 | 19.7 | 20.2 | 22.6 | 16.4 | 23.7 | 20.5 | 20.9 | 16.0 | 25.8 | 17.3 | 27.2 | 22.2 |
| Milk | 11.6 | 10.2 | 11.7 | 11.1 | 9.4 | 10.8 | 7.9 | 12.4 | 8.7 | 10.3 | 8.0 | 12.1 | 7.3 | 10.2 | 8.6 |
| Eggs | 2.4 | 3.3 | 3.5 | 3.0 | 2.0 | 1.8 | 1.1 | 1.8 | 1.2 | 1.5 | 1.1 | 1.1 | 0.8 | 1.7 | 1.6 |
| Misc. | 0.7 | -- | -- | -- | 0.5 | 0.5 | 0.2 | 0.2 | 0.2 | 0.2 | 0.2 | 0.2 | 0.2 | 0.2 | 0.2 |
| Gaza Strip | | | | | | | | | | | | | | | |
| Output - total | 100.0 | 100.0 | 100.0 | 100.0 | 100.0 | 100.0 | 100.0 | 100.0 | 100.0 | 100.0 | 100.0 | 100.0 | 100.0 | 100.0 | 100.0 |
| Crops - total | 77.5 | 77.6 | 76.6 | 78.3 | 76.1 | 73.3 | 75.5 | 73.8 | 77.0 | 77.7 | 72.4 | 75.3 | 74.8 | 72.4 | 72.0 |
| Field crops | 0.6 | 1.5 | 1.1 | 0.9 | 0.9 | 0.9 | 1.1 | 1.0 | 0.9 | 0.8 | 0.6 | 0.6 | 0.8 | 0.8 | 0.6 |
| Vegetables | 17.4 | 15.6 | 13.6 | 11.1 | 11.3 | 10.7 | 9.9 | 10.0 | 9.9 | 10.2 | 9.7 | 11.2 | 15.4 | 14.6 | 17.6 |
| Melons and pumpkins | 4.7 | 3.1 | 1.6 | 1.6 | 1.7 | 1.8 | 1.4 | 1.6 | 1.5 | 0.8 | 0.9 | 0.9 | 2.6 | 1.6 | 0.6 |
| Citrus fruits | 40.5 | 43.5 | 48.9 | 53.3 | 50.6 | 47.9 | 51.6 | 50.3 | 55.5 | 57.1 | 49.6 | 50.3 | 39.1 | 43.1 | 45.5 |
| Other fruits/olives | 14.3 | 13.9 | 11.4 | 11.3 | 11.7 | 12.1 | 11.5 | 10.9 | 9.1 | 8.8 | 11.6 | 11.8 | 16.9 | 12.3 | 7.7 |
| Livestock: | 20.5 | 20.3 | 21.1 | 20.4 | 22.7 | 25.8 | 23.9 | 25.5 | 22.3 | 21.7 | 27.3 | 24.7 | 24.8 | 27.1 | 27.7 |
| Meat | 6.8 | 7.9 | 7.7 | 8.9 | 8.5 | 9.0 | 8.5 | 7.9 | 6.9 | 6.9 | 8.8 | 10.2 | 11.9 | 13.6 | 13.2 |
| Milk | 6.2 | 5.8 | 4.8 | 4.0 | 4.9 | 6.3 | 6.0 | 6.5 | 6.0 | 5.7 | 8.2 | 7.7 | 7.5 | 6.9 | 7.2 |
| Fish | 5.1 | 3.7 | 5.7 | 4.5 | 6.6 | 7.6 | 7.0 | 7.3 | 6.6 | 6.5 | 6.8 | 1.8 | 1.5 | 2.1 | 2.0 |
| Eggs | 2.1 | 2.6 | 2.9 | 2.9 | 2.5 | 2.5 | 2.1 | 3.0 | 2.3 | 2.2 | 3.1 | 4.4 | 3.8 | 4.0 | 4.7 |
| Misc. | 0.4 | 0.3 | -- | -- | 0.2 | 0.3 | 0.4 | 0.7 | 0.4 | 0.4 | 0.5 | 0.5 | 0.4 | 0.5 | 0.6 |

Source: Derived from Table 4.6.

TABLE 4.8
Livestock in the West Bank, 1961-1966 (in thousands)

| Livestock | 1961 | 1962 | 1963 | 1964 | 1965 | 1966 |
|---|---|---|---|---|---|---|
| Cattle | 24.2 | 24.5 | 26.4 | 28.0 | 32.2 | 34.5 |
| Sheep | 188.7 | 213.2 | 146.2 | 264.5 | 322.2 | 379.0 |
| Goats | 161.5 | 190.9 | 201.0 | 223.3 | 256.1 | 272.3 |
| Broilers | 290.6 | 737.1 | 917.7 | 1,391.5 | 2,608.9 | 2,421.9 |
| Layers | 319.8 | 468.2 | 527.4 | 470.1 | 506.3 | 561.9 |

Source: Abu Howayej, Agricultural Atlas, p. 88, 92, 94, 96, 98.

egg production grew by 50 percent in the West Bank and almost doubled in the Strip. Fish catch remained basically unchanged throughout much of the period, although it decreased considerably in the last few years, probably due to security restrictions on fishing trips.

The value of livestock production constituted about one-third and one-fourth of total agricultural output in the West Bank and Gaza Strip, respectively. Meat has contributed around two-thirds of the value of the livestock branch in the West Bank, milk more than 30 percent, and eggs account for the rest. Similarly, meat has been the most important component of the livestock industry in the Strip, contributing one-third to close to one-half of its total value; milk accounted for around 25 to 30 percent, and fish fluctuated widely at one-fourth to less than one-third, but collapsed to a mere 7 percent in 1982. Egg contribution has been between 10 and 17 percent in the last few years.

In general, the livestock industry has been impeded from achieving its potential during the postwar period. First, livestock in the territories consists mainly of sheep, goats, poultry, and fish, the latter in the case of the Gaza Strip. Sheep and goats are fed on natural pastures for part of the year, especially when precipitation is adequate. The confiscation of large areas of range land and restrictions on sheep herd movements have reduced grazing areas and called for costly supplementary feed.[51] In addition, poultry and eggs have been exposed to competition from subsidized Israeli produce, driving many local farmers out of business.

Growth in agricultural output may be attributed to structural changes in the composition of crops and to improvements in inputs and production methods as well. The shift from subsistence to export, industrial, and import-substitution crops has undoubtedly raised the value of agricultural production. In addition, a few farmers have had access to a new cultivation technique through demonstration plots established by the Israelis on the West Bank;[52] improved seed varieties and new strains have become readily available to many farmers, raising output of many crops;[53] and more efficient methods of irrigation such as drip and sprinkling have been introduced to conserve scarce water. Indeed, 13,000 and 8,000 dunums were under drip and sprinkling irrigation, respectively, in the West Bank in 1979,[54] compared with 9,000 dunums under drip irrigation in the Gaza Strip.[55] Also, mechanization has been on the increase to alleviate the labor shortage problem. Israeli authorities estimated the number of tractors at 147 in the West Bank in 1967 and 36 in the Gaza Strip in 1970; by 1982 there were 2,606 tractors in the West Bank and 540 in the Gaza Strip. The use of fertilizers and insecticides has expanded, although they still are not universally utilized. The amount of fertilizer used in the West Bank was 4,200 tons in 1966,[56] which increased to 11,600 tons in 1978.[57] Plastic covers and greenhouses have been used in some 43,000 and 10,000 dunums in the West Bank and Gaza Strip in 1982, mainly for growing vegetables.[58] The overall impact of these developments has been a measurable improvement in crop productivity and higher yields per dunum.

## AGRICULTURAL COOPERATIVES

The cooperative movement grew fairly rapidly in Jordan in the 1950s and the 1960s until the war. In 1966, there were 702 cooperatives in Jordan, of which 337 were agricultural, formed to provide credit, inputs, and grading and marketing services for members.[59] The Jordan Central Cooperatives Union (JCCU), later the Jordan Cooperative Organization, was the body responsible for the administration of the movement, with the Central Auditing Union, the Cooperative Training Institute, and the Cooperative Bank as affiliates. Of the total number of cooperatives in Jordan in 1966, more than half (384) existed in the West Bank, 178 of which were agricultural.[60] On the other hand, there was no organized cooperative movement in the Gaza Strip in the prewar period.[61]

After 1967, cooperatives came under the jurisdiction of the Israeli Military Administration, and most of them became inactive since their ties to the JCCU in Amman were severed, and the services of affiliates such as the Cooperative Bank, the Central Auditing Union, and the Coopration Training Institute were no longer accessible. Israeli authorities have impeded the growth of the movement through licensing refusals and unwarranted delays in answering applications for cooperative registration. For instance, out of 43 new applications only 9 cooperatives received approval in 1979.[62] Two hundred applications for cooperatives were still pending in 1980, most for over a year and some for up to five years. From 1967 through 1981, the Israeli authorities licensed 201 cooperatives, only 42 of which were agricultural.[63] The Cooperatives Department in the West Bank was undermined in the postwar period. Before the war it consisted of three regional offices staffed with 40 employees and had six cars; at present, only 12 employees man four regional offices there with just one car at their disposal.[64]

Under current conditions, cooperatives appear to be an appropriate vehicle for promoting collective development action in such activities as agriculture, electric and hydraulic installations, education and health, etc.[65] Cooperatives have been viewed by the people of the West Bank as a means to attain needed services. Therefore, the movement "needs support, organization, and trained personnel to cultivate its potential as a mainstay in West Bank agricultural development."[66]

Extension services have been reduced in the West Bank during the postwar period. The number of employees working in district offices in 1982 was one-half of that in 1968 (65 persons); agricultural extension institutions have been cut from 9 to 5;[67] training facilities for extension personnel have been inadequate; and agricultural research activities have been moved to Israel.[68]

## AGRICULTURAL CREDIT

Before the June war, credit for West Bank agriculture was provided by the Agricultural Credit Corporation (ACC) and the Jordan Central Cooperatives Union, both of which are government institutions. Established in 1959, the ACC took over the credit extension functions of many agencies, such as the Agricultural Bank, Development Board, Rural Development Fund, and Construction and Development Bank. The ACC has granted long- and medium-term loans for the development of dry farming through terracing, land reclamation, irrigation works, livestock, farm machinery, farm construction, and other objectives,[69] in addition to a few short-term loans. The JCCU extended seasonal credit to cooperatives for the benefit of their members.

Outstanding agricultural loans from various official lending institutions before the establishment of the ACC were JD 3.3 million, of which JD 1.3 million (39 percent) was in the West Bank. The ACC assumed responsibility for those loans. Between 1960 and May 1967, the ACC disbursed additional loans for a total amount of JD 6.2 million, over one-quarter of which was granted to farmers in the West Bank; no loans were granted after the occupation. However, an amount of JD 1.7 million in ACC's outstanding loans in the West Bank was frozen due to circumstances created by occupation.

The JCCU extended loans to cooperatives for an amount of JD 3.3 million between 1960 and 1966.[70] Of this total JD 1.9 million (58 percent) was granted to cooperatives in the West Bank, serving more than 48,000 persons, or 61 percent of the total members of cooperatives in the whole of Jordan. Loans outstanding in the West Bank of JD 446,000 plus interest (fees) of JD 286,000 were frozen after the war. No loans were extended to those cooperatives in the few years immediately after the war.

After June 1967, West Bank farmers were cut off from pre-1967 sources of credit, and local and Israeli loans for agriculture were prohibitively expensive. But in the mid-1970s modest amounts of loans and grants started flowing from the Jordan Cooperative Organization (JCO) and several private voluntary organizations, subject to the approval of Israeli military authorities. Since 1979, the Jordanian-Palestinian Joint Committee has made several million dinars available to inhabitants of the West Bank on a loan and grant basis for investment in agriculture, industry, housing, services, etc., disbursed through the JCO to cooperatives. By the end of 1982, a total of JD 9 million was transferred, the bulk of which was for agricultural purposes. The amount appropriated for 1983 was JD 4 million. However, the Israeli authorities often prohibited the transfer of any funds believed to have been coming solely or jointly from PLO sources.

## PROBLEMS

Agricultural growth in the territories has been constrained by the limited amount of available land, which keeps shrinking as a result of Israeli expropriaton and by the increasing scarcity of water in the West Bank and its over-utilization in the Gaza Strip. The possibility of expanding the cultivated area, which depends to a large extent on the availability of extra water for irrigation, is very slim. Second, landholdings are still fragmented, a condition precluding the spread of mechanization in view of labor shortages in this sector.[71] Third, financial resources of investment in irrigation works, land reclamation, mechanization, and other agricultural projects are lacking.[72] Fourth, the risks involved in the more intensive use of agricultural inputs such as improved seed varieties, fertilizers, and pesticides are still great in dry farming. Fifth, there exists no organized marketing system that synchronizes production with market demands[73] and facilitates the movement of produce to wholesale and retail outlets. Sixth, certain agricultural produce, poultry and eggs in particular, has been hurt by competition from the subsidized Israeli products. All these limiting factors have severely restricted the development potentials of agriculture in the two territories.

Appendix A, an outline of a proposed plan for the development of the agricultural sector in the occupied territories, is sketched in view of the existing constraints imposed on it by the occupation authorities.

**Notes**

1. Department of Statistics, Population and Employment in Agriculture, 1967 (Amman, 1968), Table 1.

2. Danny Rubenstein, "Deluxe Annexation," New Outlook (June 1981), p. 18.

3. "Palestinian Emigration," p. 112.

4. Haselkorn, Kurz, and Wagner, Trade and Economic Links, p. 8.

5. Trudy Rubin, "Israel Seems to be Slowly Annexing the West Bank," Christian Science Monitor (August 31, 1981).

6. Rubenstein, "Deluxe," p. 18.

7. Eric Silver, "Light and Shadow," The Guardian (August 23, 1981).

8. Nafez Nazzal, "Land Tenure, the Settlements, and Peace," p. 113 in Emile A. Nakhleh, ed., A Palestinian Agenda for the West Bank and Gaza (Washington, D.C.: American Enterprise Institute for Public Policy Research, 1980); Pearson, "Economic and Social Development," p. 11-12.

9. Z. Nuseiba and J. Ja'abari, "Settlements in the Occupied Territories," Al-Quds Daily (June 5, 1977); and Department of Agriculture, Agriculture in the West Bank, 1974, p. 5. Both cited in Hisham Awartani, Agriculture in the West Bank: "A New Outlook" (Nablus: Al-Najah National University, 1978), p. 7.

10. Derived from Central Bureau of Statistics, Statistical Abstract of Israel, 1983, p. 781.

11. Peter Oakley, "The Jordan Valley: Drip Irrigation for Small Farmers," RDDC Bulletin (November 1978), p. 6.

12. Department of Statistics, Statistical Yearbook (1966), p. 123.

13. B. Abu Howayej, Agricultural Atlas of Jordan (Amman: Ministry of Agriculture, 1973), p. 102, 132, and 162.

14. Central Bureau of Statistics, Statistical Abstract of Israel, 1972, p. 655.

15. Abdul Rahman Khraisheh and Jon Ebersole, "West Bank Agricultural Cooperatives" (1980), p. 7.

16. Rural Research Centre, Statistical Bulletin for the West Bank and the Gaza Strip, Vol. 3 (Nablus: Al-Najah University, 1982), p. 88-89, 98, and 108.

17. Ibid., p. 90, 99, and 109 (for 1982); Vol. 2, p. 87, 96, and 106 (for 1981).

18. Ibid., p. 85 (Vol. 2) and p. 88 (Vol. 3).

19. Uri Davis, Antonia E.L. Maks, and John Richardson, "Israel's Water Policies," Journal of Palestine Studies (Winter 1980), p. 15; Darrel R. Elgin, "The Economy," p. 120, in Richard F. Nyrop, ed., Jordan: A Country Study (Washington, D.C.: The American University, 1980).

20. Hisham Awartani, "Agriculture," p. 17, in Nakhleh, A Palestinian Agenda; Elias H. Tuma and Haim Darin-Drabkin, The Economic Case for Palestine (London: Croom Helm, 1978), p. 60.

21. British Consulate, West Bank: Water Resources and Their Exploitation (Jerusalem, 1978), p. 10.

22. Ibid., p. 6.

23. Ibid., p. 8.

24. Darin-Drabkin, "The Economic Viability," p. 45.

25. British Consulate, West Bank, p. 8.

26. Ibid., p. 9.

27. Awartani, "Agriculture," p. 17; Reja Shehadeh, The West Bank and the Rule of Law (New York: International Commission of Jurists, 1980), p. 66.

28. British Consulate, West Bank, p. 9-10.

29. Awartani, "Agriculture," p. 17.

30. Shehadeh, The West Bank, p. 65.

31. British Consulate, West Bank, p. 11.

32. Ibid., p. 12.

33. Ibid.

34. Ibid., p. 12-13.

35. William Claiborne, "West Bank Oasis Withers: Nearby Kibutzim Flowers," International Herald Tribune (October 8, 1979).

36. Tuma and Darin-Drabkin, The Economic Case, p. 74.

37. Darin-Drabkin, "The Economic Viability," p. 45.

38. Pearson, "Economic and Social Development," p. 21.

39. Ben Shahar et al., Economic Structure, p. 39.

40. Central Bureau of Statistics, Housing, Household Equipment Support and Farm Cultivation in Occupied Areas (Jerusalem, 1968); cited in Aryeh Sheshkin, "Postwar Economics of the West Bank," New Outlook (October 1968), p. 18.

41. Ben Shahar et al., Economic Structure, p. 46.

42. Ibid., p. 45.

43. Van Arkadie, Benefits and Burdens, p. 28.

44. Remba, "Why Jordan Can Survive," p. 24.

45. "Five Years Israel Administration in Judea and Samaria," The Israeli Economist (September-October 1972), p. 243.

46. Ibid.

47. Pearson, "Economic and Social Development," p. 10.

48. Remba, "Why Jordan Can Survive," p. 24; E. Kanovsky, Economic Development of Jordan (Tel Aviv: University Publishing Projects, 1977), p. 28.

49. Aryeh Sheshkin, "Economic Structure of the West Bank," New Outlook (September-October 1967), p. 21.

50. Rural Research Centre, *Statistical Bulletin,* Vol. 3, p. 124-127.

51. Awartani, *Agriculture in the West Bank*, p. 14.

52. Tuma and Darin-Drabkin, *The Economic Case,* p. 64.

53. Awartani, *Agriculture in the West Bank,* p. 15.

54. Jelal Dawoud, "Irrigated Agriculture in the West Bank and the Effect of Israeli Water Policies," *SAMED* (October 1980), p. 32.

55. Awartani, "Agriculture," p. 21.

56. Department of Statistics, *Statistical Yearbook* (1966), p. 132.

57. Palestine National Fund, *Agricultural Statistical Bulletin for the West Bank* (Damascus: PLO, 1980), p. 46.

58. Rural Research Centre, *Statistical Bulletin*, Vol. 3, p. 130.

59. Sayigh, *The Economies,* p. 211.

60. Jordan Cooperative Organization records.

61. Pearson, "Economic and Social Development," p. 46.

62. Ibid., p. 61 (footnote 50).

63. Rural Research Centre, *Statistical Bulletin,* Vol. 2, p. 129.

64. "West Bank Cooperative Movement: Restrictions on Growth," *Al-Fajr* (October 2-November 1, 1980), p. 3; cited in Pearson, "Economic and Social Development," p. 46.

65. International Labor Office, *Report of the Director General* (Geneva, 1980), p. 154.

66. Pearson, "Economic and Social Development," p. 48.

67. Ibid., p. 61 (footnote 50).

68. UNDP, *Report of the Inter-Agency Force on Assistance to the Palestinian People* (1979), p. 42.

69. Sayigh, *The Economies,* p. 211.

70. Department of Statistics, *Statistical Yearbook* (1960 through 1966).

71. Tuma and Darin-Drabkin, *The Economic Case*, p. 64.

72. ILO, *Action Taken,* p. 41.

73. Tuma and Darin-Drabkin, *The Economic Case,* p. 64.

# 5 Manufacturing and Mining

Manufacturing and mining activity has been of minor importance in the West Bank and Gaza Strip both before and after the 1967 war. The industrial sector has constituted a small fraction of total domestic production as well as employment. Most manufacturing enterprises in the territories are workshops of the owner-operator type with little investment in machinery, and servicing mainly local demand.

## RELATIVE IMPORTANCE OF INDUSTRIAL ACTIVITY

Manufacturing and mining together contributed around 10 percent of the GDP in the whole of Jordan before the war. This sector consisted of a few large enterprises, which dominated the industrial scene, and many small establishments. More than three-quarters of the 6,838 industrial concerns in Jordan employed less than five persons in 1965; 14 percent employed between 5 and 9 employees; and the rest (9 percent) employed 10 or more persons. However, only 28 enterprises employed between 50 and 99 workers and only 21 engaged more than 100 employees[1] (see Table 5.1).

TABLE 5.1
Industrial establishments in Jordan, by employment, 1965

| Persons Employed | Number of Establishments | Percentage |
|---|---|---|
| Less than 5 | 5,263 | 77 |
| 5-9 | 979 | 14 |
| 10+ | 596 | 9 |
| Total | 6,838 | 100 |

Source: Department of Statistics, Industrial Survey, p. 156.

Specifically, manufacturing and mining contributed JD 16.2 million to a gross domestic product of JD 150.9 million in 1965 (around 11 percent). The West Bank's share of this sum was JD 4.5 million, or 28 percent. There were more than 37,000 persons engaged in industrial activity in Jordan, of whom about 46 percent were in the West Bank.

The discrepancy between the contribution of industry in the West and East Banks to their respective GDP (the West Bank contributed considerably less than the East Bank) came as a result of the concentration of large concerns in the Amman region of the East Bank. In some cases, the location of an industry was determined by the proximity of natural resources as is the case of the three largest industries in the country. Phosphate mining, petroleum refining, and cement production were all established in the East Bank, and coincidentally near Amman, because the various raw materials they depended upon were most readily available in this area. The combined share of these three enterprises in the GDP of the whole country in 1965 was JD 4.5 million. Other enterprises were established in Amman long before 1950, such as the two cigarette companies whose value added in 1965 was JD 0.743 million. The other large companies that were established in the Amman area depended on imported raw materials and could presumably have been established on either Bank. For practical reasons, it seems that investors preferred to locate their industrial investment in the Amman region. The reasons for this are obvious enough. First, the proximity of government and the various branches of the civil service is important to industry. Similarly, the Amman region is heavily populated and thus can provide sufficient manpower for industrial concerns. The infrastructure, too, is well established and offers industry easy access to ports and foreign countries through well-defined trade routes.

It should be noted that industrial development in Jordan was largely the product of the private sector, with government taking some equity in certain companies but following the preference of companies as regards the location of factories. Incentives were offered to locate in regions other than Amman but these have had no appreciable effect. In fact, not a single large industrial establishment was located beyond a thirty kilometer radius from Amman in the East Bank.

If we exclude these large companies, then the share of the West Bank industry in GDP becomes comparable to that of the East Bank, around 7.5 percent in 1965. Phosphates, oil refining, cement, and cigarettes together contributed close to 6 percent to the GDP of the East Bank and 3.4 percent of that of the whole country in 1965. In terms of output, these industries produced 28 percent of the total gross production of Jordan.

Industry contributed little to the prewar domestic economy of the Gaza Strip. Value added in industry was as small as JD 0.4 million in 1966, or 4.2 percent of GDP. It was the least important sector in the economy next to transportation.

Industrial activity has stagnated at around 6 percent of the GDP in the West Bank, and has increased to almost 11 percent in the Gaza Strip in the postwar period. But industry has remained the smallest sector in the economies of the two territories. The overall performance of the industrial sector has been greatly impeded by the lack of investment either in new plant or in the improvement of existing industries.

## PRODUCTION UNITS

The industrial census of 1965 revealed that there were 6,838 industrial establishments in the whole of Jordan, employing more than 37,000 persons. Industrial fixed assets totaled some JD 19.8 million, and annual wages were JD 5.3 million, or JD 195 per employee per annum. The West Bank contained 56 percent of industrial establishments and accounted for 46 percent of employment in 1965. The West Bank's share of fixed assets was JD 4.5 million (23 percent of the total), and wages stood at JD 1.4 million.

Generally, production units in Jordan were small and engaged on average 5.4 persons. In the West Bank, more than three-quarters of all industrial establishments employed less than 5 persons in 1965, whereas 16 percent employed from 5 to 9 persons, and 8 percent employed 10 persons or more (see Table 5.2).

Industrial establishments employing 10 persons or more weighed most in the industrial sector in Jordan in 1965. Although accounting for less than 9 percent of the total

TABLE 5.2
Industrial establishments, by employment, East and West Banks, 1965

| | East Bank | | West Bank | | Total | |
|---|---|---|---|---|---|---|
| Employment | Number | % | Number | % | Number | % |
| Less than 5 | 2,336 | 44.4 | 2,927 | 55.6 | 5,263 | 100.0 |
| 5-9 | 374 | 38.2 | 605 | 61.8 | 979 | 100.0 |
| 10+ | 286 | 48.0 | 310 | 52.0 | 596 | 100.0 |
| Total | 2,996 | 43.8 | 3,842 | 56.2 | 6,838 | 100.0 |

Source: Department of Statistics, Industrial Survey, p. 159-166.

number, these establishments engaged 45 percent of all industrial employment, used 84 percent of the sector's fixed assets, expended 87 percent of its capital outlay, paid 60 percent of its wages, and contributed 65 percent of its value added. These West Bank establishments accounted for 35 percent of total Jordanian industrial employment, 15 percent of investment in fixed assets, 36 percent of capital expenditures, 22 percent of wages, and 16 percent of value added. The average wage in these enterprises in the West Bank was considerably lower than that of the East Bank because of the seasonal nature of the work in several of these establishments (see Table 5.3).

The Amman region monopolized most industrial activity, and certainly all large-scale establishments in the East Bank. This region contained 87 percent of East Bank industrial establishments employing 10 persons or more and all those employing 50 persons or more. The average wage rate in Amman was much higher than that in the rest of the East Bank. Obviously, these figures reveal that Amman was the only industrial center in the East Bank, a fact that need not be overemphasized.

Apparently, Jerusalem, like Amman, was growing to be the major industrial center in the West Bank in the postwar period. Jerusalem contained almost one-half of all industrial establishments employing 10 persons or more in the West Bank and accounted for 57 percent of the Bank's industrial employment, 52 percent of fixed assets, 60 percent of capital outlay, 59 percent of wages, and 53 percent of value added.

There were only 21 industrial establishments employing 100 persons or more in the whole of Jordan in 1965, four of

TABLE 5.3
Data on industrial establishments employing 10 persons or more in the East and West Banks, 1965

| | East Bank | | West Bank | | Jordan | |
|---|---|---|---|---|---|---|
| | No./JD | % | No./JD | % | No./JD | % |
| Number of establishments | 286 | 48.0 | 310 | 52.0 | 596 | 100.0 |
| Employed persons | 10,893 | 64.7 | 5,954 | 35.3 | 16,847 | 100.0 |
| Fixed assets (million) | 14.1 | 84.9 | 2.5 | 15.1 | 16.6 | 100.0 |
| Capital expenditures | 0.9 | 64.3 | 0.5 | 35.7 | 1.4 | 100.0 |
| Wages (JD million) | 2.5 | 78.1 | 0.7 | 21.9 | 3.2 | 100.0 |
| Annual wage rate (JD) | 230 | 120.4 | 118 | 61.8 | 191 | 100.0 |
| Value added (million) | 8.8 | 83.8 | 1.7 | 16.2 | 10.5 | 100.0 |

Source: Department of Statistics, Industrial Survey, p. 31.

which were located in the West Bank. On the whole, industrial activity in the West Bank, and the East Bank as well, was carried out in relatively small concerns utilizing little capital per worker. Thus, average output was JD 550 per worker in 1965.

Industrial units in the Gaza Strip were, as in the West Bank, very small in terms of employment, capital, and production. The total number of industrial concerns in 1960 was 769, employing 1,782 persons, using capital of JD 0.3 million and producing JD 0.4 worth of output.[2] Hence, each establishment on the average employed 2.3 persons and used as little capital as JD 390. Production stood at no more than JD 223 per worker. Industry in the Strip was limited to repair shops, weaving, textiles, food processing, and crafts. A single citrus packing plant was the largest industrial establishment in terms of employment (75 persons) and capital (JD 125,000).[3]

Industrial establishments numbered 2,174 in the West Bank (excluding Arab Jerusalem) and 1,421 in the Gaza Strip in 1982. Only 58 percent of the total for both areas had hired employees, the rest being owner-operated. In fact, more than 95 percent of all industrial establishments in the West Bank and 94 percent of those in the Gaza Strip employed 10 persons or less; only 7 enterprises employed 100 workers or more in the West Bank and none in the Strip[4] (see Tables 5.4 and 5.5).

Two Palestinian writers, however, have come up with a much smaller number of industrial establishments in the Gaza Strip than that published in the Statistical Abstract of Israel. A survey of industries carried out in the two territories has revealed that there were 2,587 industrial enterprises in the West Bank (including Arab Jerusalem) and 430 in the Gaza Strip in the Spring of 1978.[5] No enterprises were employing more than 49 workers in the Strip, whereas 14 such enterprises existed in the West Bank, most of which were established before the occupation.[6] Another study listed individual industrial firms in the Gaza Strip by branch, name, and employment as of 1977, coming up with 411 establishments employing a total number of 2,904 workers.[7] In view of the large discrepancy between these figures, one should not place too much emphasis on the total number of existing firms, but rather the distribution of these by type of product is more illuminating.

## STRUCTURE OF INDUSTRY

Prewar industry in the West Bank consisted mostly of small workshops and crafts engaging in such activities as car repairs, carpentry, lathing, etc. The bigger industrial establishments were unevenly distributed over a wide range of

TABLE 5.4
Industrial establishments, by branch and employment, the West Bank[a] and the Gaza Strip, 1982
(revenue in IL million, current prices)

| Branch[b] | West Bank | | Gaza Strip | | Revenue | |
|---|---|---|---|---|---|---|
| | Number | Employment | Number | Employment | West Bank | Gaza Strip |
| Food, beverages and tobacco | 228 | 1,333 | 202 | 675 | 1,314 | 119 |
| Textiles and its products | 456 | 2,302 | 523 (Textiles and Leather combined) | 2,576 (Textiles and Leather combined) | 189 | 326 (Textiles and Leather combined) |
| Leather and its products | 202 | 634 | | | 50 | |
| Wood and its products | 444 | 1,144 | 212 | 927 | 95 | 112 |
| Rubber, plastics, and chemicals | 50 | 777 | -- | -- | 352 | -- |
| Nonmetallic minerals | 146 | 798 | -- | -- | 108 | -- |
| Basic metal products | 464 | 1,329 | 261 | 1,108 | 158 | 269 |
| Others | 184 | 591 | 223 | 1,002 | 122 | 152 |
| Total | 2,174 | 8,908 | 1,421 | 6,288 | 2,387 | 977 |

Source: Central Bureau of Statistics, Statistical Abstract of Israel, 1983, p. 792-793.

[a]Excluding Arab Jerusalem.
[b]Excluding quarrying.

activities such as quarrying, food processing, textiles and tricot, clothing, shoes, furniture, chemicals, nonmetallic products, and basic metals. Enterprises engaged in the production of food, beverages, and cigarettes comprised 37 percent of all the establishments employing 10 persons or more in 1965; next in importance came quarrying, which accounted for one-fifth of the total; textiles, tricot, and clothing accounted for 11 percent; basic metals, 7 percent; chemicals and nonmetallic products, 6 percent each; furniture, 4 percent; and shoes, 3 percent. About two-thirds of all industrial firms in the Gaza Strip in 1960 were producing textiles and carpets, the remaining one-third being distributed among the other kinds of firm (see Tables 5.6 and 5.7).

In the postwar period, the structure of industry in the territories has remained essentially unchanged. Major invest-

TABLE 5.5
Industrial establishments[a] in the West Bank and the Gaza Strip, by branch and employment, 1982

| Employment / Branch | West Bank | | | | Gaza Strip | | | |
|---|---|---|---|---|---|---|---|---|
| | 1-3 | 4-10 | 11-20 | 21+ | 1-3 | 4-10 | 11-20 | 21+ |
| Food, beverages, and tobacco | 143 | 72 | 9 | 7 | 154 | 40 | 5 | 3 |
| Textiles and clothing | 263 | 142 | 34 | 14 | 306 | 160 | 45 | 12 |
| Leather and its products | 135 | 65 | 1 | 1 | | | | |
| Wood and its products | 358 | 80 | 6 | -- | 128 | 75 | 4 | 5 |
| Rubber, plastics, and chemicals | 16 | 16 | 6 | 12 | -- | -- | -- | -- |
| Nonmetallic minerals | 47 | 90 | 7 | 2 | -- | -- | -- | -- |
| Basic metal products | 342 | 119 | 1 | 2 | 179 | 73 | 5 | 4 |
| Others | 146 | 33 | 3 | 2 | 102 | 112 | 6 | 3 |
| Total | 1,450 | 617 | 67 | 40 | 869 | 460 | 65 | 27 |

Source: Central Bureau of Statistics, Statistical Abstract of Israel, 1983, p. 792-793.

[a]Excluding quarrying.

ment in new plant has been notably absent; industry continued to be labor-intensive, low productivity[8] handicrafts in addition to traditional and light industries. In 1982, over one-fifth of all industrial establishments in the West Bank engaged in textiles; one-fifth in wood products; over one-tenth in food, beverages, and tobacco; and one-tenth in leather products. In terms of employment, textile firms engaged over a quarter of the work force; food, beverages, and tobacco and basic metals more than 15 percent each; wood products, 13 percent; rubber, plastics, and chemicals, 9 percent; and nonmetallic minerals, 9 percent (see Table 5.8). In the Gaza Strip, textiles and leather production accounted for 37 percent of the total number of industrial establishments in 1982; food, beverages, and tobacco and wood products accounted for 14 percent each; and basic metal products, 18 percent. In general, food, beverages, and tobacco earned the greatest amount of revenue for the West Bank in 1982 (55 percent). In

TABLE 5.6
Industrial establishments employing 10 persons or more, by branch, East and West Banks, 1965

| Branch | East Bank | | West Bank | | Total | |
|---|---|---|---|---|---|---|
| | Number | % | Number | % | Number | % |
| Mining and quarrying | 97 | 56.4 | 61 | 43.6 | 140 | 100.0 |
| Food processing | 43 | 28.7 | 107 | 71.3 | 150 | 100.0 |
| Beverage | 10 | 62.5 | 6 | 37.5 | 16 | 100.0 |
| Cigarettes | 2 | 50.0 | 2 | 50.0 | 4 | 100.0 |
| Textiles and tricot | 17 | 39.5 | 26 | 60.5 | 43 | 100.0 |
| Clothing | 13 | 61.9 | 8 | 38.1 | 21 | 100.0 |
| Shoes | 6 | 37.5 | 10 | 62.5 | 16 | 100.0 |
| Furniture | 24 | 64.9 | 13 | 35.1 | 37 | 100.0 |
| Paper | 4 | 100.0 | -- | -- | 4 | 100.0 |
| Printing | 8 | 42.1 | 11 | 57.9 | 19 | 100.0 |
| Leather and hides | 3 | 100.0 | -- | -- | 3 | 100.0 |
| Rubber | 2 | 100.0 | -- | -- | 2 | 100.0 |
| Chemicals | 8 | 30.8 | 18 | 69.2 | 26 | 100.0 |
| Nonmetal | 20 | 52.6 | 18 | 47.4 | 38 | 100.0 |
| Basic metal | 25 | 55.6 | 20 | 44.4 | 45 | 100.0 |
| Electrical | 2 | 100.0 | -- | -- | 2 | 100.0 |
| Transport equipment | 16 | 80.0 | 4 | 20.0 | 20 | 100.0 |
| Others | 4 | 40.0 | 6 | 60.0 | 10 | 100.0 |
| Total | 286 | 48.0 | 310 | 52.0 | 596 | 100.0 |

Source: Department of Statistics, Industrial Survey, p. 141.

TABLE 5.7
Industrial establishments in the Gaza Strip, by branch, employment, capital, and production, 1960

| Branch | Establishment | Employment | Estimated capital (JD '000) | Production (JD '000) |
|---|---|---|---|---|
| Textiles and weaving | 508 | 685 | 72.8 | 201.4 |
| Food, beverages, and tobacco | 89 | 462 | 218.5 | 156.3 |
| Clay | 29 | 75 | 2.6 | 4.3 |
| Handicrafts (basic metal) | 143 | 560 | 25.7 | 81.4 |
| Total | 769 | 1,782 | 319.6 | 443.4 |

Source: Dawoud, "Industry," p. 31 (adapted).

TABLE 5.8
Industrial establishments, by branch and employment, the West Bank and the Gaza Strip, 1982

| Branch | West Bank | | | | Gaza Strip | | | |
|---|---|---|---|---|---|---|---|---|
| | Number | % | Employ-ment | % | Number | % | Employ-ment | % |
| Food, beverages, and tobacco | 228 | 10.5 | 1,333 | 15.0 | 202 | 14.2 | 675 | 10.7 |
| Textile and its products | 456 | 21.0 | 2,302 | 25.8 | 523 | 36.8 | 2,576 | 41.1 |
| Leather and its products | 202 | 9.3 | 634 | 7.9 | | | | |
| Wood and its products | 444 | 20.4 | 1,144 | 12.8 | 212 | 14.9 | 927 | 14.7 |
| Rubber, plastics, and chemicals | 50 | 2.3 | 777 | 8.7 | -- | -- | -- | -- |
| Nonmetallic minerals | 146 | 6.7 | 789 | 9.0 | -- | -- | -- | -- |
| Basic metal products | 464 | 21.3 | 1,329 | 14.9 | 261 | 18.4 | 1,108 | 17.6 |
| Others | 184 | 8.5 | 591 | 6.6 | 223 | 15.7 | 1,002 | 15.9 |
| Total | 2,174 | 100 | 8,908 | 100 | 1,421 | 100 | 6,288 | 100 |

Source: Central Bureau of Statistics, Statistical Abstract of Israel, 1983, p. 792-793.

the Gaza Strip, textiles, food, and wood products contributed the most (57 percent of total revenues).

Industrial output in the two territories may be classified into four major categories: processed agricultural products produced mainly for the domestic market such as olive oil, soap, fruit and vegetable canning, cigarettes, chocolates, etc.; processed raw materials in the form of wood, paper, leather, and construction tiles and bricks; subcontracted work for Israeli firms such as clothing, metal work, electronic equipment (component assembly); and jewelry, gifts, and souvenirs for tourists.[9] All these products are manufactured in labor-intensive small workshops utilizing conventional methods of production.

Olive pressing is one of the major food processing activities in the West Bank. It is, however, seasonal in nature and its production and employment fluctuate widely in response to olive crop yields. In good years, the number of operating presses reaches as many as 300, employing more than 3,000 people; in poor seasons, as in 1974/75, the number of presses and employees declines considerably (102 presses and 633 employees).

One of the major postwar developments in the Gaza Strip has been the establishment of an industrial zone at Erez on the border with Israel. Plants in this zone are owned, operated, and managed by the Israelis who are also responsible for the marketing of production. As a result, employment opportunities have been opened in the zone for local labor on a piecework basis producing assembly parts for Israeli industries or completed products.[10] Therefore, industry has remained, basically, limited to "handicrafts, citrus packing, food processing, piecework in the form of cottage industries under sub-contract to Israeli firms, or in the form of employment at nearby Israeli companies."[11]

## SUBCONTRACTING

Many Israeli firms have been attracted by the availability of cheap unskilled and semi-skilled labor in the territories to enter into subcontracts with some of the areas' entrepreneurs. Subcontracting activity has been intensified and enlarged to include such simple goods produced mainly by manual labor such as textiles, clothing, carpets, furniture, shoes, plastics, and construction materials. The development of some of these industries has accelerated in response to increasing Israeli demand for their products. In some cases, Israeli enterprises have been providing raw materials to workshops in the West Bank and Gaza Strip, which are then shipped back to Israel in a processed form for completion. In addition, there is an increasing amount of subcontracting on repair jobs for consumer durable goods by workshops in the territories, including such items as motor vehicles, refrigerators, etc.[12]

Subcontracting has opened some employment opportunities in the territories and drawn some women into the labor force who would otherwise have remained economically inactive. On the other hand, it has so far failed to have any lasting effects on either industrial development or the structure of existing industries.[13]

## PROBLEMS AND PROSPECTS

The industrial sector has stagnated in the occupied territories during the postwar period. Industrial development in the territories has been impeded by several factors. First, local entrepreneurs and Israelis have been unwilling to invest in industrial plant because of political uncertainties. The political climate is so confused that economic ventures are considered too risky. Consequently, industrial investment has remained at a minimum with very few Palestinian-Israeli partnerships. Second, the free import of superior Israeli industrial products into the territories has exposed local products to severe competition, inhibiting new ventures and investments. Third, the high costs of production in the territories have placed industry in a weak position in the face of imports. The lack of natural resources in the areas has made industry dependent on raw materials imported either from or through Israel at inflated prices.[14] Moreover, the rising labor cost as a result of the expansion of the employment of migrant workers in Israel has contributed to the cost of production. Fourth, the absence of a domestic banking system has deprived industry of a major source of credit and investment loans, necessary for the financing of working capital and long-term requirements. In the prewar period, the Industrial Development Fund (later replaced by the Industrial Development Bank), a specialized lending institution, extended long-term loans to industry in the West Bank to an amount of JD 103,567. Credit facilities and short-term loans were provided by the commercial banking system in Jordan. These sources of finance have stopped completely since the war; but loans for JD 611,000 were disbursed through the Jordan Cooperative Organization in 1979/80 to cooperatives for industrial purposes.

Local businessmen have been reluctant to deal with Israeli banks because of the exorbitant interest rates charged on loans. In addition, all loans must be approved by the military authorities, and this often is extremely time consuming. There is also a fear of breach of confidentiality regarding financial information. Lastly, the requirement to fill out many forms in Hebrew is a language barrier that makes banking with Israeli banks difficult.[15]

There are many other obstacles facing industry in the territories. Among these are shortage of skilled manpower and entrepreneurs, limited power capacity,[16] lack of marketing channels and absence of protection policies for industry.[17] Most important has been the absence of a central authority to institute policy, promote industry, and invest in infrastructure and large-scale industries to set industrial development in motion.[18]

Under current conditions, the prospects for industrial development in the occupied territories are very slim indeed. Prerequisites for development are the elimination of certain risks and uncertainties, a commitment of large investments in infrastructure and machinery, the promulgation of policies aimed at protecting and promoting industry, the training of personnel in technical and managerial skills, and the provision of finance at appropriate terms.

## Notes

1. Department of Statistics, Industrial Survey, p. 136-139.
2. Jelal Dawoud, "Industry in the Gaza Strip," SAMED (August 1980), p. 31.
3. Ibid.
4. Hisham, Awartani, A Survey of Industries in the West Bank and Gaza Strip (Birzeit: Birzeit University Publications, 1979), p. 22-23.
5. Ibid., p. 24.
6. Ibid., p. 11.
7. Dawoud, "Industry," p. 34-52.
8. Van Arkadie, Benefits and Burdens, p. 124.
9. Bull, The West Bank, p. 26.
10. Bregman, The Economy, p. 44.
11. David W. Mize et al., An Assessment of Education in the West Bank and Gaza Strip: Analysis, Vol. 1 (Washington, D.C.: America-Mideast Educational and Training Services, 1979), p. 62.
12. Haselkorn, Kurz, and Wagner, Trade and Economic Links, p. 15.
13. UNDP, Report, p. 44.
14. Tuma and Darin-Drabkin, The Economic Case, p. 110.
15. Awartani, A Survey, p. 38.
16. Committee on Foreign Affairs, The West Bank-Gaza, p. 37.
17. Pearson, "Economic and Social Development," p. 23.
18. Ben Shahar et al. Economic Structure, p. 11.

# 6 Construction and Services

## CONSTRUCTION

Construction accounted for around 5 percent of the GDP of the West Bank and employed 20,000 to 25,000 persons[1] in the prewar period. In the Gaza Strip, it contributed 6 percent of the GDP and employed 4,000 workers.[2] Construction in the two territories was marked by the preponderance of private building, which in turn employed two-thirds of the sector's total workers[3] and absorbed as much of gross investment in the West Bank.[4] Total annual building area was of the magnitude of 100,000 square meters in each of the two territories before the war.[5]

Construction activity dropped sharply in the few years immediately after the war, but recovered and grew fairly rapidly until stagnation set in in the last few years. Its contribution to the GDP has jumped to around 15 percent in the West Bank and to considerably more than 20 percent in the Gaza Strip. Yet its employment decreased between 1970 and 1975 in the two territories, increased afterward, but never reached the 1975 level in the Gaza Strip. In 1982, the construction sector accounted for almost 11 and 9 percent of total domestic employment in the West Bank and Gaza Strip, respectively. The difference between construction's share in domestic output and employment may be explained by high labor productivity in this sector and by unpaid family labor working on weekend vacation from employment in Israel.[6]

Building starts increased from 88,000 square meters in 1968 to 1,210,000 square meters in the two territories together in 1979; by 1982 this had dropped to 810,000 square meters (see Table 6.1).

The years 1968-1979 represented a peak in construction activity. In the West Bank, building starts jumped from 67,000 to 798,000 square meters; in the Gaza Strip the rise was from 21,000 to 412,000 square meters. However, these figures plunged to 543,000 and 267,000 square meters in the West Bank and the Gaza Strip, respectively, in 1982. Almost

TABLE 6.1
Area of building, by initiating sector and purpose, the West Bank and the Gaza Strip, 1968-1982 (in thousands of square meters)

| | 1968 | 1969 | 1970 | 1971 | 1972 | 1973 | 1974 | 1975 | 1976 | 1977 | 1978 | 1979 | 1980 | 1981 | 1982 |
|---|---|---|---|---|---|---|---|---|---|---|---|---|---|---|---|
| Building completed - Grand total | 82.6 | 110.6 | 114.2 | 122.3 | 290.4 | 400.1 | 515.7 | 611.5 | 802.0 | 845.3 | 912.7 | 1019.5 | 1010.3 | 1006.9 | n.a. |
| West Bank - total | 79.0 | 83.8 | 101.7 | 109.3 | 199.0 | 279.7 | 382.5 | 490.5 | 580.4 | 627.5 | 655.3 | 718.1 | 749.7 | 694.1 | n.a. |
| Residential | 63.3 | 64.6 | 71.2 | 75.8 | 159.8 | 255.2 | 320.8 | 402.0 | 473.5 | 504.8 | 542.5 | 571.7 | 624.7 | 582.2 | 490.9 |
| Nonresidential | 5.7 | 19.2 | 30.5 | 33.5 | 39.2 | 24.5 | 61.7 | 88.5 | 106.9 | 122.7 | 112.8 | 246.4 | 125.0 | 111.9 | n.a. |
| Gaza Strip - total | 3.6 | 26.8 | 12.5 | 13.0 | 91.4 | 120.4 | 133.2 | 121.0 | 221.6 | 217.8 | 257.4 | 294.9 | 260.6 | 312.8 | n.a. |
| Residential | 3.0 | 7.5 | 8.7 | 9.2 | 74.9 | 106.9 | 126.2 | 102.5 | 193.0 | 181.4 | 210.1 | 248.1 | 217.9 | 258.6 | 304.5 |
| Nonresidential | 0.6 | 19.3 | 3.8 | 3.8 | 16.5 | 13.5 | 7.0 | 18.5 | 28.6 | 36.4 | 47.3 | 46.8 | 42.7 | 54.2 | n.a. |
| Building begun - Grand total | 87.9 | 122.3 | 146.5 | 258.4 | 499.5 | 523.7 | 692.3 | 827.3 | 944.5 | 969.6 | 1119.5 | 1209.6 | 1145.6 | 1195.7 | 809.9 |
| West Bank - total | 66.8 | 109.3 | 129.1 | 233.7 | 325.5 | 364.6 | 557.7 | 586.1 | 646.7 | 683.0 | 786.4 | 797.6 | 756.3 | 795.6 | 543.2 |
| Residential | 51.0 | 78.2 | 95.3 | 184.5 | 259.7 | 289.9 | 452.3 | 481.3 | 529.8 | 541.2 | 638.2 | 655.7 | 631.9 | 652.9 | 473.0 |
| Nonresidential | 15.8 | 31.1 | 33.8 | 49.2 | 65.8 | 74.7 | 105.4 | 104.8 | 116.9 | 141.8 | 148.2 | 131.9 | 124.4 | 142.7 | 70.2 |
| Gaza Strip - total | 21.1 | 13.0 | 16.6 | 34.7 | 124.0 | 159.1 | 134.6 | 241.2 | 297.8 | 286.6 | 333.1 | 412.0 | 389.3 | 400.1 | 266.7 |
| Residential | 3.8 | 8.5 | 11.8 | 27.0 | 106.1 | 142.9 | 124.3 | 212.4 | 243.9 | 237.1 | 276.4 | 342.5 | 327.0 | 340.8 | 233.7 |
| Nonresidential | 17.3 | 4.5 | 5.8 | 7.7 | 17.9 | 16.2 | 10.3 | 28.8 | 53.9 | 49.5 | 56.7 | 69.5 | 62.3 | 59.3 | 33.0 |

Source: Central Bureau of Statistics, Statistical Abstract of Israel (various issues).
n.a. = Not available.

all building starts have been in private residential housing, which accounted for well over four-fifths of the total area in the two territories. The concentration on housing came in part as a result of increased demand for dwellings generated by the rise in population incomes. The Arab inhabitants of the areas are culturally predisposed toward investments in home ownership. Other factors responsible for the expansion of residential construction include the lack of alternative investment opportunities, an unwillingness to invest in other branches of the economy because of the prevailing uncertainties associated with the occupational status of the territories, and the people's determination to assert their rights to the land in the face of continuous threat of confiscation. The annual supply of dwellings, therefore, has been increasing by an average of 4,721 units in the West Bank and 1,679 units in the Gaza Strip during the past few years.

## SERVICES

Service sectors together represented the major economic activity in the two territories before the war, accounting for over two-thirds and one-half of domestic product in the West Bank and the Gaza Strip, respectively. Predominant among these were public services, trade, and transportation. Since the war, the share of services has declined to less than half of the domestic product in the territories (except in 1981 and 1982 in the Strip) due to considerable curtailment in tourism and public services, among other factors. The service sectors consist of several heterogeneous activities, including transport, trade, tourism, and public services, in addition to various kinds of personal services.

### Transport

The West Bank was served by a relatively well developed road network connecting its various parts together and linking it to East Bank population centers. After the war, the transportation system was restructured to integrate the two territories into the Israeli road system. As a result, new roads were constructed connecting various areas in the territories to Israeli urban centers to facilitate the flow of goods and labor[7] and to link Jewish settlements with major roads and highways.[8] Employment in transportation stands at less than 6,400 persons in the West Bank and 5,100 persons in the Gaza Strip in 1982, compared with 4,700 and 3,500, respectively, in 1970.

**Tourism**

Tourism income in Jordan grew rapidly from about JD 3 million in 1960 to more than JD 11 million in 1966. This income soon became a major source of foreign currency, exceeding the total proceeds from commodity exports and accounting for 27 percent of the country's current account income. The number of tourists coming to Jordan rose from 132,000 in 1960 to as many as 491,000 in 1965 and 617,000 in 1966. About 60 percent of all tourists visiting the country in 1966 came from Arab countries.[9]

The tourist industry in Jordan was mainly concentrated in the West Bank, with Arab Jerusalem being the center of tourist activities. Consequently, the West Bank received more than 90 percent of the total investment of about JD 20 million in tourist facilities in the 1960s. During the 1960-1967 period, the Industrial Development Fund, the Development Board, and the Industrial Development Bank extended a total of JD 590,000 in loans for tourist purposes in Jordan, of which JD 455,000 (77 percent) was for projects in the West Bank. As a result, the West Bank contained 225 hotels on the eve of the war, compared with only 96 hotels in the East Bank, and Arab Jerusalem in particular housed most of the graded hotels (55 out of 67 classified hotels were in the West Bank, of which 45 were in Jerusalem).

In 1966, the number of travel agencies in Jordan was 87, most of which (70) were in the West Bank (60 were in Jerusalem alone). In the same year, Jerusalem contained 64 percent of the total number of souvenir shops in Jordan, 90 percent of the tourist guides, the sole tourist transportation company, tourist guides institute, and a hotel training center.

The majority of tourists coming to Jordan were mainly attracted to the historic and religious sites in the West Bank. It was estimated that around 80 percent of Jordan's total tourism income of JD 11 million was earned in the West Bank; Arab Jerusalem accounted for about JD 6 million of this income because it contained most of the holy shrines and tourist facilities and services.

The occupation of the West Bank in general and the incorporation of Arab Jerusalem into Israel in particular dealt the tourism industry a severe blow. Tourism income declined appreciably because the flow of hundreds of thousands of Arab visitors completely stopped.

Arab visitors coming to the West Bank after the war have been confined to those Palestinians working abroad who spend their vacations by staying with their families there. Therefore, the demand for tourism facilities and services has remained limited. On the other hand, foreign tourists visiting the holy places prefer to use Israeli services, which are better suited to cater to the needs of those visitors.[10] Consequently, the number of hotels in the West Bank, excluding Arab Jerusalem, stood at 18 in 1982 and received about 13,000 guests.

The hotel occupancy rate has declined from about 50 percent in the prewar period to around 20 percent since the late 1970s, a clear indication of the shift to Israeli services.

## Trade

Wholesale and retail trade accounted for considerably more than one-fifth of the domestic product in the West Bank before the war. In fact, this sector was the single most important economic activity in terms of contribution to the GDP, surpassing that of agriculture in almost every year during the 1959-1966 period. Trade activity was carried out in 6,118 outlets and employed more than 12,000 persons. Similarly, trade was one of the more important sectors in the prewar economy of the Gaza Strip. It prospered due to free import policies allowed by the Egyptian admnistration, and the city of Gaza grew to become a major trading center serving Egyptian tourists hungry for imported goods.

The value of sales in wholesale trade increased considerably in the two territories in the postwar period (statistics covering the late 1970s are not available), with food, beverages, and tobacco in the West Bank, and metals and chemicals in the Gaza Strip recording the highest rates of growth. Employment in commerce, restaurants, and hotels has increased from about 13,000 persons in the West Bank and 10,000 persons in the Gaza Strip in 1969 to 17,000 and 11,000, respectively, in 1982.

## Electricity and Water

Each municipality had its own electricity generation unit in the territories in the prewar period. But since occupation the Israeli authorities have tried, and partially succeeded, in linking these units to the Israeli grid to gain control over the supply of electricity in the territories. Therefore, the military government has refused permission for power companies to expand their production capacity, or for the construction of new and independent electrification projects in rural areas. Relentless Israeli attempts to control the independent electricity company in Arab Jerusalem through purchase or confiscation have resulted in a dispute that has received wide publicity and reached the highest court in Israel.

Ironically, the occupation authorities have insisted that Arab companies supply electricity to Israeli settlements in their areas of concession.[11]

Water resources for domestic use in the territories, like power generation, have been barely maintained at prewar levels. The military government has not only failed to invest in new water projects, but has also severely restricted the expansion of existing resources. (More than JD 100,000 in loans were granted to West Bank local authorities through the Jordan Cooperative Organization for water and electricity projects in 1979/80.) Consequently, the growing scarcity of power and water has greatly impeded economic growth by depriving industry of the much needed utilities at a reasonable cost.

## Public Services

The government of Jordan assumed responsibility for the provision of public services such as health, education, welfare, and defense in the West Bank before the war. In the Gaza Strip, UNRWA provided some of the public services, in addition to the Egyptian administration, especially in the fields of education and health.[12] This sector was relatively large in terms of contribution to the GDP, accounting for around 12 percent in the West Bank and about 25 percent in the Gaza Strip. In terms of employment, public and community services absorbed close to 16 percent of the employed labor force in the West Bank in 1961.

Budget estimates for the West Bank showed a deficit that was financed by the central government in Amman (see Table 6.2). Domestic revenues in the fiscal year 1965/66 were almost JD 11 million, more than 60 percent of which were in the form of indirect taxes, mainly customs duty. On the other hand, locally financed public expenditures reached JD 15 million, of which 12 percent were spent on development and the rest on consumption. Spending for civilian purposes absorbed one-third of total current expenditure. However, current domestic revenues fell short of current expenditures, of which defense was a major component. It should be noted that a great part of investment in capital works was directly financed by the government of Jordan. On the other hand, government current budget in the Gaza Strip was balanced; that is, current revenues totally covered consumption expenditures. When investment is added to expenditures, the budget showed a deficit of some JD 350,000. Indirect taxes in the Strip were the major source of domestic revenues, accounting for almost four-fifths of the total proceeds. Excess demand was about 8 percent of total product in the West Bank and 3 percent in the Strip, and government consumption expenditures comprised more than one-fifth of the GNP in each territory. This implies that government was instrumental in stimulating economic activity in the prewar period.

TABLE 6.2
Government budget, Jordan and the West Bank, 1965/66[1], and the Gaza Strip, 1966[2]

| | Jordan | West Bank | | Gaza Strip |
|---|---|---|---|---|
| | JD million | JD million | % | JD million |
| Domestic revenues - total | 26.7 | 10.7 | 40 | 2.9 |
| Direct taxes | 4.0 | | | 0.4 |
| Indirect taxes[a] | 16.5 | | | 2.3 |
| Other revenues[b] | 6.5 | | | 0.2 |
| Expenditures | 41.9 | 15.0 | | 3.3 |
| Consumption[c] | 35.8 | 13.2 | 37 | 2.9 |
| Investment | 6.1 | 1.8 | 30 | 0.4 |
| Deficit (surplus) | 12.5 | 4.3 | 28 | 0.4 |

Sources: (1) Adapted from Ward, Peretz, and Wilson, The Palestinian State, p. 125; (2) Bregman, Economic Growth, p. 74.

[a]A reasonable estimate of indirect taxes in the West Bank is not possible.
[b]For Jordan, this item includes post, telegraph and telephone, oil transit dues, interest and profit, revenue from pension, and miscellaneous items.
[c]For Jordan, this includes general administration, defense, justice and police, education, health services, social welfare services, communications, and other services.

Government services have expanded very slowly in comparison with the national income in the territories during the postwar period. These services are now lagging behind domestic demand, and government expenditure in general is very small. Spending for the development of economic infrastructure is extremely limited and that for the development of the production base of the economy, i.e., industry and agriculture, is totally nonexistent.[13] Therefore, economic infrastructure has been at a level below that required for the economic development of the territories; health and education especially, but also water and power services, have fallen far short of expanded demand created by population and income growth.[14]

Government consumption expenditures have grown at a modest rate, averaging less than 4 percent per annum in each territory in the postwar period; they have dramatically declined from about 15 percent of the GNP in each territory in 1968 to around 6 percent in 1982 (see Table 6.3). Hence, the role played by government in the economies has been decreasing in importance, despite considerable tax levies from the terri-

TABLE 6.3
Government consumption expenditures, the West Bank and the Gaza Strip, 1968-1982 (in 1968 prices; IL million)

| Year | West Bank Expenditures | West Bank % of GNP | Gaza Strip Expenditures | Gaza Strip % of GNP |
|---|---|---|---|---|
| 1968 | 51 | 14.8 | 19 | 14.5 |
| 1969 | 56 | 13.2 | 23 | 15.9 |
| 1970 | 64 | 13.7 | 28 | 15.0 |
| 1971 | 69 | 12.0 | 29 | 12.9 |
| 1972 | 73 | 10.2 | 30 | 10.9 |
| 1973 | 74 | 11.0 | 31 | 9.9 |
| 1974 | 77 | 8.6 | 30 | 9.5 |
| 1975 | 76 | 8.6 | 29 | 8.5 |
| 1976 | 78 | 7.7 | 30 | 7.9 |
| 1977 | 79 | 7.9 | 30 | 7.6 |
| 1978 | 80 | 7.0 | 31 | 7.5 |
| 1979 | 84 | 7.6 | 30 | 6.6 |
| 1980 | 84 | 6.4 | 29 | 6.5 |
| 1981 | 86 | 7.2 | 29 | 6.3 |
| 1982 | 86 | 6.6 | 29 | 6.3 |

Source: Central Bureau of Statistics, Statistical Abstract of Israel (various issues).

tories. It is true that the Israeli authorities have retained the tax structure under the Jordanian law in the West Bank, except Arab Jerusalem where higher Israeli taxes apply, which entails a lower tax burden than in Israel. But the incidence of taxation borne by the population in the territories has been greatly modified as a result of the increasing links with the Israeli economy.[15] First, the Israeli system of customs duty has been applied to imports from the outside world[16] in order to make up for the low indirect tax in the West Bank,[17] putting, in the process, a further burden on consumers. Second, Arab inhabitants working in Israel have been subject to various wage deductions, many of which neither revert to the territories nor accrue to individuals. Third, businesses now pay a value added tax assessed on turnover at a rate of 12 percent, which poses, along with rising prices and labor costs, extra problems for small enterprises.[18] Consequently, the Israelis have continued to collect taxes under provisions of the Jordanian and Israeli laws, spending only a portion of the proceeds in the territories and transferring the rest to the Israeli treasury.[19]

Local authorities, mainly municipalities, in the West

Bank developed various community services before the war. Municipal budgets on the whole were not balanced; combined current expenditures (excluding repayment of loans and interest) in the fiscal year 1965/66 were JD 1.4 million, whereas current revenues totaled just JD 1.2 million. Municipal spending was for running public utilities and services, in addition to investment in the expansion of those services. Revenues of municipalities were derived from taxes, fees, property tax, licensing and other fees, sales of power, water, and services. Some of these revenues, notably fuel tax, were collected by the central government on behalf of municipalities. Loans granted before the war to local authorities in the West Bank by the Municipal and Village Loans Fund, a specialized government lending institution, amounted to JD 1.9 million, one-half of the total amount of loans extended to all local authorities in the whole of Jordan (see Table 6.4). These loans were invested in the construction of school buildings, clinics, water, power, and sewage systems, roads, day care centers, housing, slaughterhouses, vegetable markets, public buildings, bus depots, animal markets, garbage disposal facilities, and hospitals.

The overall income and expenditure of towns in the occupied territories have been balanced in the postwar period. Current revenues have been more than enough to cover current expenditures in every year after the occupation in the Gaza

TABLE 6.4
Loans extended by the Municipal and Village Loans Fund, Jordan and the West Bank, 1956-1967

| | Jordan | | West Bank | |
|---|---|---|---|---|
| Year | (JD '000) | % | (JD '000) | % |
| Before 1960 | 872.1 | 100.0 | 417.6 | 47.9 |
| 1960 | 356.3 | 100.0 | 162.1 | 45.5 |
| 1961 | 260.0 | 100.0 | 122.3 | 47.0 |
| 1962 | 272.6 | 100.0 | 161.8 | 59.4 |
| 1963 | 312.0 | 100.0 | 197.8 | 63.4 |
| 1964 | 572.5 | 100.0 | 260.8 | 45.6 |
| 1965 | 354.7 | 100.0 | 167.9 | 47.3 |
| 1966 | 437.0 | 100.0 | 170.0 | 38.9 |
| 1967[a] | 274.2 | 100.0 | 192.7 | 70.3 |
| Total | 3,711.4 | 100.0 | 1,853.0 | 49.9 |

Source: Cities and Villages Development Bank, Amman, Jordan.

[a]Until May.

Strip, except in the last two years and in 1979/80, which showed a small deficit; current revenues in the West Bank have fallen short of current expenditures since 1978/79. However, total income of towns in the territories has exceeded total expenditures in almost all years since 1973/74, showing a modest surplus in their annual budget.

In the postwar period, local authorities in the territories have continued to derive their income from property tax, fuel tax, various fees, and other sources, which are collected through the military administration. Loans and grants from this administration constituted a very small portion of total revenues, 1 and 4 percent in the West Bank in 1981/82 and 1982/83, respectively; and 4 and 12 percent in the Gaza Strip in the same years. However, the most important component of income is the one generated by establishments, that is, water and electricity. Current expenditures constitute the bulk of total town expenditures, accounting for 81 and 80 percent of total expenditures in the West Bank in 1981/82 and 1982/83; and 72 and 74 percent in the Gaza Strip in the same years. Current expenditures cover such items as general administration, sanitation, engineering and technical department, guarding and security and fire extinguishing, running costs of water and electricity, and repayment of loans. Total current expenditures of towns comprised one-third of general government consumption expenditure in the Strip and over one-fourth in the West Bank in 1982.

Investment expenditures of local authorities accounted for 11 and 26 percent of total expenditures in the West Bank and Gaza Strip, respectively, in 1982/83. However, the government of Jordan has been a major source of finance, directly or indirectly, for various local authorities' investment projects in the West Bank. Loans advanced to local authorities in the West Bank by Jordan have totaled some JD 3.7 million since June 1967 (see Table 6.5). These funds have been invested in the construction of new projects and the expansion of old ones such as electricity, water and sewage, commercial centers, school buildings, industrial centers, public buildings, and other development projects.

The budgets of the municipalities in the territories will continue to be constrained by lack of sufficient authority to raise additional income through taxation. Consequently, municipalities have to rely on the small number of loans and grants offered by the military government, Jordan, and other Arab countries (strictly controlled by the Israeli authorities) to finance current and capital expenditures.[20] These sums are not enough to satisfy the needs of an expanding population for various public services such as water, power, health, and education.

TABLE 6.5
Jordanian loans granted to West Bank municipalities and village councils, by source, 1967-1981 (thousand dinars)

| Year | Commercial Banks in Jordan[a] | Government of Jordan | Government of Jordan Executive Office[b] | Total |
|---|---|---|---|---|
| 1967 | -- | 88 | -- | 88 |
| 1968 | -- | 9 | -- | 9 |
| 1969 | -- | 6 | -- | 6 |
| 1970 | -- | -- | -- | -- |
| 1971 | -- | 25 | -- | 25 |
| 1972 | -- | 48 | -- | 48 |
| 1973 | 444 | 97 | -- | 541 |
| 1974 | 851 | 137 | 252 | 1,240 |
| 1975 | 495 | 151 | 117 | 763 |
| 1976 | 135 | 35 | 30 | 200 |
| 1977 | 100 | 170 | 26 | 296 |
| 1978 | -- | 277 | 26 | 303 |
| 1979 | 124[c] | 16 | 11 | 151 |
| 1980 | -- | -- | -- | -- |
| 1981 | -- | -- | 3 | 3 |
| Total | 2,149 | 1,059 | 465 | 3,673 |

Source: Cities and Villages Development Bank.

[a]Guaranteed by the government of Jordan.
[b]Loans to villages disbursed from fees collected on goods crossing bridges into Jordan.
[c]Includes an amount of JD 24,000 whose date is not known.

## Notes

1. See Tuma and Darin-Drabkin, The Economic Case, p. 66; and Bregman, Economic Growth, p. 69. In their Economic Structure, Ben Shahar et al. put the figure at 12,500 persons, p. 52.
2. Bregman, Economic Growth, p. 69.
3. Ben Shahar et al., Economic Structure, p. 52.
4. Kanovsky, The Economic Impact, p. 143.
5. Bregman, Economic Growth, p. 67.
6. Tuma and Darin-Drabkin, The Economic Case, p. 66.
7. Abdul-Ilah Abu-Ayyash, "Israeli Regional Planning

Policy in the Occupied Territories," *Journal of Palestine Studies* (Winter-Spring 1976), p. 103.

8. Ibid., p. 102.

9. Department of Statistics, *Statistical Yearbook* (1960 through 1966).

10. Ben Shahar et al., *Economic Structure*, p. 122.

11. Pearson, "Economic and Social Development," p. 35.

12. Bregman, *Economic Growth*, p. 73.

13. C.A.C.I., *The Economic Implications of a Middle-East Peace Settlement*, Vol. II (1978), p. 9-10 (draft version).

14. Committee on Foreign Affairs, *The West Bank-Gaza*, p. 34.

15. Van Arkadie, *Benefits and Burdens*, p. 98.

16. Ibid.

17. Ann Mosley Lesch, *Israel's Occupation of the West Bank: The First Two Years* (Santa Monica: The Rand Corporation, 1970), p. 25.

18. Sarah Graham-Brown, "The Structural Impact of Israeli Colonization: The West Bank and Gaza," *MERIP Reports* (January 1979), p. 12.

19. Lesch, *Israel's Occupation*, p. 25.

20. Committee on Foreign Affairs, *The West Bank-Gaza*, p. 42.

# 7
# Foreign Trade, Balance of Payments, and Capital Movement

## FOREIGN TRADE

Before the June 1967 war, foreign trade was dominated by the prevalence of agricultural exports, industrial imports, and by a large import surplus. Exports (including re-exports) totaled JD 10 million in Jordan in 1966, of which 40 percent was agricultural.[1] Phosphate exports constituted about 30 percent of Jordan's total exports in the same year, or about one-half of its nonagricultural exports.[2] The West Bank's exports to foreign countries amounted to JD 2.1 million in 1966 and constituted one-fifth of Jordan's total, or 29 percent if phosphates are excluded. The West Bank's agricultural exports stood at JD 1.4 million, or more than one-third of the total for the entire country; industrial exports represented 11 percent of Jordan's total, but double this figure if phosphates are once again excluded. The West Bank exported such items as fruits, vegetables, processed food, limestone, marble, soap, and other light industrial products. Arab countries were the major market for these products. Citrus dominated the Gaza Strip's exports, accounting for 90 percent of its total of JD 2.6 million (1966), the remaining 10 percent being mainly re-export goods.[3]

Jordan imported JD 68 million of manufactured goods and foodstuff in 1966,[4] and the West Bank's share of this stood at JD 20 million, or almost 30 percent of the total. The West Bank, like the East, was a net importer of foodstuff and manufactured products, with the bulk of such imports (90 percent) being manufactured goods and raw materials; agricultural imports accounted for the remaining JD 2 million.[5] The Gaza Strip's import level stood at JD 10 million on the eve of the war, and consisted mostly of foodstuff, consumer goods, and raw materials.[6]

In addition to the above trade figures for the West Bank, there was also a certain amount of internal trading activity between the East and West Banks. In 1966 the West Bank exported JD 2 million worth of goods to the East Bank, JD 1.6

million of which was agricultural.[7] Total West Bank exports to all other countries amounted to JD 4 million in the same year, three-quarters of which were agricultural. Imports from the East Bank were valued at more than JD 4 million, 93.0 percent of which were manufactured products and raw materials.[8] This brings total West Bank imports to JD 24 million in 1966 and leaves a deficit in the balance of trade of some JD 20 million. Similarly, trade deficit in the Gaza Strip was more than JD 7 million. Trade deficit in the territories was compensated by tourism earnings, remittances, transfer payments by UNRWA and other foreign agencies, and, in the case of the West Bank, by excess government demand.[9]

The territories' foreign trade in the postwar period has been reoriented as a result of several Israeli measures adopted to increase their economic links with Israel, making it in a few years their major trading partner. First, trade with the East Bank (and to a lesser extent with other Arab countries) was resumed soon after the war across the "open bridges." The resumption of the flow of agricultural produce across the bridges on the Jordan River helped solve the problem of marketing the West Bank's agricultural surplus that would otherwise have undersold subsidized Israeli farm produce. Second, tight quotas were maintained on agricultural products that could be exported from the territories to Israel to protect its farmers from competition, leading finally to the restructuring of crops grown in the areas so as to minimize competition with Israeli farmers. Third, Israeli products were permitted to flow freely into the territories without any restrictions, exposing in the process the local industry to severe competition. Finally, a system of tariffs, customs duty, and other restrictions was placed on goods imported through Israel, effectively limiting trade with the outside world.

Israel has progressively become the territories' dominant trading partner, receiving 54 and 82 percent of the total West Bank and Gaza Strip exports, respectively, in 1982 (see Table 7.1). On the other hand, Jordan has remained the second largest market for the territories' products, absorbing 46 and 16 percent of the West Bank's and Gaza Strip's total exports, respectively, in the same year. The relative importance of the West Bank's exports to Jordan has generally declined, with some fluctuations in the postwar period because of the weakening position of Jordan as its trading partner and variation in crop production. Conversely, the Strip's exports to and through Jordan, although far from stable, increased modestly during the same period. Exports to other countries have constituted a negligible fraction (0.9 percent) of the West Bank's total exports in 1982; exports dropped sharply from 53 percent of those of the Strip in 1971 to as little as 3 percent in 1982. The reason for this dramatic decline lies in

TABLE 7.1
Imports and exports, the West Bank and the Gaza Strip, 1971-1982 (in percentages)

| | 1971 | 1972 | 1973 | 1974 | 1975 | 1976 | 1977 | 1978 | 1979 | 1980 | 1981 | 1982 |
|---|---|---|---|---|---|---|---|---|---|---|---|---|
| West Bank | | | | | | | | | | | | |
| Imports | | | | | | | | | | | | |
| Total | 100.0 | 100.0 | 100.0 | 100.0 | 100.0 | 100.0 | 100.0 | 100.0 | 100.0 | 100.0 | 100.0 | 100.0 |
| From Israel | 79.8 | 82.5 | 89.4 | 89.6 | 86.6 | 89.7 | 89.9 | 86.5 | 85.8 | 86.8 | 88.5 | 87.8 |
| From Jordan | 4.8 | 4.6 | 3.0 | 2.4 | 2.2 | 1.5 | 1.7 | 2.0 | 1.4 | 1.4 | 1.7 | 2.1 |
| From other countries | 15.4 | 12.9 | 7.6 | 8.0 | 9.2 | 8.8 | 8.4 | 11.5 | 12.8 | 11.8 | 9.8 | 10.1 |
| Exports | | | | | | | | | | | | |
| Total | 100.0 | 100.0 | 100.0 | 100.0 | 100.0 | 100.0 | 100.0 | 100.0 | 100.0 | 100.0 | 100.0 | 100.0 |
| To Israel | 52.4 | 49.6 | 72.0 | 70.1 | 64.0 | 62.5 | 62.1 | 54.5 | 60.4 | 57.8 | 62.5 | 53.8 |
| To Jordan | 46.2 | 49.6 | 27.3 | 29.2 | 32.0 | 34.8 | 37.0 | 44.5 | 39.0 | 41.3 | 36.8 | 45.8 |
| To other countries | 1.4 | 0.8 | 0.7 | 0.7 | 4.0 | 2.7 | 0.9 | 1.0 | 0.6 | 0.9 | 0.7 | 0.4 |
| Gaza Strip | | | | | | | | | | | | |
| Imports | | | | | | | | | | | | |
| Total | 100.0 | 100.0 | 100.0 | 100.0 | 100.0 | 100.0 | 100.0 | 100.0 | 100.0 | 100.0 | 100.0 | 100.0 |
| From Israel | 84.9 | 88.8 | 91.2 | 89.2 | 94.5 | 91.3 | 92.9 | 90.7 | 89.3 | 89.0 | 91.1 | 90.9 |
| From Jordan | 0.1 | 0.1 | 0.1 | 0.1 | 0.1 | -- | -- | -- | -- | -- | -- | -- |
| From other countries | 15.0 | 11.1 | 8.7 | 10.7 | 5.4 | 8.7 | 7.1 | 9.3 | 10.7 | 11.0 | 8.9 | 9.1 |
| Exports | | | | | | | | | | | | |
| Total | 100.0 | 100.0 | 100.0 | 100.0 | 100.0 | 100.0 | 100.0 | 100.0 | 100.0 | 100.0 | 100.0 | 100.0 |
| To Israel | 35.1 | 47.3 | 58.2 | 60.8 | 63.8 | 64.3 | 60.2 | 65.8 | 67.5 | 76.2 | 82.8 | 81.5 |
| To Jordan | 11.9 | 10.2 | 10.5 | 18.4 | 20.0 | 23.4 | 30.4 | 27.1 | 25.2 | 17.7 | 13.5 | 15.7 |
| To other countries | 53.0 | 42.5 | 31.3 | 20.8 | 16.2 | 12.3 | 9.4 | 7.1 | 7.3 | 6.1 | 3.7 | 2.8 |

Source: Derived from Central Bureau of Statistics, Statistical Abstract of Israel (various issues).

the fact that much of the citrus fruits, the main export item in the Strip, has been exported through Israel to outside markets.

Israel has been the main source of imports for the territories, supplying 88 and 91 percent of total West Bank and Gaza Strip imports, respectively, in 1982. The West Bank's imports from Jordan declined from 5 percent in 1971 to 2 percent in 1982; those from other countries dwindled from 15 percent to 10 percent during the same period. The Strip has never been a market for Jordanian goods; imports from other countries accounted for 15 percent of the total in 1971, but they decreased to 9 percent in 1982.

Obviously, the territories have increasingly become an exclusive market for Israeli exports and are the largest single importer of Israeli goods second only to the United States. In 1982, Israeli exports to the territories were valued at $639 million, or 11 percent of its total exports, including diamonds (13 percent excluding diamonds). By contrast, Israeli exports to the United States reached $1.1 billion in 1982, of which $418 million were in diamonds. If diamond exports are excluded, the U.S. total would be close to that of the territories, both topping the list as recipients of Israeli exports.

Total value of exports equaled 21 and 38 percent of GNP of the West Bank and Gaza Strip, respectively, in 1982. Agricultural produce comprised about one-quarter of total exports of the West Bank and the Gaza Strip in the same year. About 16 percent of the West Bank's exports to Israel and 11 percent of the Strip's exports are agricultural products, which means that most of the territories' exports to Israel are manufactured goods. Fruits, especially citrus, and vegetables have been shipped to Israel either for consumption, processing, or re-exporting. About 13 percent of West Bank fruit exports and 58 percent of its vegetables have been destined for Israel and overseas in 1981/82, compared to more than one-third each for the Strip in the same period (see Tables 7.2 and 7.3).

Most of the territories' industrial exports to Israel are goods subcontracted by Israeli firms. In many instances, those firms supply workshops in the territories with the necessary raw materials, which in turn produce semifinished manufactured goods shipped to Israel for finishing.[10] Products produced on a subcontracting basis include such items as textiles, clothing, wood and leather products, and construction materials in the form of building bricks and floor tiles.[11] Other industrial products exported to Israel are carpets, especially from the Gaza Strip, furniture, and handicrafts.[12]

Jordan, as the second largest market for the territories' exports, received two-thirds of total agricultural exports of each territory and two-fifths of total West Bank industrial

TABLE 7.2
Exports of Israel, 1967-1982 ($ million)

| Year | Gross Exports | Exports to West Bank and Gaza Strip | Percent of Gross Exports |
|---|---|---|---|
| 1967 | 569.0 | 14.6 | 2.6 |
| 1968 | 690.1 | 50.9 | 7.4 |
| 1969 | 797.2 | 67.9 | 8.5 |
| 1970 | 852.6 | 73.9 | 8.7 |
| 1971 | 1,060.0 | 102.4 | 9.7 |
| 1972 | 1,284.0 | 137.0 | 10.7 |
| 1973 | 1,653.3 | 194.3 | 11.8 |
| 1974 | 2,127.8 | 302.1 | 14.2 |
| 1975 | 2,308.4 | 367.7 | 15.9 |
| 1976 | 2,807.2 | 392.7 | 14.0 |
| 1977 | 3,544.0 | 462.3 | 13.0 |
| 1978 | 4,311.3 | 390.0 | 9.0 |
| 1979 | 5,043.7 | 497.4 | 9.9 |
| 1980 | 6,109.1 | 571.6 | 9.4 |
| 1981 | 6,337.5 | 667.4 | 10.5 |
| 1982 | 5,920.5 | 639.0 | 10.8 |

Source: Central Bureau of Statistics, Statistical Abstract of Israel, 1983, p. 214.

TABLE 7.3
Israeli exports, by main country of destination, 1978-1982 ($ million)

| Country | 1978 | 1979 | 1980 | 1981 | 1982 |
|---|---|---|---|---|---|
| Belgium and Luxembourg | 208.2 | 218.6 | 236.5 | 206.9 | 232.2 |
| Germany, F.R. | 340.4 | 418.7 | 541.9 | 413.7 | 366.9 |
| United Kingdom | 282.6 | 394.5 | 465.8 | 472.8 | 417.0 |
| France | 180.1 | 246.9 | 299.3 | 301.3 | 258.6 |
| United States | 685.2 | 749.1 | 886.9 | 1220.8 | 1119.2 |
| Hong Kong | 308.0 | 247.2 | 251.1 | 216.8 | 179.8 |
| Japan | 181.4 | 223.4 | 229.9 | 206.1 | 193.4 |
| West Bank and Gaza Strip | 390.0 | 497.4 | 571.6 | 667.4 | 639.0 |
| United States without diamond exports | 309.4 | 408.5 | 432.4 | 715.0 | 701.7 |

Source: Central Bureau of Statistics, Statistical Abstract of Israel, 1981, p. 209 and 213; and 1983, p. 229-230.

exports in 1982. Viewed from a slightly different perspective, most of the West Bank's exports to Jordan have been in the form of manufactured goods (67 percent); those of the Strip have been almost exclusively agricultural produce. Jordan was the recipient of 81 percent of the total West Bank fruit exports, excluding olives, and 63 percent of the Strip's in 1981/82. Over one-fifth of the vegetable exports and over 90 percent of the melon and pumpkin exports of the West Bank went to Jordan in the same year. Industrial exports to Jordan have been confined to processed agricultural products such as olive oil, soap, and tomato paste, in addition to handicrafts and souvenirs.

Jordan has maintained a free trade policy toward the West Bank, and to a lesser extent the Gaza Strip, throughout the postwar period. No customs duty, tariffs, and other barriers have been placed on trade with the West Bank, permitting the flow of goods, especially agricultural, across the bridges to continue unimpeded. However, processed agricultural and industrial products are subject to Arab boycott laws to which Jordan subscribes. According to these laws, the import of products that partially or totally use raw materials originating in Israel or imported through Israeli intermediaries and facilities is prohibited. On the other hand, Israel has stimulated exports to Jordan through special incentives offered to these exporters who turn in their export earning dinars in exchange for Israeli currency through official channels. Some territory exporters may have shipped some Israeli products across the river to take advantage of these incentives.

The territories' exports to the rest of the world have remained very small. The West Bank has exported only a small amount of handicrafts (less than 1 percent of total industrial exports) to other countries; the Gaza Strip shipped 10 percent of its total agricultural exports (mainly citrus) overseas to markets in Europe. However, a sizable portion of the territories' trade with Israel is re-exported to the rest of the world through Israeli intermediaries.[13]

Total imports of the West Bank amounted to more than two-fifths of its GNP in 1982, whereas those of the Gaza Strip were much higher at 64 percent in the same year. The value of imports in the territories has been growing fairly rapidly in the past few years due to inflation and the associated deterioration in the value of the Israeli pound, among others. The territories are a heavy importer of manufactured goods; industrial goods accounted for 88 percent of total imports of each in 1982. Israel has increasingly become the major source of the territories' imports. The predominant position Israel has in trade has been significantly strengthened by Israeli abolition of most restrictions of the flow of goods between Israel and the territories, and their isolation from outside markets by a system of trade barriers imposed on all imports from countries other than Israel. These arrangements have guaranteed the free and unchallenged entry of Israeli goods into the areas' markets, deforming as a result their economies and retarding the development of certain sectors.

Israel has been providing the territories with most of their needs of manufactured, as well as agricultural, products. For instance, Israel's share in total industrial imports was 88 percent in the West Bank and 92 percent in the Gaza Strip, and its share in total agricultural imports was 88 percent in the West Bank and 85 percent in the Strip in 1982. The areas' industrial imports from Israel consist of consumer goods, durable and nondurable, construction materials, and raw materials for the domestic industry. Agricultural imports from Israel include fruits, vegetables, and poultry and eggs, some of which are subsidized by the Israeli government and hence undersell domestic production and hurt local farmers.

The territories' imports from both Jordan and other countries have been declining to negligible proportions. The West Bank imports from Jordan manufactured products such as paper, printed materials, films, textiles, and cotton goods.[14] The deterioration of Jordan's share in the West Bank's total imports was caused by high tariffs and tight security checks and restrictions placed on goods shipped from Jordan, thereby providing an impediment to the flow of trade.[15] Thus, the "open bridges" policy, hailed in several quarters as a generous Israeli gesture serving the interests of the territories, turned out to be open in the direction that serves only Israel's interests. Initially, the West Bank's agricultural produce was moved to Jordan across the bridges to ease the immediate economic difficulties created by the war. At the same time, this arrangement relieved the occupation authorities of the burdensome task of finding an outlet for this output without hurting subsidized Israeli farmers who are politically powerful. Afterward, these bridges have been open eastward only, and westbound traffic, on the other hand, has been handicapped by various sorts of barriers, restrictions, and checks.

Imports from overseas have decreased from 15 percent of all imports for the West Bank and the Gaza Strip in 1971 to 10 and 9 percent, respectively, in 1982. The world has provided the West Bank with 10 percent of its manufactured imports and 11 percent of its agricultural imports in 1982, whereas it has supplied the Gaza Strip with 8 and 15 percent, respectively, during the same year. The decline in the importance of imports from other countries has been a direct result of stiff tariffs imposed upon such imports, placing those countries in a disadvantaged position relative to that of Israel.

The territories' balance of trade has shown a huge annual deficit. Trade deficit equaled more than one-fifth of the

West Bank's GNP and exceeded one-fourth of that of the Strip in 1982. However, most of the trade deficit in the territories is attributed to the exceedingly high imports from Israel, which enjoys a handsome surplus in its balance of trade with each of the two territories. Similarly, trade with overseas countries has resulted in a modest surplus in favor of those countries. Jordan is the only country that has been a net importer of the territories' products, giving rise to a surplus in their favor. The deficit in the balance of trade has been financed by wages earned by migrant workers in Israel, in addition to remittances transferred from abroad[16] and the surplus with Jordan.

In short, Israel has emerged as the main beneficiary of the territories' redirected trade relationships. The application of Israeli customs barriers to the territories soon after the war has given Israel the best of two worlds: restricting the areas' exports, especially competitive agricultural produce, to Israel under various pretexts and at the same time severely limiting their access to world markets. Hence, the areas have become open for uncontested Israeli competition (see Tables 7.4 and 7.5).

## BALANCE OF PAYMENTS

The territories suffered a considerable deficit in their current account, which reached JD 12 million for the West Bank and JD 3 million for the Gaza Strip in 1966. Commodity trade was entirely resposible for this deficit, contrary to services that, thanks to tourism, recorded a substantial surplus of more than JD 11 million and about JD 5 million in the West Bank and the Strip, respectively. This surplus in the balance of services, however, covered less than one-half of the deficit in commodity trade. The current account deficit was financed by remittances from the Jordanian government, in the case of the West Bank, and from UNRWA and other institutions. Such transfers allowed the two territories to maintain a large deficit in their balance of commodity trade.[17]

The balance of payments in the two territories has continued to show a chronic deficit in commodity trade, exports of services surplus and an overall deficit in the current account (see Tables 7.6 and 7.7). The major debit item has been commodity imports, which continued to climb at a rate faster than that of exports, and accounted for three-quarters and four-fifths of total imports in the West Bank and Gaza Strip, respectively, in 1982. On the other hand, wages earned by Arab workers employed mainly in Israel have thus far been the most important credit component of the balance of payments in the two territories. These wages constituted 54 percent of total exports of the West Bank and 50 percent of those of the

Gaza Strip, and more than 90 percent of services exports in each territory in 1982. However, commodity and services exports fell short of total imports, giving rise to a deficit in current account. This deficit is financed by unilateral payments from abroad, in the form of remittances and transfers from Jordan, other Arab countries, and UNRWA. As a result, the balance of payments has shown a net surplus in the Gaza Strip but continued to show a net deficit in the West Bank over the last few years.

## CAPITAL MOVEMENT

It is difficult to estimate the magnitude of risk capital that has been flowing between the territories and other countries because much of this capital is unofficially transferred. But evidence suggests that capital was transferred out of the territories in significant amounts in the late 1960s and early 1970s as a result of the risks involved with investment in their economies. This process, however, has been reversed since 1972 with an improved economic climate in the territories, and outside capital started flowing into their economies, especially in the West Bank.[18] The source of this capital, although not exactly known, is probably Jordan and other Arab countries. Risk capital has been moving out of the Gaza Strip in the past several years, a fact that might point to the narrowing range of investment opportunities in its economy.

Capital movement into the territories has taken various forms: visitors' spending, settlement of the export surplus, Jordanian payment of salaries for 6,000 former civil servants and teachers and payment of the rent on public buildings in the West Bank, Jordanian grants and loans to local authorities, loans and grants disbursed by the Jordanian-Palestinian Joint Committee to local authorities and cooperatives, remittances, etc. (see Table 7.8).

All loans and grants extended to local authorities and cooperatives in the territories are subject to approval by the military government. The Israelis have been known to deny petitions from communities where the mayor is seen as "uncooperative." Moreover, private voluntary organizations that are believed to be sympathetic to Palestinian aspirations have faced difficulties in securing approval for their projects.[19] Finally, the Israelis have blocked any funds suspected of being totally or partially provided through the PLO. Consequently, it is estimated that as much as JD 21 million has been transferred to the territories without the consent or knowledge of the authorities since 1979. However, not all monies accrued to Arab inhabitants are brought into the territories. There is ample evidence to suggest that much of the

TABLE 7.4
Imports, exports, and foreign trade balance, the West Bank, 1971-1982 (IL million)

| | 1971 | 1972 | 1973 | 1974 | 1975 | 1976 | 1977 | 1978 | 1979 | 1980 | 1981 | 1982 |
|---|---|---|---|---|---|---|---|---|---|---|---|---|
| **Imports** | | | | | | | | | | | | |
| Total | 285.1 | 413.5 | 555.7 | 881.8 | 1,463.4 | 1,970.6 | 2,809.8 | 4,406.2 | 9,055 | 20,955 | 29,805 | 105,450 |
| From Israel - total | 227.4 | 341.1 | 496.7 | 790.0 | 1,297.3 | 1,766.9 | 2,526.1 | 3,813.2 | 7,771 | 18,194 | 44,095 | 92,546 |
| Agricultural produce | 39.7 | 56.2 | 84.5 | 125.9 | 205.1 | 290.8 | 431.2 | 638.1 | 1,179 | 2,985 | 6,658 | 11,123 |
| Industrial products | 187.7 | 284.9 | 412.2 | 664.1 | 1,092.2 | 1,476.1 | 2,094.9 | 3,175.1 | 6,592 | 1,529 | 37,537 | 8,143 |
| From Jordan - total | 13.9 | 18.9 | 16.5 | 21.3 | 31.4 | 29.9 | 48.7 | 87.5 | 127 | 279 | 852 | 2,235 |
| Agricultural produce | 4.8 | 3.9 | 3.9 | 3.4 | 0.9 | 1.5 | 2.9 | 5.5 | 10 | 26 | 21 | 106 |
| Industrial products | 9.1 | 15.0 | 12.6 | 17.9 | 30.5 | 28.4 | 45.8 | 82.0 | 117 | 253 | 831 | 2,129 |
| From other countries - total | 43.8 | 53.5 | 42.5 | 70.5 | 135.7 | 173.8 | 235.0 | 505.5 | 1,157 | 2,482 | 4,858 | 10,669 |
| Agricultural produce | 7.7 | 12.6 | 8.2 | 13.2 | 49.1 | 71.2 | 70.7 | 24.1 | 91 | 165 | 311 | 1,343 |
| Industrial products | 36.1 | 40.9 | 34.3 | 57.3 | 85.6 | 102.6 | 164.3 | 481.4 | 1,066 | 2,317 | 4,547 | 9,326 |
| **Exports** | | | | | | | | | | | | |
| Total | 148.0 | 216.4 | 242.6 | 409.6 | 690.5 | 986.4 | 1,250.9 | 2,435.8 | 3,726 | 9,814 | 23,945 | 50,667 |
| To Israel - total | 77.6 | 107.3 | 174.7 | 287.3 | 442.2 | 616.6 | 777.4 | 1,327.4 | 2,291 | 5,674 | 14,968 | 27,260 |
| Agricultural produce | 11.9 | 14.4 | 35.6 | 54.9 | 66.3 | 107.6 | 166.7 | 292.4 | 468 | 1,386 | 2,575 | 4,257 |
| Industrial products | 65.7 | 92.9 | 139.1 | 232.4 | 375.9 | 509.0 | 610.7 | 1,035.0 | 1,823 | 4,288 | 12,393 | 23,003 |
| To Jordan - total | 68.4 | 107.3 | 66.2 | 119.5 | 220.6 | 342.8 | 462.7 | 1,085.0 | 1,479 | 4,057 | 8,806 | 23,195 |
| Agricultural produce | 17.4 | 45.7 | 25.4 | 34.5 | 70.7 | 98.3 | 224.0 | 442.6 | 524 | 1,079 | 2,812 | 7,762 |
| Industrial products | 51.0 | 61.6 | 40.8 | 85.0 | 149.9 | 244.5 | 238.7 | 642.4 | 955 | 2,978 | 5,994 | 15,433 |
| To other countries - total | 2.0 | 1.8 | 1.7 | 2.8 | 27.7 | 27.0 | 10.8 | 23.4 | 25 | 83 | 171 | 212 |
| Agricultural produce | -- | -- | -- | -- | 18.6 | 18.8 | -- | -- | -- | -- | -- | -- |
| Industrial products | 2.0 | 1.8 | 1.7 | 2.8 | 9.1 | 8.2 | 10.8 | 23.4 | 25 | 83 | 171 | 212 |
| **Excess of imports over exports** | | | | | | | | | | | | |
| Trade with Israel | 149.8 | 233.8 | 322.0 | 502.7 | 855.1 | 1,150.3 | 1,748.7 | 2,485.8 | 5,480 | 12,520 | 29,127 | 65,286 |
| Trade with Jordan | -54.5 | -88.4 | -49.7 | -99.2 | -189.2 | -312.9 | -414.0 | -997.5 | -1,352 | -3,778 | -7,954 | -20,960 |
| Trade with other countries | 41.8 | 51.7 | 40.8 | 68.7 | 107.0 | 146.8 | 224.2 | 482.1 | 1,132 | 2,399 | 4,687 | 10,457 |
| Total | 137.1 | 197.1 | 313.1 | 472.2 | 772.9 | 984.2 | 1,558.9 | 1,970.4 | 5,260 | 11,141 | 25,860 | 54,783 |

Source: Central Bureau of Statistics, Statistical Abstract of Israel (various issues).

TABLE 7.5
Imports, exports, and foreign trade balance, the Gaza Strip, 1971-1982 (IL million)

| | 1971 | 1972 | 1973 | 1974 | 1975 | 1976 | 1977 | 1978 | 1979 | 1980 | 1981 | 1982 |
|---|---|---|---|---|---|---|---|---|---|---|---|---|
| <u>Imports</u> | | | | | | | | | | | | |
| Total | 184.4 | 270.1 | 350.0 | 611.9 | 1,117.7 | 1,485.9 | 2,478.0 | 3,462.9 | 5,613 | 13,789 | 35,762 | 75,808 |
| From Israel - total | 156.5 | 239.8 | 319.5 | 545.7 | 1,055.9 | 1,355.9 | 2,301.5 | 3,142.4 | 5,015 | 12,267 | 32,591 | 68,911 |
| Agricultural produce | 26.0 | 36.4 | 59.6 | 73.9 | 148.1 | 182.6 | 343.3 | 447.7 | 683 | 1,628 | 3,859 | 7,659 |
| Industrial products | 130.5 | 203.4 | 259.9 | 471.8 | 907.8 | 1,173.3 | 1,958.2 | 2,694.7 | 4,332 | 10,639 | 28,732 | 61,252 |
| From Jordan - total | 0.2 | 0.2 | 0.3 | 0.7 | 1.0 | 0.4 | 0.1 | -- | -- | -- | -- | -- |
| Agricultural produce | 0.2 | 0.2 | 0.3 | -- | 0.1 | -- | -- | -- | -- | -- | -- | -- |
| Industrial products | -- | -- | -- | 0.7 | 0.9 | 0.4 | 0.1 | -- | -- | -- | -- | -- |
| From other countries - total | 27.7 | 30.1 | 30.7 | 65.5 | 60.8 | 129.6 | 176.4 | 320.5 | 598 | 1,522 | 3,171 | 6,897 |
| Agricultural produce | 1.1 | 1.2 | 0.6 | 6.6 | 18.5 | 52.1 | 84.9 | 35.9 | 72 | 138 | 263 | 1,338 |
| Industrial products | 26.6 | 28.9 | 30.1 | 58.9 | 42.3 | 77.5 | 91.5 | 284.6 | 526 | 1,384 | 2,908 | 5,559 |
| <u>Exports</u> | | | | | | | | | | | | |
| Total | 102.8 | 134.7 | 181.2 | 273.8 | 526.3 | 823.2 | 1,387.7 | 2,125.5 | 3,077 | 7,820 | 21,626 | 44,301 |
| To Israel - total | 36.1 | 63.7 | 105.5 | 166.6 | 335.9 | 529.0 | 835.5 | 1,399.6 | 2,076 | 5,955 | 17,903 | 36,090 |
| Agricultural produce | 9.2 | 12.0 | 29.7 | 27.0 | 47.8 | 76.9 | 181.7 | 300.7 | 465 | 1,202 | 2,594 | 4,020 |
| Industrial products | 26.9 | 51.7 | 75.8 | 139.6 | 288.1 | 452.1 | 653.8 | 1,098.9 | 1,611 | 4,753 | 15,309 | 32,070 |
| To Jordan - total | 12.2 | 13.8 | 19.1 | 50.3 | 105.4 | 192.8 | 422.0 | 575.3 | 775 | 1,382 | 2,927 | 6,941 |
| Agricultural produce | 12.2 | 13.8 | 19.1 | 50.3 | 105.4 | 192.8 | 421.5 | 574.4 | 775 | 1,381 | 2,914 | 6,937 |
| Industrial products | -- | -- | -- | -- | -- | -- | 0.5 | 0.9 | -- | 1 | 13 | 4 |
| To other countries - total | 54.5 | 57.2 | 56.6 | 56.9 | 85.0 | 101.4 | 130.2 | 150.6 | 226 | 483 | 796 | 1,270 |
| Agricultural produce | 54.5 | 57.2 | 56.6 | 56.9 | 85.0 | 101.4 | 130.2 | 150.6 | 226 | 483 | 796 | 1,270 |
| Industrial products | -- | -- | -- | -- | -- | -- | -- | -- | -- | -- | -- | -- |
| <u>Excess of imports over exports</u> | | | | | | | | | | | | |
| Trade with Israel | 120.4 | 176.1 | 214.0 | 379.1 | 720.0 | 826.9 | 1,466.0 | 1,742.8 | 2,939 | 6,312 | 14,688 | 32,821 |
| Trade with Jordan | -12.0 | -13.6 | -18.8 | -49.6 | -104.4 | -192.4 | -421.9 | -575.3 | -775 | -1,382 | -2,927 | -6,941 |
| Trade with other countries | -26.8 | -27.1 | -25.9 | 8.6 | -24.2 | 28.2 | 46.2 | 169.9 | 372 | 1,039 | 2,375 | 5,627 |
| Total | 81.6 | 135.4 | 169.3 | 338.1 | 591.4 | 662.7 | 1,090.3 | 1,337.4 | 2,536 | 5,969 | 14,136 | 31,507 |

Source: Central Bureau of Statistics, <u>Statistical Abstract of Israel</u> (various issues).

TABLE 7.6
Balance of payments, the West Bank and the Gaza Strip, 1965 and 1966

| | West Bank | | | | | | | | Gaza Strip |
|---|---|---|---|---|---|---|---|---|---|
| | 1965[1] | | 1965[2] | | 1965 | | 1966 | | 1966[1] |
| | JD million | % of Jordan | JD million | % of Jordan | JD million | % of Jordan | JD million | % of Jordan | JD million |
| Exports of goods | 2.0 | 20 | 2.5 | 25 | 2.5 | 25 | 2.1 | 20 | 2.6 |
| Exports of services | 11.4 | 42 | 11.0 | 40 | 11.5 | 42 | 13.1 | 42 | 4.7 |
| Total exports | 13.4 | 63 | 13.5 | 36 | 14.0 | 38 | 15.2 | 37 | 7.3 |
| Imports of goods | 23.6 | 42 | 32.1 | 50 | 22.2 | 40 | 25.8 | 38 | 10.2 |
| Imports of services | 1.3 | 16 | | | 1.5 | 18 | 1.7 | 17 | -- |
| Total imports | 24.9 | 39 | 32.1 | 50 | 23.7 | 37 | 27.5 | 36 | 10.2 |
| Deficit in current account | 11.5 | -- | 18.6 | -- | 9.7 | -- | 12.3 | -- | 2.9 |
| Transfer payments | | | | | | | | | |
| Individuals | 6.4 | 70 | 5.9 | 65 | 6.4 | 70 | 7.4 | 70 | 0.7 |
| UNRWA | 3.6 | 60 | -- | -- | 3.0 | 50 | 2.8 | 50 | 2.2 |
| Total | 10.0 | 66 | 5.9 | 39 | 9.4 | 62 | 10.2 | | 2.9 |
| Net deficit[a] | 1.5 | -- | 12.7 | | 0.3 | -- | 2.1 | -- | -- |

Sources: (1) Ben Shahar et al., Economic Structure, p. 31; (2) Ward, Peretz, and Wilson, The Palestinian State, p. 124; Derived from Department of Statistics, External Trade Statistics (Amman, 1965); Central Bank of Jordan, Fourth Annual Report (Amman, 1967), Tables (17), (19), and (20); Central Bank of Jordan, Monthly Statistical Bulletin (March 1970), Table (14).

[a]Covered by the government of Jordan.

TABLE 7.7
Balance of payments, the West Bank and the Gaza Strip, 1968, 1974, and 1978-1982 (IL million)

| | 1968[a] | 1974 | 1978 | 1979 | 1980 | 1981 | 1982 |
|---|---|---|---|---|---|---|---|
| West Bank | | | | | | | |
| Exports of goods | 118 | 424 | 2,517 | 3,940 | 10,168 | 24,850 | 52,208 |
| Exports of services | 58 | 600 | 2,824 | 5,504 | 12,288 | 28,772 | 70,496 |
| thereof: wages | 15 | 531 | 2,573 | 5,066 | 11,224 | 26,346 | 65,790 |
| Total exports | 176 | 1,024 | 5,341 | 9,444 | 22,456 | 53,622 | 122,704 |
| Imports of goods | 238 | 892 | 4,423 | 907.9 | 21,003 | 49,929 | 105,546 |
| thereof: government | 60 | 283 | 1,631 | 305.4 | 7,379 | 17,161 | 37,057 |
| Imports of services | 7 | 9 | 35 | 60 | 139 | 297 | 646 |
| Total imports | 298 | 1,175 | 6,054 | 12,133 | 28,382 | 67,090 | 142,603 |
| Deficit in current account | 122 | 151 | 713 | 2,689 | 5,926 | 13,468 | 19,899 |
| Unilateral transfers | 183 | 100 | 856 | 1,355 | 3,084 | 6,568 | 11,616 |
| Net deficit (surplus) (Net capital movement) | (61) | 51 | (143) | 1,334 | 2,842 | 6,900 | 8,283 |
| Gaza Strip | | | | | | | |
| Exports of goods | | 274 | 2,141 | 3,109 | 7,944 | 21,930 | 44,697 |
| Exports of services | | 337 | 1,667 | 3,623 | 8,380 | 21,446 | 50,311 |
| thereof: wages | | 308 | 1,537 | 3,389 | 7,804 | 20,077 | 47,324 |
| Total exports | | 611 | 3,808 | 6,732 | 16,324 | 43,376 | 95,008 |
| Imports of goods | | 616 | 3,595 | 5,621 | 13,807 | 35,808 | 75,865 |
| Imports of services | | 127 | 751 | 1,430 | 3,606 | 8,536 | 19,243 |
| thereof: government | | 8 | 33 | 56 | 130 | 278 | 604 |
| Total imports | | 743 | 4,346 | 7,051 | 17,413 | 44,344 | 95,108 |
| Deficit in current account | | 132 | 538 | 319 | 1,089 | 968 | 100 |
| Unilateral payments | | 63 | 734 | 1,058 | 2,604 | 6,178 | 12,279 |
| Net deficit (surplus) (Net capital movement) | | 69 | (196) | (739) | (1,515) | (5,210) | (12,179) |

Source: Central Bureau of Statistics, Statistical Abstract of Israel, 1970, 1975, and 1983.

[a] The West Bank and Gaza Strip combined.

TABLE 7.8
Net capital transfer into the West Bank and the Gaza Strip, 1968-1982 (IL million)

| Year | West Bank | Gaza Strip | Total |
|---|---|---|---|
| 1968 | -- | -- | -61.4 |
| 1969 | -- | -- | -41.7 |
| 1970 | -39.3 | -54.0 | -93.3 |
| 1971 | -79.1 | -50.7 | -129.8 |
| 1972 | -56.3 | -71.9 | -128.2 |
| 1973 | 25.6 | 32.9 | 58.5 |
| 1974 | 149.0 | 83.4 | 309.0 |
| 1975 | 245.6 | 160.0 | 405.6 |
| 1976 | 167.4 | -179.5 | -12.1 |
| 1977 | 467.1 | 52.3 | 519.4 |
| 1978 | -143.0 | -196.0 | -339.0 |
| 1979 | 1,317.0 | -722.0 | 595.0 |
| 1980 | 2,842.0 | -1,515.0 | 1,327.0 |
| 1981 | 6,900.0 | -5,210.0 | 1,690.0 |
| 1982 | 8,283.0 | -12,179.0 | -3,896.0 |

Source: Extracted from the balance of payments in Central Bureau of Statistics, Statistical Abstract of Israel (various issues).

export surplus with Jordan, salaries of many former Jordanian civil servants and remittances, is banked or invested in real estate in Amman. Figures for the amounts involved are not available, especially for West Bankers who hold Jordanian passports and thus may invest in the East Bank without restriction.

It is equally difficult to estimate the amounts of capital transferred out of the territories into Jordan. It is believed, however, that residents of the West Bank have been investing considerable sums in land, apartment buildings, and, lately, in securities, in Amman. Monetary sources in Jordan have estimated that about 10 to 15 percent of the total deposits in commercial banks in Jordan belong to West Bank residents.[20] In addition, many West Bank businessmen "have become increasingly inclined to move part or all of their capital to Jordan (or other Arab countries), where profit expectations are much higher."[21] It is believed that this trend is increasing.[22] The following summary itemizes sources of money flow between the West Bank and Jordan in 1979.

| | Inflow to West Bank (JD Million) | Outflow from West Bank (JD Million) |
|---|---|---|
| Summer Visitors | 15.0 | 1.5 |
| Export Surplus | 16.0 | 3.0 |
| Jordanian Government Transfers | 4.2 | 2.0 |
| Joint Arab Money | 5.3 | 0.0 |
| UNRWA | 3.4 | 0.0 |
| Remittances | 60.0 | 30.0 |
| Totals | 103.9 | 36.5 |

Source: Abu Hijleh, Studies, p. 24.

Note: The net money that flowed into the West Bank of some JD 67 million amounted to one-fifth of Jordan's foreign currencies reserves.[23]

## Notes

1. Department of Statistics, External Trade Statistics (Amman, 1966), p. 13-22.
2. Ibid.
3. Ben Shahar et al., Economic Structure, p. 32.
4. Department of Statistics, External Trade, p. 42-47.
5. Economic Planning Authority, Survey, p. 26-28.
6. Ben Shaher et al., Economic Structure, p. 32.
7. Economic Planning Authority, Survey, p. 27-28; cited in Hilal, The West Bank, p. 161.
8. Ibid.
9. Kanovsky, The Economic Impact, p. 143.
10. Haselkorn, Kurz and Wagner, Trade and Economic Links, p. 14.
11. Van Arkadie, Benefits and Burdens, p. 84.
12. Bregman, The Economy, p. 43.
13. Van Arkadie, Benefits and Burdens, p. 82.
14. Ibid., p. 8.
15. Bregman, Economic Growth, p. 88.
16. Bregman, The Economy, p. 52.
17. Van Arkadie, Benefits and Burdens, p. 26.
18. Haselkorn, Kurz, and Wagner, Trade and Economic Links, p. 45.
19. Gordon Roberts, "Israel Curbs the Agencies," Middle East International (March 13, 1981), p. 6.
20. A. Abu Hijleh, Studies in the Economies of the Occupied Territories (Amman: Central Bank of Jordan, 1981), p. 18.
21. Awartani, A Survey, p. 39.
22. Ibid.
23. Abu Hijleh, Studies, p. 25.

# 8
# Currency, Banking, Prices, and Savings and Investment

At present, the West Bank and the Gaza Strip are without a capital market, a monetary policy, an indigenous banking system, and above all without a currency of their own. As a result, the Arab inhabitants of the areas have tended, probably for lack of acceptable alternatives, to hoard most of their savings in the form of cash, mostly in hard currencies.

## CURRENCY

The West Bank has not been brought into the mainstream of the Israeli monetary system. The Jordanian dinar has remained, along with the Israeli currency, the legal tender. Conversely, the Gaza Strip is less monetarily independent and the Israeli pound is the legal tender, although the Jordanian dinar and Egyptian pound are also circulated. Soon after the war, the Israeli authorities set an exchange rate for the dinar against the Israeli pound at a level much below its real value. As a result, Jordan complained to the International Monetary Fund (IMF), which in turn sent a mission to the area, which investigated the situation and suggested an appropriate exchange rate for the dinar. In August 1967, the Israelis decided to maintain a dual currency system in the area, except for Arab Jerusalem, whereby Jordanian and Israeli currencies are both circulated.

The continued use of the Jordanian dinar has proved beneficial to West Bank Arab inhabitants because it is much healthier than the Israeli pound. Indeed, the territory has enjoyed some monetary autonomy due to the "limited penetration of Israeli banks, the continued circulation of the dinar and the fact that financial links remain with Amman."[1] In addition, the continued circulation of the dinar was instrumental in reactivating business activity and restoring trade with the East Bank of the Jordan River.[2] Similarly, this arrangement has provided Israel with a much needed source of hard currency.

The Jordanian dinar has been accumulated into the Israeli treasury through various means: the settlement of territories' import surplus with Israel; conversion into pounds at generous rates; payments for customs duty by those Arab inhabitants crossing the bridges into the West Bank; and the money spent by those visiting Israel. A small fraction of the dinars in circulation in the West Bank is paid for imports from Jordan, the rest is kept by the areas' Arab inhabitants in the form of cash. The areas' Arab inhabitants have preferred to hold to the relatively stable dinar rather than the Israeli pound, which has been subject to successive and substantial devaluations in the past several years. Consequently, the Israeli pound is held only to the extent that is needed for the settlement of transactions concluded with or through Israel.[3]

The limited current use of the banking system has made currency the most important means of payment.[4] Currency, the Jordanian dinar and other foreign currencies in particular, constitutes the major component of the money supply in the area. On the eve of the war, the money supply in the West Bank was estimated at about JD 20 to 25 million, out of a total of JD 67 million for the whole of Jordan. After the war, remittances from Palestinian inhabitants working abroad, the government of Jordan's money transfers to former civil servants and local authorities, and transfers by UNRWA and other parties, in addition to export surplus with the East Bank, have substantially increased the stock of the dinar and foreign currencies.[5] The total amount of Jordanian dinars in circulation in the West Bank, including those held by Israel, was put at JD 40 to 50 million in 1975, or more than one-third of Jordanian currency held by the public and one-quarter of Jordan's money supply.[6] Dinars in circulation in the West Bank in 1982 were estimated at 28.0 percent of Jordanian currency and less than one-fifth of Jordan's money supply. The circulation of a significant portion of Jordan's money supply outside the jurisdiction of official Jordanian monetary authorities, which can be partly used to finance trade deficit with the West Bank, could create tremendous pressures on Jordan's foreign reserves and destabilize the dinar should Israel choose to convert its accumulated dinars into other currencies.[7]

## BANKING AND CREDIT

There existed 31 branches of Arab and British banks in the West Bank on the eve of the war, employing 485 persons and paying JD 236,000 in annual salaries. Total assets of those branches were more than JD 15 million in June 1967, accounting for over one-fifth of total assets of Jordan's commercial banking system. At the same time, the aggregate balance sheet of those branches showed total deposits of JD 14 million (26 percent of total deposits in Jordan), total credit facilities of about JD 10 million (close to one-fourth of Jordan's total), and cash in vaults of JD 600,000.

Immediately after the war, Israeli authorities closed branch banks in the territories and confiscated cash in their vaults. The Jordanian government on its part reacted by formally declaring the closure of these branches, freezing their deposits and credit facilities, including some JD 3.5 million in loans granted by governmental specialized lending institutions, and abolishing all transactions concluded after June 6, 1967. Bank closures caused hardships for the economies of the territories, at least in the short run. This decision denied depositors their right to withdraw their money in a time of great need and made it extremely difficult for banks to collect their debts, in the process shaking confidence in the banking system; as a result economic activity had to carry on without recourse to banking services. In the longer term, the Arab inhabitants have preferred to hoard their savings in the form of cash and much of the remittances has been kept in the East Bank. As a result, savings have not been channeled into the much needed investment in infrastructure and development projects. Limited credit has handicapped commercial and industrial activities and confined business to the family level.

Negotiations to reopen the banks in the West Bank between Israeli and Jordanian monetary officials were held through the offices of the International Monetary Fund. But no agreement was reached and negotiations were broken off; the banks remained closed although they continued to pay salaries for their employees and rents for their premises in the West Bank. Points of disagreement were first, Israeli insistence on the formation of special bodies to manage bank branches in the West Bank, thereby implying a break with head offices in Amman; and second, Jordanian refusal to give branches in Arab Jerusalem a special legal status different from that in the rest of the West Bank. In the Gaza Strip, the Bank of Palestine was closed for a long period despite relentless efforts by its owners to get it reopened. The Israeli authorities have demanded that the Bank's liquidity be increased by one million Israeli pounds and that the owners bring forward a certificate attesting that the Bank's money deposited in Egypt is free of any restriction. The extra cash was indeed put up but Egypt's response to the second demand was slow, and this gave Israel a pretext to stall the entire issue. It should be noted, however, that the Israeli authorities taxed the interest earned on the Bank's money in Egyptian banks. Eventually, the Bank was reopened under the condition that it deal only in Israeli currency.

The Jordanian monetary authorities permitted deposits in

West Bank branches to be gradually withdrawn against balances those branches maintained at their headquarters in Amman. Whenever these balances were completely withdrawn, the Jordanian treasury deposited amounts equal to any additional withdrawals at the bank within one week of payment. At the same time, the government of Jordan continued its freeze on the JD 3.5 million in credits owed to specialized lending institutions. In January of 1977, all restrictions on the withdrawal of deposits were removed. However, banks have not been able to collect a major portion of their debts in the area, and outstanding credit there remained at JD 4.4 million at the end of 1980, most of which originated before the war.

Israeli authorities have allowed Israeli banks to open branches in the territories, and there are now several of them there. These banks lend money to Arabs, charging the same interest rate as in Israel. But loans are granted upon the approval of the military administration and guaranteed by the Israeli government.[8] These Israeli banks have so far failed to attract the business of the areas' inhabitants. In fact, local deposits have remained at a minimum level, just enough to cover transactions with Israel or foreign parties.[9] Thus, Israeli banks have played only a minor role in financing trade and development in the territories. It remains true that most business transactions are carried out in cash without the services offered by banks.[10]

Israeli banks in the territories have not sustained prewar levels of operation because the Arab inhabitants have been reluctant to deal with them. Among the reasons for this are the economic and political uncertainty associated with military occupation, political objections to cooperation with the occupying power, the people's preference for the healthier and more stable Jordanian dinar, high interest rates,[11] and the uncommitted attitude of the Israeli banks to serving the interests of the territories.[12] As a result, moneychangers have filled part of the vacuum created by the absence of local financial institutions and played an increasingly important role in facilitating business transactions.[13] In addition, several banks in Amman have authorized certain people in various cities and towns in the West Bank to receive deposits (and extend limited credit) and to transfer them to Amman. The scale of such operations, however, is still very limited and the amounts involved did not exceed JD 1 million by the end of 1982.

## PRICES

Prices have been rising at an alarming rate in the territories since occupation. In 1971 the consumer price index in the West Bank and Gaza Strip stood at 126 and 128, respectively; by 1982 these figures had jumped to 4,200 and 4,294. (Until the end of 1975, the base year was July 1968-June 1969; thereafter, 1976 became the base year.)

In 1980 the Consumer Price Index showed an annual increase of 139 percent in the West Bank, and 156 percent in the Gaza Strip. By 1982, the Index had declined to 107 in the West Bank, and 115 in the Gaza Strip (see Table 8.1). Average price levels of food, transport, and household maintenance were consistently the highest in the areas throughout the past decade. Economic links with Israel have made the territories highly susceptible to the high rate of inflation in Israel. For the most part, Israeli inflation levels seem to have been transmitted into the territories through several ways, among them high wages earned by the areas' inhabitants working in Israel and imports of Israeli goods. Both of these increased appreciably the demand for various consumer goods and gave rise to a prices and wages spiral, whereby real purchasing power is eroded.

TABLE 8.1
Consumer Price Index, Israel, the West Bank, and the Gaza Strip, 1971-1982

| | Israel | | West Bank | | Gaza Strip | |
|---|---|---|---|---|---|---|
| Year | CPI | Increase (%) | CPI | Increase (%) | CPI | Increase (%) |
| 1971 | 118.8[a] | 12.0 | 125.9[b] | -- | 128.1[b] | -- |
| 1972 | 134.1 | 12.9 | 148.1 | 17.6 | 153.1 | 19.5 |
| 1973 | 160.9 | 20.0 | 179.9 | 21.6 | 190.3 | 24.3 |
| 1974 | 224.8 | 39.7 | 256.5 | 42.6 | 294.3 | 54.7 |
| 1975 | 313.1 | 39.3 | 367.4 | 43.2 | 452.3 | 53.8 |
| 1976 | 411.2[c] | 31.3 | 114.9[d] | 14.9 | 113.2[d] | 13.2 |
| 1977 | 134.6 | 34.6 | 156.3 | 36.0 | 151.5 | 33.8 |
| 1978 | 202.7 | 50.6 | 235.1 | 50.4 | 216.4 | 42.8 |
| 1979 | 361.4 | 78.3 | 395.3 | 68.1 | 373.0 | 72.4 |
| 1980 | 834.9 | 131.0 | 946.2 | 139.4 | 954.7 | 156.0 |
| 1981 | 216.8[e] | 116.8 | 2,025.2 | 140.0 | 200.5 | 109.5 |
| 1982 | 477.7 | 120.3 | 4,199.5 | 107.4 | 4,294.0 | 114.6 |

Source: Central Bureau of Statistics, Statistical Abstract of Israel (various issues).

[a]Base: 1969 = 100.0
[b]Base: July 1968-June 1969 = 100.0
[c]Base: end of 1976 = 100.0
[d]Base: January 1976 = 100.0
[e]Base: 1980 = 100.0

## SAVINGS AND INVESTMENT

Disposable private income from all sources has risen in the territories during the postwar period, both in current and real terms. At the same time, private consumption has also increased, although at a lower rate than that of income, resulting in a considerable accumulation of monetary reserves. Private savings as a percentage of disposable income have grown: in the West Bank, the percentage rose from 12 percent in 1968 to 19 percent in 1982; in the Gaza Strip between the same years, the rise was from 15 to 35 percent (see Table 8.2). The principal reason for this increase in private savings has been the political and economic uncertainties regarding the future of the territories.[14] These risks have discouraged investment in economic activity and encouraged residents to accumulate cash in Jordanian dinars and other foreign currencies.

TABLE 8.2
Gross disposable private income, private consumption, and savings, the West Bank and the Gaza Strip, 1968-1982
(current prices; IL million)

| | West Bank | | | Gaza Strip | | |
|---|---|---|---|---|---|---|
| Year | G.D.I.[a] | P.C.E.[b] | P.S.[c] | G.D.I.[a] | P.C.E.[b] | P.S.[c] |
| 1968 | 400 | 354 | 46 | 167 | 142 | 25 |
| 1969 | 493 | 452 | 41 | 198 | 174 | 24 |
| 1970 | 570 | 496 | 74 | 262 | 205 | 57 |
| 1971 | 776 | 635 | 141 | 352 | 270 | 82 |
| 1972 | 1,161 | 908 | 253 | 539 | 405 | 134 |
| 1973 | 1,368 | 1,144 | 224 | 789 | 547 | 242 |
| 1974 | 2,351 | 1,808 | 543 | 1,072 | 802 | 270 |
| 1975 | 3,353 | 2,857 | 496 | 1,612 | 1,285 | 327 |
| 1976 | 4,854 | 4,006 | 848 | 2,281 | 1,642 | 639 |
| 1977 | 6,408 | 5,655 | 753 | 3,349 | 2,714 | 635 |
| 1978 | 11,831 | 8,912 | 2,919 | 5,333 | 3,952 | 1,381 |
| 1979 | 20,366 | 17,012 | 3,354 | 10,155 | 6,943 | 3,212 |
| 1980 | 51,077 | 40,990 | 10,087 | 23,631 | 16,385 | 7,246 |
| 1981 | 102,449 | 90,155 | 12,294 | 56,805 | 36,609 | 20,196 |
| 1982 | 237,112 | 192,631 | 44,481 | 124,646 | 80,540 | 44,106 |

Source: Central Bureau of Statistics, Statistical Abstract of Israel (various issues).

[a]Gross Disposable Income
[b]Private Consumption Expenditure
[c]Private Savings

Investment has played a minor role in the economic development of the territories in the postwar period. Total investment, although increased, remained at a much lower level than private savings during much of the period since 1968. In the last five years it has accounted for about 20 percent of the GNP in the West Bank, and close to 25 percent in the Gaza Strip. In the early years of occupation, the average stood at about 12 percent. In terms of total resources used, investment averaged about one-sixth of total gross disposable private income plus import surplus, compared with about 10 percent in the early 1970s.

Private sector investment has been responsible for the increased level of gross investment. The relative importance of private investment has constantly increased to around 90 percent of gross investment in both the West Bank and the Gaza Strip. Private investment, which is financed by private savings, has remained well below the level of private savings in each year since 1968 in the Gaza Strip and in most years in the West Bank. This confirms the idea that the people tend to hoard their money or invest abroad, or both, rather than invest in local economic activity.[15] Similarly, private Israeli capital has been severely restricted in the territories due to economic and political risks, despite the existence of incentives for such investment.

Private investment has for the most part been used to construct residential buildings and to buy consumer durable goods, such as cars, television sets, etc. Construction has absorbed more than four-fifths of private investment, whereas machinery, transport, and other equipment have accounted for only the remaining fifth. Growth in investment in durable goods is evidenced by the increase of the number of households that possess private cars, refrigerators, washing machines, etc. (see Table 8.3).

Public investment as a percentage of total investment has increasingly declined to a negligible proportion, around 10 percent in the West Bank and 15 percent in the Gaza Strip in the last five years. Investment by the military government in the expansion of public services has been extremely modest and investment by municipalities has remained constrained by their scarce budgetary resources and by the several restrictions imposed upon them by the Israeli authorities.[16] As a result, public services such as health, education, water, power, etc., have failed to satisfy current demand, and the economic infrastructure necessary for economic development has stagnated[17] (see Table 8.4).

So far government, local authorities, and residents have not been making the right kind of investment and in quantities sufficient to modernize the local economy and to sustain economic growth. Heavy investment is badly needed in various economic sectors to develop the economy and to reduce its

TABLE 8.3
Households possessing durable goods, the West Bank and the Gaza Strip, selected years (percent of all households)

| | West Bank | | | | | Gaza Strip | | | |
|---|---|---|---|---|---|---|---|---|---|
| Commodity | 1961 | 1967 | 1975 | 1979 | 1981 | 1967 | 1975 | 1979 | 1981 |
| Radio | 30.0 | 58.0 | 84.6 | 79.4 | 80.2 | 50.0 | 90.6 | 91.7 | 89.8 |
| Electric refrigerator | 1.8 | 4.8 | 27.5 | 41.3 | 51.5 | 3.0 | 22.5 | 49.3 | 66.2 |
| Washing machine | 1.7 | -- | 15.9 | 19.8 | 27.4 | -- | 6.1 | 11.2 | 15.8 |
| Television set | -- | 1.8 | 10.0 | 46.7 | 60.7 | 3.0 | 7.5 | 54.2 | 69.6 |
| Private car | n.a. | -- | 2.7 | 4.3 | 6.3 | -- | 3.4 | 5.2 | 6.7 |

Sources: For 1961: Department of Statistics, First Census, Vol. 3, p. 64-65; for 1967: Bregman, Economic Growth, p. 24; for other years: Central Bureau of Statistics, Statistical Abstract of Israel, 1983, p. 771.

dependence on foreign factors, notably employment in Israel. The absence of such investment will undoubtedly diminish prospects for economic development in the areas and accelerate the integration of their economies into that of Israel.

The general trends of the currency, banking, and investment possibilities in the West Bank and Gaza Strip are not hard to summarize. A condition of confusion and disorientation has been more than evident, with the areas' Arab inhabitants being obliged to dispense with customary banking and investment facilities, and to resort to a cash economy. One result of this has been the lack of financial structures that could facilitate sufficient investment to modernize and boost economic growth. Credit facilities and the desire to invest in industry have been lacking due to a number of factors, all of which emanate from the policies (or lack of them) of the occupying force. The great danger, already alluded to, is that the economies of the territories will ossify yet further and thus become more prone to an overdependence on the Israeli economy. A more local disincentive for productive investment has been the largely negative effects of dependence on an Israeli economy that is unstable and prone to damaging bouts of inflation.

**TABLE 8.4**
**Investment in the West Bank and the Gaza Strip, 1968-1982 (current prices; IL million)**

| | 1968 | 1969 | 1970 | 1971 | 1972 | 1973 | 1974 | 1975 | 1976 | 1977 | 1978 | 1979 | 1980 | 1981 | 1982 |
|---|---|---|---|---|---|---|---|---|---|---|---|---|---|---|---|
| **West Bank** | | | | | | | | | | | | | | | |
| Gross domestic capital formation | 25 | 51 | 64 | 87 | 147 | 208 | 409 | 683 | 884 | 1,279 | 2,347 | 4,709 | 9,976 | 20,919 | 46,462 |
| Government and local authorities | 13 | 19 | 20 | 20 | 26 | 31 | 60 | 112 | 100 | 93 | 221 | 453 | 732 | 1,750 | 5,511 |
| Private sector | 12 | 32 | 44 | 67 | 121 | 177 | 349 | 571 | 784 | 1,186 | 2,126 | 4,256 | 9,244 | 19,819 | 40,951 |
| thereof: Building and construction work | 9 | 19 | 25 | 42 | 84 | 128 | 269 | 461 | 668 | 1,014 | 1,656 | 3,333 | 7,555 | 16,143 | 33,297 |
| Machinery, transport, and other equipment | 3 | 13 | 19 | 25 | 37 | 49 | 80 | 110 | 116 | 172 | 470 | 923 | 1,689 | 3,046 | 7,654 |
| **Gaza Strip** | | | | | | | | | | | | | | | |
| Gross domestic capital formation | 11 | 24 | 25 | 36 | 77 | 130 | 212 | 341 | 538 | 709 | 1,237 | 2,574 | 5,059 | 12,945 | 26,558 |
| Government and local authorities | 4 | 15 | 16 | 19 | 28 | 39 | 64 | 118 | 114 | 122 | 237 | 349 | 619 | 1,263 | 3,069 |
| Private sector | 7 | 9 | 9 | 17 | 49 | 91 | 148 | 223 | 424 | 587 | 1,000 | 2,225 | 4,440 | 11,682 | 23,489 |
| thereof: Building and construction work | 5 | 4 | 4 | 7 | 25 | 58 | 98 | 150 | 334 | 435 | 817 | 1,965 | 3,926 | 10,326 | 20,600 |
| Machinery, transport, and other equipment | 2 | 5 | 5 | 10 | 24 | 33 | 50 | 73 | 90 | 152 | 183 | 260 | 514 | 1,356 | 2,889 |

Source: Central Bureau of Statistics, Administered Territories Statistics Quarterly (various issues).

**Notes**

1. Van Arkadie, Benefits and Burdens, p. 106.
2. Ibid., p. 104.
3. Bull, The West Bank, p. 60.
4. Bregman, Economic Growth, p. 95.
5. Bull, The West Bank, p. 41.
6. Van Arkadie, Benefits and Burdens, p. 105-106.
7. Ibid.
8. Bull, The West Bank, p. 60.
9. Awartani, A Survey, p. 37.
10. Bregman, Economic Growth, p. 103.
11. Lesch, Israeli's Occupation, p. 24.
12. Tuma and Darin-Drabkin, The Economic Case, p. 69.
13. Van Arkadie, Benefits and Burdens, p. 104.
14. Bregman, Economic Growth, p. 21.
15. Van Arkadie, Benefits and Burdens, p. 107.
16. Committee on Foreign Affairs, The West Bank-Gaza, p. 7.
17. Ibid., p. 34.

# 9 Israeli Policies Affecting the Economies of the Territories

The occupation of the two territories brought such government agencies as health, education, agriculture, public works, and the administration of justice under direct Israeli control.[1] This, in addition to direct military rule, has given Israel the chance to completely reshape the economies of the territories in such a way as to serve Israeli interests. Israeli control over the economy of the two territories has been more or less total; moreover, the areas' populations, for lack of sovereignty, "have not participated in the political process that has set the major economic policies affecting them or that has supervised the overall implementation of these policies."[2] Therefore, it has not been at all possible for the Arab inhabitants to make the kind of economic decisions that would either satisfy domestic needs or promote development of the economy.

Israeli economic policies have been geared toward bringing the two territories into economic dependence and, in some respects, integrated into the Israeli economy. Shortly after occupation, the Israeli authorities adopted several measures that have had profound effects on the economies of the territories. Labor from the territories was recruited to work in the Israeli economy; Israeli goods flowed freely into the territories' markets; and products from the territories were allowed in the Israeli market initially on a limited, but later on a wider, basis.[3] These policies exposed the economies of the West Bank and Gaza Strip to "powerful market forces resulting from the differences in wage levels and economic structure between the territories and Israel, forces which acted mainly through the labor market and the commodity market."[4]

Israeli policies discourage investment in infrastructure essential to the development of the economies of the territories. The military government, which maintains an absolute right to veto any project, has consistently denied approval for economic and infrastructure projects in the development of local financial institutions, power generation capacity, water for irrigation and other economic development schemes.[5] Projects submitted by municipalities whose officials take an independent line from that of Israel, or by private voluntary organizations who are keen to develop the territories' needs, or those financed by Arab funds, are often rejected by the military government.[6] Apparently, the Israelis feel that "agricultural development outside of exports to Jordan and industrial productivity beyond component work for Israeli firms threaten Israeli sectors, the State's balance of payments and its labor supply."[7]

## POLICIES AFFECTING ECONOMIC SECTORS

Agriculture in the territories, especially in the West Bank, can compete successfully in Israeli markets. Therefore, the Israeli Ministry of Agriculture issued, immediately after the war, directives for West Bank agriculture with the aim of reducing its dependence on trade with the East Bank of Jordan and introducing crops that complement, rather than compete with, Israeli produce, have export markets overseas, or serve the food processing industry in Israel. Subsequently, crop structure was adjusted to serve these objectives: substituting crops needed by Israel for those exported to the East Bank; restricting the cultivation of certain consumer crops such as melons and some vegetables and expanding production of tobacco, sesame, and other industrial crops; promoting winter vegetables for export to Europe.[8] At present, the Israeli Ministry of Agriculture determines the acreage and crops that can be grown in the territories to avoid necessary competition with Israeli farm produce[9] and to meet the needs of the Israeli economy. In addition, prospects for agricultural growth have thus been greatly reduced as a result of such Israeli policies and measures as the curtailment of extension services, discouragement of agricultural cooperatives, rejection of irrigation projects, expropriation of land, and control of water resources.[10]

Israeli water policy in the West Bank has been dictated by two major considerations: first, to ensure sufficient supply of irrigation and domestic water for Jewish settlements; and second, to preserve water resources in Israel because a good proportion of this water is drawn from aquifers under the western side of the West Bank. Uncontrolled drilling and pumping of water in the West Bank can seriously deplete this valuable resource.[11] Hence, the Israelis have been withholding permits for the sinking of new wells for irrigation and the few that have been sunk since occupation have been for domestic use. Pumping from already existing wells has been metered and strictly regulated. By contrast, no restrictions have been placed on the drilling of wells for Jewish settlers in the area nor in their water consumption. In addition, Jewish settlers have taken over wells that they categorize as absentee property.[12] The Israeli water policy has in effect deprived local farmers from needed water to maintain and expand agricultural production, probably driving many of them out of farming and transforming them into wage laborers in the Israeli economy, increasing in the process the territory's dependence on Israel for agricultural produce.[13]

The expropriation law was changed to facilitate the takeover of property by the military authority. At present, the military government may order the use of force to evacuate an owner of confiscated land if he refuses to do so within the period determined by the area commander. Jewish settlers or any other party whom the military government approves can expropriate land quietly without announcing its intention or obtaining permission from civil bodies. Local courts are not empowered to review decisions as to expropriation or as to the compensation for the land that has been expropriated.[14] In addition, the military commander in the territory has declared vast areas of land "closed areas," requiring a special permit for anyone to enter or leave.[15]

The territories serve as a source of some raw materials and a manufacturer of assembly parts to Israeli industry.[16] Israeli policy toward industry in the territories emphasizes two aspects: it encourages, through financial incentives, Israeli firms to set up industry in the areas,[17] and vigorously promotes industrial exports to Jordan and other Arab countries.[18] At the same time, the territories constitute an open market for Israeli manufactured goods, competing with an unprotected and less developed domestic industry and retarding its development prospects. Israeli firms have been induced to subcontract some work in the areas by the availability of cheap labor, especially women, forcing their industry to specialize in the production of components.

Israel has taken over all government functions in the territories, yet investment in public services has fallen far short of local requirements. The Israeli authorities have maintained the attitude that the areas' revenues and expenditures should be balanced.[19] Consequently, public investment has been constrained by the limited availability of local revenues; these revenues are barely sufficient to maintain current levels of service. The military authority has kept tight controls over local authorities and their finances. It requires prior approval for the transfer of any outside funds for municipalities, cooperatives, or charitable societies. The Israeli authorities have used their veto power over the transfer of such funds in order to reward and punish municipalities and organizations working in the area. "Cooperative" localities and organizations can expect speedy processing and approval for their projects, whereas those that are not so cooperative face long delays and perhaps eventual rejection.

In 1968, the Israeli authorities started allowing West Bankers to work in the Israeli economy. In the years following this decision, the rapidly expanding Israeli economy grew short of labor, and Arabs from the territories were encouraged to seek employment in Israel, especially in unskilled or semiskilled jobs. Arab workers now work in Israel on a daily basis; that is, the short distance between their homes and places of work allows them to commute. These workers, however, are not authorized to reside or stay overnight in Israel and are required to have a renewable work permit. The flow of this labor into Israel is restricted when the Israeli economy is in recession and unemployment is high. This labor exchange has caused severe labor shortages in some sectors of the local economies and has pushed up wages, raising thereby the costs of production of goods made in the territories.

**TRADE POLICIES**

Soon after occupation the Israeli authorities permitted the flow of the territories' goods eastward to the East Bank of Jordan and other Arab countries. Initially the "open bridges" policy solved the problem of disposing of the West Bank's surplus agricultural produce without adversely affecting Israeli farm produce, and afterward ensured outside markets for those agricultural products* that can compete in Israeli markets.[20] Exports to Arab and other countries are encouraged through incentives provided that foreign currency proceeds are converted to Israeli pounds (or sheqels). Jordan's industrial imports from the territories have been confined to domestically produced goods using local materials or those imported through Jordan.** Israel has isolated the areas from overseas markets by imposing its system of tariffs on all imports from those countries, whether imported directly or through Israeli intermediaries. Imports from Jordan were initially subjected to licensing requirements and customs duty, but later this was dropped on selected agricultural products.

----------

*Jordan has imposed a packaging requirement on West Bank produce as part of its policy to upgrade agriculture. This has hurt agricultural exports to Jordan due to the lack of packaging facilities in the West Bank, especially because Israel prohibits the return of empty boxes.

**Jordan, at a certain time, levied customs duty on goods coming from the territory and disbursed the proceeds to village councils there in the form of grants and loans to finance community projects.

The Israeli authorities have opened the border between the occupied territories and Israel for the free flow of goods in both directions, except when these goods compete with Israeli products. Israeli exports are allowed into the territories without restrictions. These exports have been placed in a privileged position in comparison with overseas exports because Israeli goods are tariff free and incur lower transportation costs. As a result, the territories have become a protected market for Israeli industrial and agricultural products. Indeed many farmers in the areas have not been able to compete with subsidized Israeli agricultural produce, especially poultry and eggs, which has been dumped in local markets.

On the other hand, the areas' exports to Israel have been impeded by several restrictions imposed by the Israeli authorities. Immediately after the war, the Israelis imposed restrictions on the sale of West Bank farm produce in Israel in order to protect its agriculture. West Bank farmers wishing to sell their produce in Israel were required to have a special permit, health checks on processed foods, and a certificate that the import would not cause any surpluses in Israel.[21] Later, these restrictions were kept on a selective basis, thereby limiting the flow of competitive produce. At present, the Israeli agricultural board determines the crops that can be shipped to Israeli and overseas markets. Agricultural exporters are required to follow detailed and strict procedures in order to get access to Israeli markets.* A system of permits has been instituted that determines the time when the product will be allowed into Israel, the amounts allowed to be exported, and requires the name of the Israeli wholesale market to which it may be sold and the description of the truck transporting the produce.[22] Normally, the Israeli authorities inform their officer for marketing in the military government of weekly amounts of produce allowed to enter Israel who in turn allocates them among the different districts of the West Bank and for issuing permits.[23] Much of the Gaza Strip's agricultural produce is shipped to Israel and sold through Israeli marketing channels in overseas markets.

Israeli policies have blatantly steered the territories toward a state of dependency on Israel; after almost fifteen years of occupation, the economies of the West Bank and the Gaza Strip still lack indigenous economic and financial institutions necessary for setting development programs and channeling savings and investment into various economic

----------

*Farmers need a permit for each truckload, which is usually granted by leaders of Israeli-sponsored village leagues who charge a fee on a per ton basis, making the process costly and time consuming.

sectors. As a result, investment in industrial development and economic infrastructure has remained conspicuously absent. Economic growth experienced in the postwar period has been for the most part attributable to exogenous factors, that is, wages earned in Israel and remittances, and not to a solid indigenous production base.

## Notes

1. Shehadeh, The West Bank, p. 69.
2. Van Arkadie, Benefits and Burdens, p. 40.
3. Ibid., p. 38.
4. Ibid.
5. Pearson, "Economic and Social Development," p. 33-34.
6. Ibid., p. 35-36.
7. Ibid., p. 33-34.
8. Lesch, Israel's Occupation, p. 35.
9. Pearson, "Economic and Social Development," p. 34.
10. Ibid.
11. British Consulate, West Bank, p. 12.
12. Shehadeh, The West Bank, p. 66.
13. Ibid.
14. Ibid., p. 108.
15. Ibid., p. 110.
16. Pearson, "Economic and Social Development," p. 35.
17. Ibid.
18. Awartani, A Survey, p. 51.
19. "Five Years," p. 243.
20. Van Arkadie, Benefits and Burdens, p. 33.
21. Lesch, Israel's Occupation, p. 34.
22. Shehadeh, The West Bank, p. 67.
23. Khraisheh and Ebersole, West Bank, Appendix 3, p. 2.

# 10
# Future of the Territories

The political future of the West Bank and Gaza Strip is uncertain and is dependent on the outcome of any peace negotiations that might get underway. Should peace negotiations break down it is likely either that the status quo will continue or Israel will annex the territories. On the other hand, should negotiations be concluded successfully, the territories may be given an autonomous status for a transition period of three or five years after which their final status would be determined. Future economic conditions in the territories will thus be greatly molded by political developments.

## STATUS QUO SCENARIO

The Israelis may choose to leave things as they are now in order to preserve the Jewishness of their state, among other reasons. The combined population of the two territories was 1,223,800 persons at the end of 1982, of whom 747,500 were in the West Bank* and 476,300 in the Gaza Strip. The total Jewish and non-Jewish population of Israel was 4,063,600 persons at the end of the same year (the non-Jewish population stood at 690,000). Thus, the population of the territories comprised 30 percent of the total population of Israel, and over one-third of its Jewish population. The average rate of population increase during the 1972-1982 period was 1.7 percent for the West Bank and 2.8 percent for the Gaza Strip. By contrast, the rate was 2.2 percent for Israeli Jews and 4.0 percent for Israeli non-Jews for the same period. Assuming the same 11-year population rate of growth, the combined population of the West Bank and Gaza Strip will reach 1.8 million persons at the end of the century, or more than one-third the Jewish population of Israel. When non-Jews in Israel are added to the population of the occupied territo-

----------

*Excluding Arab Jerusalem.

ries, the total non-Jewish population in the whole of Palestine will constitute 63 percent of the Jews there at the end of the century. These demographic considerations may compel the Israeli government to maintain the status quo in the territories so as to protect their own supremacy in the face of growing numbers of non-Jewish inhabitants. Alternatively, the Israelis could force the Arab people out of the territories and thereby maintain the demographic balance.

Currently, economic growth in the territories has depended in great measure on wages earned from employment in the Israeli economy. But the high economic growth rates experienced in the early 1970s have slowed down considerably. Investment in productive sectors of the local economies has been at a level much below that necessary to expand production to meet increased domestic demand created by population and income growth. Therefore, the territories have increasingly depended on imports, mainly Israeli, for both income and consumption purposes.[1] At present, the economies of the areas are administered in such a way as to serve the Israeli interests, and the continuation of the prevailing conditions would more likely reinforce this trend.

The continuation of the occupation status would eventually bring the economies of the territories into closer orbit of the larger and more sophisticated Israeli economy, supplying it with labor, raw materials, and component parts, and in return importing from it a wide range of manufactured goods. The GDP grew at an average rate of 7 and 1 percent annually in the West Bank and Gaza Strip in the last five years. Similarly, the average annual growth rate of the GNP was 6 and 3 percent, respectively, for the West Bank and Gaza Strip for the same years. It is likely that both GDP and GNP in both territories would continue to rise but at a much slower rate due to increased demand for territory labor and higher wage rates in Israel.[2] However, the extremely high rates of inflation are likely to offset much of this growth.

The size of the labor force in the territories would undoubtedly grow as a result of population growth and a higher participation rate in economic activity, which is currently at 19 and 18 percent of the total population in the West Bank and Gaza Strip, respectively. The level of education has risen in the territories in the postwar period, and it is expected to remain at a similarly high level in the future. The proportion of those attending school was about one-third of the total population of each territory in 1982-83. Coupled with this is the fact that several universities were established in the territories during occupation. Therefore, the level of skills of the population is expected to rise considerably, and as a result the supply of skilled labor will increase. Because domestic investment in productive sectors of the local economies has been extremely small and demand in Israel has exclusively been for unskilled and semi-skilled occupations, employment opportunities for skilled labor will remain very slim indeed, and these economies will continue to lose the skilled segment of the population through emigration, thereby diminishing prospects for economic growth.

Under current conditions the Arab inhabitants of the areas would continue working in the Israeli economy at an increasing rate in response to higher wages there and because of restricted employment opportunities in the areas themselves. This would raise domestic wage rates, decreasing as a result the employment rate in traditional activities,[3] and at the same time increasing dependence on Israel for growth in national product in the territories. Political uncertainties would continue to discourage productive investment by the Arab inhabitants and Israelis alike, further limiting demand for skilled labor and managerial talents and accelerating their emigration to Jordan and other Arab countries. Employment in agriculture is expected to decline as more farm workers would seek employment in Israel, whereas industrial employment might rise moderately, especially in subcontracting enterprises.[4]

Agriculture remains the major economic sector in the West Bank and Gaza Strip. West Bank agriculture is heavily dependent on rainfall, which exhibits wide annual fluctuations; an increase in production of dry farming, although possible through improvements in techniques, remains highly uncertain. Irrigated areas cover a small fraction of the total cultivated land, and expansion of agricultural output through the more efficient use of existing water resources and the irrigation of additional areas could increase the total amount of available land. At present, the only possibilities for increased agricultural production lie in the improvement of production methods and the better use of existing water resources because Israeli authorities control water in the West Bank. In the Gaza Strip it appears that the utilization of water resources has reached its limits, and any further expansion in agricultural output hinges on the development of new water resources. Therefore, in the absence of investment for the development of irrigation projects, the prospects for agricultural growth in the territories remain very slim.

Under the current conditions, no significant changes can be expected in industrial activity. Future growth in industry would likely come from those activities that are related to subcontracting with Israeli firms. Other segments of the industrial sector would continue to suffer from Israeli competition. The structure of industry would remain basically unchanged and limited to production of light manufactured goods, textiles and clothing, crafts, food packing, and the like. Industrial development in the territories requires capital investment in plant and the promotion of export markets; neither condition would likely be satisfied under Israeli occupation.

Construction has been the fastest growing sector in the domestic economies and now comes next to agriculture in terms of contribution to production. The Arab inhabitants have been willing to invest in residential construction for cultural and financial reasons already outlined. Under the present conditions, the rapid growth experienced by the construction sector in the past decade would more likely be impeded by Israeli practices and policies in the areas.

Many services have suffered immensely since occupation, notably tourism and finance. These services are not likely to experience any measurable growth as long as current conditions remain. Public investment in social infrastructure has constituted only a small fraction of the GNP in the territories. Municipal investment in utilities and social services has been severely limited by restrictions imposed by Israeli authorities on sources of finance and investment activity. As a result, several social and economic public services have barely kept pace with current requirements. Under the prevailing conditions, it seems likely that public services would grow at a lower rate than that of population and income.

Trade relationships established in the 1970s are likely to continue; that is, the territories would remain almost totally dependent on imports from and through Israel; Israel and Jordan would remain as first and second markets for their exports. Exports to overseas markets would be channeled through Israeli intermediaries.

## Required Finance

The continuation of the occupation status of the territories has made it imperative that investment be made in various economic sectors to revitalize the economy. A program for economic and social development in the areas is called for to create new employment opportunities and to "serve the humanitarian purpose of making life under military occupation more tolerable,"[5] and to encourage people "in their determination to stand firm and to retain their identity."[6] Until now, the territories have received a negligible amount of foreign aid, and Jordan appears to be the only country that has been channeling financial resources into the areas for development purposes. However, Israel may object to such a program and demand the final say in activities in which money is invested. To overcome these objections the contribution of as many countries as possible should be welcomed and supervision might be vested in an international body. It need not be overemphasized, however, that the local population should play a pivotal role in the planning and administration phases of this scheme.

A water resources development program in the territories can be initiated to expand the irrigated area in the West Bank and the Gaza Strip by 80,000 to 100,000 dunums each, and commencing a decade of agricultural growth of no less than 8 percent per annum.[7] What is needed in the West Bank is the installation of a capital system of irrigation to save already available resources to irrigate an additional 60,000 to 80,000 dunums of land[8] plus a deep well program and complementary storage and distribution facilities to augment water resources for the irrigation of another 60,000 to 80,000 dunums.[9] The cost of both parts of this program is about $500 per dunum, or a total of between $60 and $80 million in 1977 prices over a five-year period.[10] The only possible increase in water resources in the Gaza Strip appears to be through desalination of sea water. A plant with water production capacity sufficient to irrigate additional 100,000 dunums would need investment in the range of $75 to $100 million, again in 1977 prices.[11]

Investment in industry is urgently needed in the two territories, although the amounts required are not easily determined. Probably a sum of about $400 million over a five-year period would be required to update existing plants and establish new medium-scale ones. At present, due to political uncertainties, entrepreneurs have so far been unwilling to invest in industrial plant. The odds remain against any changes in these attitudes. Therefore, investment should be committed to the modernization of existing industries and in the establishment of new ones, especially those that produce for the local market. The effect of such a program is to reactivate some industrial activities and at the same time encourage the Arab inhabitants to invest in this sector, especially if some industrial investment was made jointly between them and foreign enterprises or through soft or interest-free loans.

Aid is needed for the development of infrastructure such as roads, communications, water, power, etc., in addition to health, education, and social welfare services. Investment of about $60 million each year and for five years would probably raise those services to a level sufficient to meet current and potential demands and prepare the ground for the revitalization of economic activity.

Thus the total amount of capital needs for the revitalization of economic activity in the areas would run in the neighborhood of $1.0 billion in current prices to be spent over a five-year period, or around $200 million each year. This cost would be covered by Arab and foreign governments and agencies, which would secure approval of the Israelis for carrying out these programs.

## ANNEXATION SCENARIO

Israeli annexation of the two territories remains a distinct possibility. Should Israel choose to do so, Israeli laws could be extended over the areas, and their residents would be forced to hold Israeli citizenship. The economic implications of such a decision are manifold. First, the economies of the two territories would be totally integrated into the bigger and technically more advanced Israeli economy. Second, trade transactions would exclusively be concluded with or through Israel. Third, the flow of areas' labor into the Israeli economy would be likely to slow down, and the domestic labor force would find more employment in the areas as a result of an influx of Israeli investment. Fourth, irrigated agriculture would probably expand rapidly, although old and new Israeli settlers stand to reap the benefits. And finally, the higher Israeli income taxes would be borne by the population and the unstable Israeli pound would become the only legal tender in the territories.

Arab reaction to outright annexation of the territories to Israel would culminate in measures that would have grave economic consequences. The first thing to expect is the complete closure of the bridges across the Jordan River for all kinds of traffic. As a result, trade as well as monetary and fiscal links between Jordan and other Arab countries on the one hand and the West Bank and Gaza Strip on the other would be totally cut off. In addition, emigration of the areas' Arab inhabitants to Jordan and other Arab countries would come to a sudden halt, raising in effect the rate of population growth to no less than 3.5 percent per annum. Remittances from Palestinian inhabitants working in Arab countries would probably be substantially curtailed because money transfers would have to be made through foreign channels and those workers would not be able to visit the areas.

The net economic effect of an annexation of the territories to Israel is extremely difficult to predict. The economies of the territories would undoubtedly be greatly influenced by whatever accompanying policies and measures the Israelis choose to undertake. One would surmise that the economic conditions in the areas and living standards of their inhabitants would tend to resemble those of the non-Jewish population in Israel, considerably worse off than the levels achieved by the Jews.

## AUTONOMY SCENARIO

The third possible alternative concerning the future of the occupied territories is to provide full autonomy to their Arab inhabitants for a transitional period of no more than five years after which they will be granted the right to self-determination. During this period the Arab inhabitants of these areas shall freely elect a self-governing authority to replace the existing Israeli military government (see Appendix B). Such authority should have the powers to create a local planning body to "handle the present and future needs in development design."[12] In addition, it must have control over the resources and should be "recognized as the official responsible government body for the negotiation and administration of foreign loans and grants."[13] It should also be charged with the responsibilities for the development of economic infrastructure to promote economic self-reliance that would eventually lead to Palestinian self-determination.

After the transition period, the Palestinians shall determine the final status of the West Bank and the Gaza Strip. They may choose to establish an independent state of their own or an autonomous unit linked with Jordan in some type of federation. Regardless of the final choice of the Palestinians, it should be pertinent at the outset to sketch the assumptions under which such a unit might function. First, the proposed entity is presumed to incorporate both the West Bank and the Gaza Strip, roughly within their pre-1967 boundaries. Second, Arab Jerusalem would again become the capital of the new entity without necessarily partitioning it and an agreement could be worked out with Israel as to all matters of mutual interest. Third, the West Bank and the Gaza Strip would be linked together by a corridor extending from the southern part of the West Bank to the Strip. Fourth, Arab refugees already living in the territories would be resettled permanently there, and refugees now residing in other countries who wish to return to the new entity would be allowed to do so. Fifth, the proposed entity would be established within a framework of a comprehensive political settlement and, therefore, would maintain friendly relations with its neighbors. In this respect, relations with Jordan would be most intimate due to historical ties and common economic interests,[14] in addition to the fact that Jordan is the entity's "nearest Arab neighbor, the gateway to the Arab world and the sea."[15] Finally, the creation of a Palestinian entity is in the interests of all parties involved, and foreign governments would be willing to come forth with a generous aid program.

The self-governing authority may find it necessary to take some immediate measures to prepare for economic development in the future entity, among which are the organization and administration of a monetary system; reopening of commercial banks and licensing new ones; establishment of financial institutions and a development board; stimulating and controlling agricultural and industrial commodity imports and exports with protection for producers; reopening and improving the port of Gaza into a deep water port; reopening Kalandia airport in Arab Jerusalem; and improving and expanding public transportation, including the road corridor between the West Bank and the Gaza Strip.[16]

The areas would have to receive those Palestinians now living abroad and wishing to return. Estimates of the number of refugees who may choose to relocate in the territories vary considerably and range between 1,200,000 and 500,000 over a five-year period, although the lower figure is the more likely one. In addition, there exist now no less than 400,000 refugees living in camps in the territories who need to be resettled permanently. Thus, the self-governing authority is faced with the formidable task of absorbing new immigrants by providing them initially with food, shelter, and clothing as well as temporary jobs, then integrating them into society by placing them in permanent jobs and housing.[17] The resettlement of close to one million refugees requires a considerable investment in housing, infrastructure, and in economic activity to create additional employment and services.

The self-governing authority would find the task of increasing employment opportunities to absorb new immigrants and growth in the indigenous labor force far from easy. Currently, there are around 100,000 laborers working, legally and illegally, in Israel, and it is convenient to expect that they would continue doing so in the early years of the self-rule because they remain needed in the Israeli economy. Should this employment be suddenly curtailed for any reason, the supply of domestic labor would immediately increase beyond the absorptive capacity of the economy. It is true that much of this labor is of the type that can be employed in public and private construction,[18] but the scope of these projects might not be sufficient to absorb a pool that has been so much enlarged by immigrants and former commuters.

The return of 500,000 refugees is expected to be accomplished over a five-year period, averaging 100,000 persons annually. If the labor participation rate of this population was 20 percent of the total, this would require an additional 20,000 jobs annually to absorb immigrants. Jobs in public works, services, and housing would be the major source of employment in the early stages of self-rule. Later, investment in the expansion of agriculture, industry, and services would create additional employment opportunities in the economy.

Agriculture is the mainstay of the economy of the new Palestinian unit. Water resources have been the major limiting factor in agricultural production, the development of which should expand output and employment in this sector. Total readily available water resources in the West Bank are estimated at 400 million cubic meters, of which 100 million are underground water, 50 brackish, 50 run-off, and 200 in the Yarmouk River as allocated by the Johnston Plan.[19] At present, water consumption for all purposes is at a much lower level than that available, making the possibilities for the expansion of irrigation very real. In the Gaza Strip underground water is mostly used for irrigation, and the only possibility for increasing water resources there is through the construction of desalination plants to supply additional water for irrigation.

Industry could be developed by expanding and modernizing existing plants and establishing new industries as well. However, due to the smallness of the local market, industries cannot be established at a scale large enough to produce efficiently unless exports to foreign markets are assured. In addition, domestic industry needs to be protected from Israeli competition through selective tariff barriers. The development of industry would eventually strengthen the economy and reduce its dependence on Israeli sources of supply. The restoration of banking services would provide industry with necessary credit for production and export.

The construction sector, including residential and public works, would grow rapidly during the transition period. Heavy investment in economic and social infrastructure would accelerate growth in this sector. Added to this is the housing requirement to settle 900,000 refugees. Assuming that the average family size is 6.6 persons, this means that there is a need for an extra 136,300 housing units during the transition period. The building needs per person are estimated at 10 square meters for living purposes.[20] Thus, the required building area needed to settle 27,260 households annually is put at 272,600 square meters, excluding improvements in housing condition and new housing needs of the present population.

Private services in the new entity are expected to rise rapidly during the transition phase. Development of tourism depends to a large extent on the kind of arrangement reached on Jerusalem and the amount of investment available for the tourist industry. Other services such as transport, commerce and trade, reopened commercial banks, etc., stand to gain from the autonomy status, increasing in the process their share in employment. Public services would increase in relative importance, reflecting expanded investment in social services and employment in the civil service.

Israel is the territories' major trading partner, supplying at present about 90 percent of their imports. A self-governing authority would serve the interests of its people by redirecting those links away from Israel toward other markets in the Middle East and elsewhere. This can be achieved through a policy of protection and subsidies to some industrial activity against Israeli competition, diversification of sources of imports, and the development of exports markets in other Arab countries.[21] Such a policy calls for the application of external tariffs to trade with Israel to eliminate the privileged position enjoyed by its products vis-a-vis products of other countries.[22]

## Cooperation

There are a few possible areas in which the autonomy authority, Jordan, and Israel could cooperate. Each of these three units has its own peculiarities, but each has a small domestic market, and needs to export, and a limited natural resource base. Regional cooperation might prove economically advantageous to these units. They may be economically linked together within a framework of a permanent regional cooperation authority.[23] Industrial development in the whole region may emphasize selective specialization based on imported inputs by each entity in the group, whereas "large-scale industries may be established with certain division of labor between the different integrated economies to serve all of them as one enlarged market."[24] A trade federation or union resembling the European Economic Community might serve in organizing and coordinating trade relations between the new entity, Jordan and Israel.[25] However, selective tariffs would probably be required in each unit to protect local and infant industries. Water resources could be developed on a regional basis because many of these resources are jointly used, and cooperation in this sphere is called for to determine the share of each country and regulate use. Tourism is another area where cooperation through packaged tours to main attractions in these entities may be needed.

## Required Finance

The self-governing unit needs a considerable amount of capital to develop its social and economic infrastructure, resettle refugees and expand productive activities. The availability of the required finances would greatly reduce the period required to reach viability.[26] The amount of capital needed during the transition phase is impossible to estimate, but it is possible to arrive at an approximate figure. Three categories of investment are required during the five-year transition period, namely capital for economic and social infrastructure, resettlement, and productive activities.

Tuma and Darin-Drabkin attempted in The Economic Case for Palestine[27] and in other related papers,[28] to come up with a comprehensive investment program for the establishment of a Palestinian state in the West Bank and Gaza Strip. They estimated investment in national infrastructure for an additional one million people at $1.5 billion in 1975 prices.[29] This investment includes $300 million for a power generation plant; $270 million for roads, including a link road between the West Bank and Gaza; $70 million for the development of the Gaza port; $300 million for water development projects, including a desalination plant for $200 million; $200 million for natural resources development, particularly minerals in the Dead Sea; $100 million for tourism; and $260 million for social infrastructure such as health, education, and other public services.[30] However, most of these investments will remain unchanged even if the population to be served by them is only half a million; hence, it will be assumed that the $1.5 billion ($2.2 billion in current prices) would be the amount required for this type of investment.

It was estimated earlier that there would be a demand for 136,300 additional dwellings for refugee resettlement. The building area required for a single household is 66 square meters at a cost of $220 per square meter (cost of public housing in Jordan), or $14,520 for each unit. Thus, the total cost of new dwellings for resettlement is about $2.0 billion, plus as much as another $2.0 billion for the physical and social infrastructure to serve these human settlements.[31] In addition, there will be a need to invest some $1.5 billion more in improvements of living conditions of the existing population,[32] bringing total construction costs close to $5.5 billion.

Estimates of investment required in various economic sectors of the economy depend on many factors, among which are the level of technology and the number of additional jobs created in each branch. Average investment in economic activity has been computed at $7,500 per employee in 1975 prices.[33] Additional job opportunities needed in the economy should be numerous enough to absorb immigrants and the growth in the labor force due to population increase. The population of the two territories together reached 1,223,800 persons by the end of 1982. Assuming that the transition period would commence at the beginning of 1986, projected population at the end of 1985 would then be close to 1.32 million people, and at the end of 1990, 1.9 million people.* The labor force at the end of 1985 is expected to reach 251,000 workers, or 19 percent of the total population; this figure would reach 380,000 workers (20 percent of the total population) by the end of the transition period. Thus, total investment required to create 129,000 new jobs in various economic activities would be $1

----------

*Yearly rates of population growth for 1982-1985 are calculated at 2.1 percent for the West Bank and 3.1 percent for the Gaza Strip; for 1985-1990 the rate is 3.5 percent for both territories. The inflow of immigrants is assumed to be even during the transition period and within the year; their natural rate of increase is estimated at 3 percent annually.

billion in 1975 prices, or about $1.5 billion in 1985 prices. There is an additional need for investment to update existing employment sources of about $3,500 per worker,[34] for the 251,000 persons domestically employed at the end of 1985, or a total of around $500 million.

To sum up, total capital needed for the creation of a Palestinian unit may be summarized as follows:

| | $ Million |
|---|---|
| Social and Economic Infrastructure | 2,200 |
| Public Housing and Related Facilities | 5,500 |
| Economic Branches | 2,200 |
| Total | 9,700 |

A total of about $10 billion required to set up a Palestinian entity on the West Bank and Gaza Strip over a five-year period, or $2 billion annually, is a very modest amount indeed.

Capital could come from several sources and in the form of aid, loans, and grants. These sources may include foreign governments, international financial institutions, international bodies such as UNRWA, foreign private firms, Israel by way of aid and compensation for Palestinian property seized, domestic savings, and Arab countries. Arab states in particular have a moral responsibility to support the Palestinian people in their quest for self-detemrination manifested in a state of their own.

**Economic Viability**

A Palestinian entity established in the West Bank and Gaza Strip would contain an area of about 6,000 square kilometers and a population of about 2 million by the end of the transition period. The resources of this entity would be limited, its domestic market small, and its level of development low.[35] Consequently, one asks whether such an entity would be economically viable.

There are no agreed upon criteria to determine viability, and economic viability of a certain country cannot be easily measured. If viability is a function of available natural resources, then Japan would be considered not especially viable; if it denoted self-sufficiency, very few countries in the world would aspire to this status; if it is measured by independence from foreign aid, practically no non-oil producing country in the third world satisfies this measure; if viability is the ability of the economy to attain high growth rates, then many countries would qualify.

A Palestinian entity can be viable on the basis of its human and natural resources, as well as on foreign aid that might be at its disposal. The people of Palestine compare favorably with other peoples of the region, including Israel, in terms of skills, enterprise, and ability. This high caliber of manpower is one of the crucial factors in achieving economic viability.[36] The ratio of Palestinian university graduates to total population is the highest in the region and is similar to that of Israel.[37] Many highly trained Palestinians manage the economies of many Arab countries, without whom many of these countries would not have reached their present levels of viability. Human resources will undoubtedly be a key factor in building a healthy economy in a Palestinian entity. In addition, there is sufficient land and water resources that are capable, with a little development and efficient use, of supporting the population.[38]

Very few developing countries in the world can claim independence from foreign aid. A case in point is Israel (and indeed Jordan, too), which has been one of the major recipients of foreign aid in the world. Between 1950 and 1973, Israel received vast amounts of money totaling more than $18 billion, mostly in the form of American loans and grants, contributions from world Jewry, Israeli bond sales, and German government reparation payments.[39] The U.S. granted Israel a sum of $1.5 billion in assistance, making it the first on a per capita basis as a recipient of American aid.[40] Following the 1973 war, American assistance jumped to more than $2.5 billion in economic and military aid in 1974, and since then it has averaged about $2.0 billion per annum.[41] In 1981 and 1982, American aid to Israel exceeded $2.5 billion in each year. Thus, Israel has been receiving each year more than $750 in American aid for every one of its citizens. Israel has raised around $4.5 billion in bonds since the beginning of the bond drive in 1951.[42] The annual proceeds of these bonds cover more than one-third of the Israeli development budget.[43] Despite the inflow of these huge amounts of money, the Israeli nondefense current account deficit reached $4.7 billion in 1982; its foreign debt, long and short term, stood at more than $23 billion in 1982, or $5,700 per capita. If, despite this influx of capital Israel is still considered economically viable, then any country with much less foreign aid might also be regarded so. A Palestinian entity could count on substantial amounts of foreign aid, especially during the transition period, to help in reaching economic viability in a short period of time.

The new unit should be able to marshall foreign aid and domestic savings into productive investments, enabling the economy to grow at levels comparable with those achieved by its neighbors. Palestinians either working or living abroad will be instrumental in the economic development of the new entity through direct investment in economic activities, remittances, and tourism. In the final analysis, this entity can be economically viable as a result of a combination of factors such as trained manpower, efficient utilization of natural resources, increased exports, high rates of investment, and above all the determination of its people.

**Notes**

1. C.A.C.I., The Economic Implications, p. 9-15.
2. Haselkorn, Kurz, and Wagner, Trade and Economic Links, p. 87.
3. Ibid., p. 41.
4. Ibid., p. 31.
5. "A Development Plan for the Palestinians," Middle East International (December 1976), p. 18.
6. Ibid.
7. Committee on Foreign Affairs, The West Bank-Gaza, p. 48.
8. Ibid., p. 30.
9. Ibid.
10. Ibid., p. 48.
11. Ibid., p. 49.
12. Pearson, "Economic and Social Development," p. 23.
13. Committee on Foreign Affairs, The West Bank-Gaza, p. 3.
14. Walid Khalidi, "Thinking the Unthinkable: A Sovereign Palestinian State," Foreign Affairs (June 1978), p. 703.
15. Ibid.
16. Ibrahim Matar, Economic Dimensions of the Self-Governing Authority for the West Bank and Gaza Strip (1979); cited in Pearson, "Economic and Social Development," p. 42-43.
17. C.A.C.I., The Economic Implications, p. 9-13.
18. Van Arkadie, Benefits and Burdens, p. 148.
19. Darin-Drabkin, "The Economic Viability," p. 53.
20. Ibid., p. 49.
21. Van Arkadie, Benefits and Burdens, p. 146.
22. Ibid., p. 147.
23. Darin-Drabkin, "The Economic Viability," p. 53.
24. Tuma and Darin-Drabkin, The Economic Case, p. 107-108.
25. See Elias H. Tuma and H. Darin-Drabkin, "The Low Cost of Creating a Palestinian State," New Outlook (December 1976), p. 37; Rami G. Khouri, "Israel's Imperial Economics," Journal of Palestine Studies (Winter 1980), p. 78; Ward, Peretz, and Wilson, The Palestinian, p. 120; and Tuma and Darin-Drabkin, The Economic Case, p. 108.
26. Ward, Peretz, and Wilson, The Palestinian, p. 119.
27. Chapters 6 and 7.
28. Darin-Drabkin, "The Economic Viability"; Tuma and Darin-Drabkin, "The Low Cost"; Elias H. Tuma, "The Economic

Viability of a Palestinian State," Journal of Palestine Studies (Spring 1978).

29. Tuma and Darin-Drabkin, The Economic Case, p. 87.
30. Ibid.
31. Darin-Drabkin, "The Economic Viability," p. 50.
32. Ibid.
33. Ibid., p. 52.
34. Ibid.
35. Tuma and Darin-Drabkin, "The Low Cost," p. 36.
36. Darin-Drabkin, "The Economic Viability," p. 46.
37. Tuma and Darin-Drabkin, "The Low Cost," p. 37.
38. Ibid.
39. Ann Crittenden, "Israel's Economic Plight," Foreign Affairs (Summer 1979), p. 1006.
40. Ibid., p. 1012.
41. Ibid., p. 1012-1013.
42. Ibid.
43. Ibid.

# Appendix A
# A Proposed Plan for Agricultural Development in the Occupied Territories

The following is a proposed plan to develop the agricultural sector in the occupied territories, drawn within the currently prevailing constraints associated with occupation. The plan aims to achieve the following specific objectives:

- Expansion of the cultivated area by developing new land.
- Expansion of dry-land tree culture.
- Expansion of the labor capacity of agriculture.
- Efficient use of available water resources to irrigate additional areas.
- Support of the livestock and poultry branches of agriculture.
- Establishment of new communities in agricultural areas.
- Reduction of food imports from Israel.

This plan proposes to raise agricultural return to levels sufficient to reactivate Arab farmers' interests in agriculture by providing them with financial and technical support. Agricultural development in the occupied territories is as much social and political as it is economic. Thus, agricultural investment in the territories cannot be measured solely by expected tangible results; rather, other factors such as Arab farmers' commitments to their land, its protection against confiscation, and its economic feasibility should also be taken into account. Accordingly, the investment required to achieve these goals should not be totally borne by local farmers.

This plan calls for the extension of soft loans to the territories' Arab farmers to cover part of the needed capital

----------

*Based on: Hisham M. Awartani, A Proposed Plan to Develop Agriculture in the West Bank and Gaza Strip, 1982-1983 (Nablus: Al-Najah National University, 1982); and Awartani, "Agriculture."

and subsidies, especially for dry farming and poultry production, to make these enterprises rewarding. There follows an outline of the measures and projects contained in the Plan.

1. **Planning Bodies.**
   It is necessary to establish an administrative structure to oversee development activities in the territories. In this context:
   - 1-a. The Jordanian-Palestinian Joint Committee should act as the supreme planning board.
   - 1-b. An agricultural planning board should be established. Its membership should consist of technical staff, many of whom should be inhabitants of the territories.

2. **Agricultural Credit.**
   Loans should be provided to Arab farmers to finance feasible and technically sound projects. This calls for:
   - 2-a. The appointment of agricultural specialists, as consultants, affiliated with main cooperatives in various districts but functionally supervised by JCO in Amman. These specialists and their assistants should be entrusted with the tasks of preparing feasibility and technical studies for agricultural projects and following up those implemented.
   - 2-b. The establishment of district committees to evaluate submitted projects.
   - 2-c. The formation of a central committee to approve loans for feasible projects.

3. **Cooperatives.**
   There is a need to support the cooperatives movement and enhance its role through:
   - 3-a. Registration of new cooperatives at JCO only, without recourse to registration at the Cooperatives Department in the territories.
   - 3-b. Encouraging cooperatives to provide a wide range of agricultural services, especially those that lie beyond the individual farmer's economic and technical means such as pesticide spraying, seed bed preparation, mechanical pruning, harvesting, etc. In addition, cooperatives can help in the provision of members with fertilizers and feed at subsidized prices.
   - 3-c. Periodic financial and administrative evaluation of main cooperatives to increase their efficiency.
   - 3-d. Improving auditing standards by assigning the task to independent and reliable accounting firms.
   - 3-e. Pre-service training for cooperative managers and

agricultural specialists.

3-f. Training for cooperative leaders.

4. **Extension and Agricultural Education.**

Agricultural skills should be enhanced to serve the needs of the areas' agricultural development. This can be achieved through:

4-a. In-service training of extension personnel in cooperation with FAO.

4-b. Reevaluation of agricultural education at Arroub Agricultural School and Khadourie Agricultural Institute to identify their needs and formulate programs relevant to development designs.

5. **Marketing.**

Agriculture suffers immensely from unfair competition with subsidized Israeli produce and complicated export procedures across the bridges. Coupled with this is the low level of marketing services such as grading, packing, transportation, storage, and other services. Necessary measures to facilitate the flow of agricultural produce should be adopted, among which are:

5-a. Establishment of an agricultural marketing office located in Amman to regulate the flow of surplus produce, get export permits from the Jordanian authorities and stimulate exports to Arab countries.

5-b. Reassessment and simplifying of current export procedures to Jordan.

6. **Projects Related to Land.**

It is necessary to expand the cultivated area by developing new land and helping farmers improve returns on agricultural activity, especially in dry farming. This calls for:

6-a. Establishment of twelve mechanized units to develop new land at a rate of 10,000 dunums annually. These units should be equipped with all necessary equipment and provide their services at subsidized prices. Ownership and management of these units should be entrusted to already existing cooperatives, or those established for this specific purpose in districts where they are lacking. However, services should be rendered to all farmers, members and nonmembers alike.

6-b. Construction of farm roads at a rate of 100 kilometers per annum to connect farms with neighboring highways.

6-c. Reconstruction of wells existing in developed land and drilling new ones to collect rainwater for livestock watering and pesticide spraying.

6-d. Appointment of a specialist in water and soil to supervise land development units and screen spring and well conditions.

7. **Water.**
Possibilities for expanding existing water resources are extremely limited due to occupation policies and practices. It is only possible to use already available water resources more efficiently to irrigate additional land. This necessitates:
7-a. Improvement of the efficiency of existing artesian wells, the negligence of which has raised the cost of water pumping and kept the amount of water produced by the wells below the ceiling imposed by the Israeli authorities. Efficiency can be augmented by cleaning or deepening some wells and repairing or installing submersible pumps on others.
7-b. Construction of irrigation ponds to hold water pumped from wells for use in irrigation and dissolution of fertilizers and chemicals.
7-c. Disseminiation of modern irrigation techniques such as dripping and sprinkling to save on water and labor.
7-d. Replacement of Al-Fara's Canal by a pipeline to increase its irrigation efficiency by reducing conveyance losses.

8. **Fruit Trees.**
An expansion of dry land tree culture and improvement of tree productivity is called for. This objective necessitates the following measures:
8-a. Conducting a comprehensive survey of existing seedling tree nurseries to suggest ways and means to improve the quality of their seedlings.
8-b. Expansion of production of seedling tree nurseries.
8-c. Distribution of olives and other fruit seedlings at subsidized prices.
8-d. Expansion of almond tree culture in rough terrain because it needs minimum effort and maintenance.
8-e. Expansion of vertical growing of grapes, which could increase productivity threefold over the conventional method currently used. This can be achieved by offering subsidies and loans to farmers willing to use this technique.

9. **Fertilization.**
Fertilizers are widely and effectively used in the production of irrigated vegetables, a few field crops and citrus products. But the use of fertilizers in dry

farming, especially in olives, has been very limited due to high costs and lack of awareness on the part of farmers of the effectiveness of this practice. Therefore, fertilizers should be disseminated to farmers on a large scale through:

9-a. Subsidization of prices of chemical fertlizers to be distributed to all farmers by various cooperatives.

9-b. Demonstration of olive tree fertilization.

10. **Pruning of Aged Trees.**
Many fruit trees have been underpruned because of the high costs of manual pruning and the scarcity of modern power pruning equipment. Pruning has had profound effects on raising productivity and reducing picking costs. Therefore, tree pruning should be carried out regularly by the mechanical services units owned by cooperatives at subsidized prices.

11. **Weed Control.**
Manual weeding is extremely expensive and plowing is inapplicable in most dry farming areas where topography does not permit the use of tractors. Necessary measures should be taken to minimize the cost of plowing by using alternative methods. This calls for:

11-a. Establishment of twenty mechanical service units in dry farming areas to economize on land preparation and modern weed and pest control operations. These units should provide basic agricultural services such as plowing, discing, seeding, spraying, pruning, and harvesting to dry farmers, and be affiliated, when possible, with cooperatives.

11-b. Utilization of small tractors in plowing tree areas, which, along with related equipment, should be attached to the mechanical service units.

11-c. Controlling weeds by chemicals, especially in dry farming areas, at subsidized prices.

12. **Pest Control.**
Spraying equipment is beyond the financial and technical means of individual farmers. This calls for the organization of a collective campaign to control such pests as the fruit fly, peacock eye, stem algae, etc. It is suggested that cooperatives with mechanical service units carry out this campaign at subsidized fees.

13. **Protected Agriculture.**
Plastic covers and greenhouses are used exclusively by wealthy farmers due to the high costs involved. To extend the area of protected agriculture, loans should be

granted to farmers willing to use these techniques.

14. **Poultry.**

Local production covers only 40 percent of domestic demand, the rest is imported from Israel. The poultry industry has been hurt by competition from subsidized Israeli produce and should, therefore, be supported to withstand this competition. Several measures should be adopted, among which are:

14-a. Establishment of a modern hatchery for broilers with a monthly capacity of 90,000 chicks to supply poultry farms with part of their requirement.

14-b. Financial support for producers in the form of subsidized feed prices and soft loans to feed factories to enable them to extend credit to farmers.

14-c. Provision of loans to establish new poultry farms and update existing ones.

14-d. Establishment of four regional laboratories to control poultry and other animal diseases.

15. **Sheep and Goats.**

The number of sheep and goats has declined considerably during occupation because of the continuous confiscation of pastures. The following measures can help expand production and improve efficiency:

15-a. Development of natural pastures that have suffered from negligence and overgrazing. This can be achieved by restricting grazing on newly seeded pastures, blocking, and rotation.

15-b. Encouragement of fodder production on private farms.

15-c. Encouragement of lamb fattening projects by providing farmers with loans to cover a portion of installation costs as well as the costs of lambs and fodder.

15-d. Prolonging lambing season over the year by the use of hormones, increasing in the process the incidence of twinnings.

15-e. Encouragement of breeding of superior quality sheep in confined places through loans granted to farmers and fodder subsidies.

16. **Cows.**

Most of the cows in the occupied territories are of the inferior <u>Baladi</u> type, which cannot compete with Israeli breeds. As a result, many cattle farmers have been driven out of business. There is an urgent need to increase productivity and reduce production costs, which can be achieved by the following:

16-a. Reduction of concentrated feed costs by granting financial support to feed factories.

16-b. Introduction of artificial insemination in cattle breeding at subsidized prices. This calls for the establishment of five units for artificial insemination affiliated with the main cooperatives.

16-c. Extension of loans to acquire improved breeds of cows.

17. **Food Industries.**

It is necessary to establish food processing industries to absorb surplus agricultural production and replace imports from Israel. This would improve and stabilize prices and open additional job opportunities in the territories. Steps involved in this process are as follows:

17-a. Conducting feasiblity studies for certain food industries such as olive pressing, olive oil packing, vegetable canning, etc.

17-b. Financing feasible projects.

18. **Other Projects.**

Farmers should be encouraged to submit certain projects at a later date, which would be evaluated and supported if feasible. Among these might be:

18-a. A study of the conditions of the fishing industry in the Gaza Strip to determine development priorities.

18-b. Allocating funds for other projects.

## SUMMARY OF PROJECTS

The following is a list of projects and associated costs included in the plan for the development of agriculture in the occupied territories. Amounts are in JD.

| Code | Project | Support | Loans | Adm. Costs |
|---|---|---|---|---|
| 1 | **Planning Bodies** | -- | -- | -- |
| 1-a | Jordanian-Palestinian Joint Committee | -- | -- | -- |
| 1-b | Agricultural Planning Board | -- | -- | -- |
| 2 | **Agricultural Credit** | | | (40,700) |
| 2-a | Agricultural Specialists | -- | -- | 19,000 |
| | Staff | -- | -- | 10,000 |
| | Transportation | -- | -- | 6,000 |
| | Office | -- | -- | 3,000 |
| 2-b | District Committees | -- | -- | 2,000 |
| 2-c | Central Committee | -- | -- | 700 |
| 3 | **Cooperatives** | | | (13,500) |
| 3-a | Registration of new cooperatives | | | |
| 3-b | Encouraging cooperatives to provide agricultural services | -- | -- | -- |
| 3-c | Periodic evaluation of main cooperatives | -- | -- | 500 |
| 3-d | Improving auditing standards | -- | -- | -- |
| 3-e | Preservice training | -- | -- | 7,000 |
| 3-f | Training cooperative leaders | -- | -- | 6,000 |
| 4 | **Extension and Agricultural Education** | -- | -- | (30,000) |
| 4-a | In-service training | -- | -- | 15,000 |
| 4-b | Reevaluation of agricultural schools | -- | -- | 15,000 |
| 5 | **Marketing** | | | (500) |
| 5-a | Agricultural marketing office | | self financing | |
| 5-b | Reassessment of current export procedures | -- | -- | 500 |
| 6 | **Land** | (487,000) | (960,000) | (7,000) |
| 6-a | Twelve mechanized units at JD 80,000 and new land development (50% of total cost) | 350,000 | 960,000 | -- |

| Code | Project | Support | Loans | Adm. Costs |
|---|---|---|---|---|
| 6-b | Construction of farm roads (50% of total cost) | 120,000 | -- | -- |
| 6-c | Reconstruction of wells (50% of total cost) | 17,000 | -- | -- |
| 6-d | Specialist in soil and water | -- | -- | 7,000 |
| 7 | **Water** | (250,000) | (550,000) | -- |
| 7-a | Improving wells efficiency (60% of total cost) | -- | 150,000 | -- |
| 7-b | Construction of irrigation ponds (50% of total cost) | 50,000 | 100,000 | -- |
| 7-c | Dissemination of modern irrigation techniques (50% of total cost) | 200,000 | 300,000 | -- |
| 7-d | Replacement of Al-Fara's Canal | outside sources | | |
| 8 | **Fruit Trees** | (205,000) | (235,000) | (1,000) |
| 8-a | Survey of nurseries | -- | -- | 1,000 |
| 8-b | Expansion of production of nurseries | -- | 50,000 | -- |
| 8-c | Distribution of fruit seedlings (30% of total cost) | 78,000 | -- | -- |
| 8-d | Almond trees culture | 2,000 | -- | -- |
| 8-e | Vertical growing of grapes (50% of total cost) | 125,000 | 185,000 | -- |
| 9 | **Fertilization** | (50,000) | (6,000) | -- |
| 9-a | Price subsidies (JD 5/ton) | 50,000 | -- | -- |
| 9-b | Demonstration on olive trees fertilization | -- | 6,000 | -- |
| 10 | **Pruning of aging trees** | (2,000) | -- | -- |
| 11 | **Weed Control** | (25,000) | (305,000) | -- |
| 11-a | Mechanical service units (20 units, 60% of total cost) | -- | 300,000 | -- |
| 11-b | Acquisition of small tractors (included in 11-a) | -- | -- | -- |
| 11-c | Weed control by chemicals | 25,000 | 5,000 | -- |
| 12 | **Pest Control** (50% of pesticides cost plus JD 2,000 cost of picking damaged fruits) | (6,000) | -- | -- |
| 13 | **Protected Agriculture** (50% of total cost) | -- | (800,000) | -- |

| Code | Project | Support | Loans | Adm. Costs |
|---|---|---|---|---|
| 14 | **Poultry** | (192,000) | (400,000) | (40,000) |
| 14-a | Hatchery (67% of total cost) | -- | 50,000 | -- |
| 14-b | Subsidies and loans to farmers | 192,000 | 150,000 | -- |
| 14-c | Loans for new poultry farms (50% of total cost) | -- | 200,000 | -- |
| 14-d | Laboratories (4 units) | -- | -- | 40,000 |
| 15 | **Sheep and Goats** | (12,000) | (230,000) | (22,000) |
| 15-a | Development of natural pasture | -- | -- | 22,000 |
| 15-b | Fodder production | 2,000 | -- | -- |
| 15-c | Lamb fattening (50% of total cost) | -- | 170,000 | -- |
| 15-d | Prolonging lambing season | 5,000 | -- | -- |
| 15-e | Breeding superior quality sheep (50% of total cost) | 5,000 | 60,000 | -- |
| 16 | **Cows** | | | |
| 16-a | Reduction of concentrated feed cost | 20,000 | -- | -- |
| 16-b | Artificial insemination | -- | -- | 8,000 |
| 16-c | Improved breeds (50% of total cost) | -- | 60,000 | -- |
| 17 | **Food Industries** | -- | (200,000) | (12,000) |
| 17-a | Feasibility studies | -- | -- | 12,000 |
| 17-b | Financing feasible projects | -- | 200,000 | -- |
| 18 | **Other Projects** | (100,000) | (300,000) | (300) |
| 18-a | Studies of fish industry | -- | -- | 300 |
| 18-b | Others | 100,000 | 300,000 | -- |
| | Total | 1,349,000 | 4,046,000 | 175,000 |
| | Grand Total | | 5,570,000 | |

The plan sketched in the preceding sections requires external finances in the form of direct support, loans, and administrative costs of about JD 5.6 million, without which it becomes extremely difficult to develop the agricultural sector in the occupied territories.

# Appendix B
# Israeli Proposals on the Powers, Responsibilities, and Structure of the Self-Governing Authority

The main points of Israel's proposals as submitted by the Government of Israel in the course of negotiations with Egypt and the United States were as follows:

I. **Scope, Jurisdiction, and Structure of the Self-Governing Authority (SGA)-Administrative Council**

(a) "The Camp David Accords (CDA), set forth the establishment of a self-governing authority (Administrative Council) that will comprise one body representing the Arab inhabitants of the West Bank and Gaza, who will choose this body in free elections, and it will assume those functional powers that will be transferred to it."

(b) "The members of the Administrative Council will be able, as a group, to discuss all subjects within the council's competence, appointing among themselves the spheres of responsibility for the various functions. Within the domain of its assigned powers and responsibilities, the council will be responsible for planning and carrying out its activities."

II. **Power of the SGA (Administrative Council)**

(a) "Under the terms of the CDA, the parties have to reach an agreement on the powers and responsibilities of the authority. Israel's detailed proposals include a list of powers that will be given to the authority and that, by any reasonable and objective criterion, represents a wide and comprehensive range of fields of operation. Without any doubt, the transferring of these powers constitutes the bestowal of full autonomy, in the full meaning of that term."

(b) "The powers to be granted the authority under these proposals are in the following domains:

1. "ADMINISTRATION OF JUSTICE - Supervision of the administrative system of the courts in the areas, dealing with matters connected with the prosecution system, with the registration of companies, partnerships, patents, trade-marks, etc."
2. "EDUCATION AND CULTURE - Operation of the network of schools in the areas, from kindergartens to higher education, supervision of cultural, artistic and sporting activities."
3. "HEALTH - Supervision on hospitals and clinics, operation of sanitary and other services related to public health."
4. "HOUSING AND PUBLIC WORKS - Constructing houses for the inhabitants and public works projects."
5. "MUNICIPAL AFFAIRS - Matters concerning municipalities and their effective operation."
6. "RELIGIOUS AFFAIRS - Provision and maintenance of religious facilities for all religious communities among the Arab inhabitants of the West Bank and the Gaza Strip."
7. "AGRICULTURE - All branches of agriculture and fisheries, nature reserves and parks."
8. "FINANCE - Budget of the Administrative Council and allocations among its various divisions, taxation."
9. "CIVIL SERVICE - Appointment and working conditions of the council's employees. Today the civil service of the inhabitants of the West Bank and the Gaza Strip, within the framework of the military government civilian administration numbers about 12,000 persons."
10. "LABOR AND SOCIAL WELFARE - Welfare, labor and employment services including the operation of labor exchanges."
11. "TRANSPORTATION AND COMMUNICATIONS - Maintenance and coordination of transport, road traffic, meteorology, local postal and communication services."
12. "LOCAL POLICE - Operation of a strong local police force and the maintenance of prisons for criminal offenders sentenced by the courts in the areas."
13. "INDUSTRY, COMMERCE AND TOURISM - Development of industry, commerce, workshops and tourist services."

Israel's practices in the occupied Arab territories have been in contradiction with every one of the powers listed above in an apparent attempt to impose its version of autonomy. For instance, thousands of Arabs are detained indefinitely on political grounds; school curriculum is changed and textbooks are distorted; schools and universities are frequently closed; professors are deported; more than two thousand books are banned; housing permits, especially in Arab Jerusalem, are denied; private property is continuously expropriated for the establishment of Jewish settlements; elected mayors are dismissed; and municipalities are denied the right to execute urgent projects. In fact, what has been once described as "creeping annexation" has quickened today into a full gallop.

# Bibliography


Abu-Ayyash, Abdul-Ilah. "Israel Regional Planning Policy in the Occupied Territories." Journal of Palestine Studies (Winter-Spring 1976).

Abu Hijleh, A. Studies in the Economies of the Occupied Territories. Amman: Central Bank of Jordan, 1981. (Arabic)

------. The Industrial Sector in the Occupied Territories and the Effects of Israeli Occupation. Amman: Central Bank of Jordan, 1981. (Arabic)

Abu Howayej, B. Agricultural Atlas of Jordan. Amman: Ministry of Agriculture, 1973.

Abu Kishk, Bakir. Arab Industry in the Occupied Territories. Jerusalem: Al-Multaka Al-Fikri Al-Arabi, 1981. (Arabic)

------. "Industry in the West Bank and the Gaza Strip." SAMED (October 1981). (Arabic)

Abu Lughod, I. "Educating a Community in Exile: The Palestinian Experience." Journal of Palestine Studies (Spring 1973).

"A Development Plan for the Palestinians." Middle East International (December 1976).

Awartani, Hisham. Agriculture in the West Bank - A New Outlook. Nablus: Al-Najah National University, 1978.

------. A Proposed Plan to Develop Agriculture in the West Bank and the Gaza Strip, 1982-83. Nablus: Al-Najah National University, 1982. (Arabic)

------. A Survey of Industries in the West Bank and Gaza Strip. Birzeit: Birzeit University Publications, 1979.

Ben-Meir, Alan. "Israel in the War's Long Aftermath." Current History (January 1981).

Ben Shahar, Haim; Berglas, Eitan; Mundlak, Yair; and Sadan, Ezra. Economic Structure and Development Prospects of the West Bank and Gaza Strip. Santa Monica: The Rand Corporation, 1971.

Black, Ian. "Military Government Wants Hebron Area Villages Hooked to Grid." The Jerusalem Post (March 14, 1980).

Bregman, Arie. Economic Growth of the Administered Areas, 1968-1973. Jerusalem: Bank of Israel, 1975.

------. The Economy of the Administered Areas, 1974-1975. Jerusalem: Bank of Israel, 1976.

British Consulate. West Bank: Water Resources and their Exploitation. Jerusalem, 1978.

Bull, Vivian A. The West Bank--Is It Viable? Lexington, Mass.: Lexington Books, 1975.

"Business Notes: Administered Areas." The Israel Economist (August-September 1970).

C.A.C.I. The Economic Implications of a Middle East Peace Settlement: Migration Projections, Vol. II (Draft). Arlington, Virginia, 1978.

Campbell, D. R. "Jordan: The Economics of Survival." International Journal (Winter 1967-1968).

Central Bureau of Statistics. Administered Territories Statistics Quarterly. Jerusalem, various issues.

------. Census of Population of the West Bank of the Jordan, Gaza Strip and Northern Sinai and Golan Heights. Jerusalem, 1967.

------. Housing Conditions, Household Equipment, Welfare Assistance and Farming in the Administered Areas. Jerusalem, 1968.

------. Statistical Abstract of Israel. Jerusalem, various issues.

Central Bank of Jordan. Fourth Annual Report. Amman, 1967.

------. Monthly Statistical Bulletin. Amman, various issues.

Claiborne, William; and Cody, Edward. The West Bank: Hostage of History. Washington, D.C.: Foundation for Middle East Peace, 1980.

------. "West Bank Oasis Withers: Nearby Kibutzim Flowers." International Herald Tribune (October 8, 1979).

Clawson, M.; Landsberg, H. H.; and Alexander, L. T. The Agricultural Potential of the Middle East. New York: American Elsevier Publishing Co., 1971.

Collard, Elizabeth; and Wilson, R. The Economic Potential of an Independent Palestine. London: Middle East Economic Digest, 1975.

Committee on Foreign Affairs, U.S. House of Representatives. The West Bank - Gaza Economy: Problems and Prospects. Washington: U.S. Government Printing Office, 1980.

Crittenden, Ann. "Israel's Economic Plight." Foreign Affairs (Summer 1979).

Darin-Drabkin, Haim. "The Economic Viability of a Palestinian State in the West Bank and Gaza Strip." New Outlook (April 1978).

Davis, Uri; Maks, Antonia E.L.; and Richardson, John. "Israel Water Policies." Journal of Palestine Studies (Winter 1980).

Dawoud, Jelal. "Industry in the Gaza Strip." SAMED (August 1980). (Arabic)

------. "Irrigated Agriculture in the West Bank and the Ef-

fect of Israeli Water Policies." SAMED (October 1980). (Arabic)
Department of Statistics. Agricultural Census, 1953. Amman, n.d.
------. Employment Survey in Establishments Engaging (5) Persons or More, 1975. Amman, 1976. (Arabic)
------. External Trade Statistics. Amman, 1965 and 1966.
------. First Census of Population and Housing, Vols. 1, 2, and 3. Amman, 1964.
------. Housing Census, 1952. Amman, n.d. (Arabic)
------. Industrial Survey, 1965. Amman, 1967. (Arabic)
------. Population and Employment in Agriculture, 1967. Amman, 1968. (Arabic)
------. Statistical Yearbook. Amman, various issues.
------. Study of Labor Force, 1966. Amman, 1968. (Arabic)
------. The Contribution of the West Bank in Jordan's Economy. Amman, 1969. (Arabic)
------. The National Accounts, 1959-1967. Amman, n.d.
Economic Planning Authority. Economic Survey of the West Bank (Summary). Jerusalem: Prime Minister's Office, 1967.
Effrat, Elisha. "Settlement Pattern and Economic Changes of the Gaza Strip, 1947-1977." Middle East Journal (Summer 1977).
"Five Years Israel Administration in Judea and Samaria." The Israel Economist (September-October 1972).
Graham-Brown, Sarah. "The Structural Impact of Israeli Colonization: The West Bank and Gaza." MERIP Reports (January 1979).
Gubser, Peter. West Bank and Gaza Economic and Social Development: Now and the Future. Washington, D.C.: The Middle East Institute, 1979.
Hagopian, E.; and Zahlan, A. B. "Palestine Arab Population: The Demography of the Palestinians." Journal of Palestine Studies (Summer 1974).
Haselkorn, Avigdor; Kurz, Mordecai; and Wagner, Abraham. Trade and Economic Links in the Transition Phase: The West Bank and Gaza Strip. Marina del Rey: Analytical Assessments Corporation, 1978.
Hilal, Jamil. The West Bank: Its Social and Economical Structure, 1948-1974. Beirut: Palestine Liberation Organization, 1974. (Arabic)
Horowitz, David; and Hinden, Rita. Economic Survey of Palestine. Tel Aviv: Economic Research Institute of the Jewish Agency for Palestine, 1938.
Hughes, Edward. "Israel's Unsettling Settlement." Readers Digest (May 1980).
International Labor Office. Action Taken on the Resolutions Adopted by the International Conference at its 64th Session, Supplement to the Report of the Director-General. Geneva, 1979.

------. Report of the Director-General, Appendices. Geneva, 1980, 1981, and 1983.

Istanbuli, Dawoud; Arafa, Abdel Rahman; and Azeh, Yusef. The Agricultural Situation in the Occupied Territories and Necessity for Development. Jerusalem: Al-Multaka Al-Fikri Al-Arabi, 1981. (Arabic)

Joint Economic Committee, U.S. Congress. The Political Economy of the Middle East 1973-1978. Washington, D.C.: Government Printing Office, 1980.

Kanovsky, E. Economic Development of Jordan. Tel Aviv: University Publishing Projects, 1977.

------. The Economic Impact of the Six Day War. New York: Frederick A. Praeger, 1970.

------. "Is Jordan's Economy Dependent on the West Bank." The Israel Economist (October-November 1967).

------. "The Economic Aftermath of the Six Day War." The Middle East Journal (Summer 1968).

Kearney, Vincent S. "Israel Economic Paradox." America (November 10, 1979).

Khalidi, Walid. "Thinking the Unthinkable: A Sovereign Palestinian State." Foreign Affairs (June 1970).

Khouri, Rami G. "Israel's Imperial Economics." Journal of Palestine Studies (Winter 1980).

Khraisheh, Abdul Rahman; and Ebersole, Jon. "West Bank Agriculture Co-operatives " (August 1980).

Konikoff, A. Transjordan: An Economic Survey. Jerusalem: Economic Research Institute of the Jewish Agency for Palestine, 1946.

Lesch, Ann. "Israeli Settlements in the Occupied Territories." Journal of Palestine Studies (Autumn 1977).

------. Israel's Occupation of the West Bank: The First Two Years. Santa Monica: The Rand Corporation, 1970.

Mazur, M. Economic Growth and Development in Jordan. Boulder: Westview Press, 1979.

MEED. "Postwar Economic Difficulties in Jordan." MEED (May 22, 1970).

Middle East Research and Information Project. "A Survey of Israeli Settlements." MERIP Reports (September 1977).

Migdal, Joel S. Palestinian Society and Politics. New Jersey: Princeton University Press, 1980.

Mize, David, et al. An Assessment of Education in the West Bank and Gaza Strip (Preliminary Findings, Vol. 1: Analysis). Washington, D.C.: America-Mideast Educational and Training Services, 1979.

Mosleh, Rose. "Industry in the West Bank, 1967-1979." Palestinian Affairs (February 1980). (Arabic)

Nakhleh, Emile A., ed. A Palestinian Agenda for the West Bank and Gaza. Washington, D.C.: American Enterprise Institute for Public Policy Research, 1980.

------. The West Bank and Gaza: Toward the Making of a Palestinian State. Washington, D.C.: American Enterprise Institute for Public Policy Research, 1979.

Nuseiba, Z.; and Ja'abari, J. "Settlement in the Occupied Territories." Al-Quds Daily (June 5, 1977).

Nyrop, Richard F. Israel: A Country Study. Washington, D.C.: The American University, 1979.

------. Jordan: A Country Study. Washington, D.C.: The American University, 1980.

Oakley, Peter. "The Jordan Valley: Drip Irrigation for Small Farmers." RRDC Bulletin (November 1978).

------. "Palestinian Emigration and Israeli Land Expropriation in the Occupied Territories." Journal of Palestine Studies (Autumn 1973).

Pearson, Robert. "Economic and Social Development on the West Bank and Gaza Strip: Some Policy Considerations." (January 1981).

Plascov, Avi. A Palestinian State? Examining the Alternatives. London: International Institute for Strategic Studies, 1981.

Palestine National FUND, Central Bureau of Statistics. Agricultural Statistical Bulletin for the West Bank. Damascus: PLO, 1980.

Royal Scientific Society. Continued Exploitation in Spite of the World, Israeli Colonization of the West Bank. Amman, 1980.

------. Information on Resources of the Occupied West Bank. Amman, 1979.

------. The Significance of Some West Bank Resources to Israel. Amman, 1979.

Remba, Oded. "Why Jordan Can Survive." The New Middle East (March 1969).

Roberts, Gordon. "Israel Curbs the Agencies." Middle East International (March 13, 1981).

Rubinstein, Danny. "Deluxe Annexation." New Outlook (June 1981).

Rubin, Trudy. "Israel Seems to be Slowly Annexing the West Bank." Christian Science Monitor (August 31, 1981).

------. "Israel Tries to Outflank West Bank Leadership." Christian Science Monitor (August 28, 1981).

Rural Research Centre. Statistical Bulletin for the West Bank and Gaza Strip. Nablus: An-Najah National University, 1981 and 1982.

Ryan, Sheila. "Israeli Economic Policy in the Occupied Areas: Foundations of a New Imperialism." MERIP Reports (January 1974).

------. "Political Consequences of Occupation." MERIP Reports (January 1979).

Salem, Jamal. The Agricultural Sector and Water Resources in the West Bank. Amman: Royal Scientific Society, 1980. (Arabic)

Sayigh, Yusif A. The Economies of the Arab World, Development Since 1945. London: Croom Helm, 1978.

Shaath, Nabeel. "High Level Palestinian Manpower." Journal of Palestine Studies (Winter 1972).

Shehadeh, Raja. The West Bank and the Rule of Law. New York: The International Commission of Jurists, 1980.

Sheshkin, Aryeh. "Economic Structure of the West Bank." New Outlook (September-October 1967).

------. "Post-War Economies of the West Bank." New Outlook (October 1968).

Silver, Eric. "Light and Shadow." The Guardian (August 23, 1981).

Simpson, Dwight James. "Israel After Thirty Years." Current History (January 1979).

Sinai, Anne; and Pollack, Allen. The Hashemite Kingdom of Jordan and the West Bank: A Handbook. New York: American Academic Association for Peace in the Middle East, 1977.

Tinnin, David B. "The Economic Sword over Israel." Fortune (May 5, 1980).

Tuma, Elias H.; and Darin-Drabkin, Haim. The Economic Case for Palestine. London: Croom Helm, 1978.

------. "The Low Cost of Creating a Palestinian State." New Outlook (December 1976).

------. "The Economic Viability of a Palestine State." Journal of Palestine Studies (Spring 1978).

United Nations Development Program. Report of the Inter-Agency Task Force on Assistance of the Palestinian People (April 1979).

Van Arkadie, Brian. Benefits and Burdens: A Report on the West Bank and Gaza Strip Economies Since 1967. New York: Carnegie Endowment for International Peace, 1977.

Ward, Richard C.; Peretz, Don; and Wilson, Evan. The Palestine State: A Rational Approach. Port Washington, N.Y.: Kennikat Press, 1977.

Waschitz, Yosef. "Commuters and Entrepreneurs." New Outlook (October-November 1975).

Zahlan, Antoine. "The Economic Viability of a West Bank State." Middle East International (December 1976).

Zananiri, Elias. "Jiftlik Farmers: Refugees in their own Homeland." Al-Fajr (July 13, 1980).

Zarhi, Sha'ul. "Economics of Refugee Settlement." New Outlook (December 1967).

------. "The Occupied Territories - Economic Liability." (Parts I and II) New Outlook (January-February and March 1977).

# Index

For Product Safety Concerns and Information please contact our EU representative GPSR@taylorandfrancis.com Taylor & Francis Verlag GmbH, Kaufingerstraße 24, 80331 München, Germany

**Batch number: 10725937**

Printed by Printforce, the Netherlands